POINTING OUR THOUGHTS

NEIL L. RUDENSTINE

POINTING OUR THOUGHTS

REFLECTIONS ON HARVARD AND

HIGHER EDUCATION ✦ 1991–2001

FOREWORD BY HANNA HOLBORN GRAY

HARVARD UNIVERSITY
CAMBRIDGE · MASSACHUSETTS

Frontispiece: The Memorial Hall tower, destroyed in a 1956 fire, was rebuilt in 1999, and stands as a symbol of the University's renewal and restoration of its campus. A new student dining hall and commons are now also part of Memorial Hall.

Contents

The Professions, Communities, and Public Service

Thinking Internationally

The Worlds of Harvard

An Education

Foreword

THE PRESENT VOLUME stands as a healthy corrective to
the familiar complaint pervading contemporary critiques of
higher education which contends that we have seen a sad decline
in the stature and role of the university president. Once upon a
time, it is said, giants strode the academic earth bestowing on it
their gifts of eloquence and moral fervor, inspiring the public with
their views on weighty issues of the day, exemplifying a wisdom
and authority that offered beacons to the social order.

By contrast, today's president is pictured as an administrative
manager more concerned with money-raising than with learning,
a cautious conciliator of diverse constituencies more intent on
placating than provoking, a spokesman for the corporate interests
of the university rather than the leader of an autonomous community of principled commitment.

This commonly repeated perception has taken on a life of its
own as a kind of emblematic shorthand for decrying the ills of, or
expressing the anxieties associated with, the developments surrounding universities in our time. Institutions have become ever
more complex and diffuse. The pace of discovery in knowledge
and its technologies has been ever more accelerated. The profu-

sion (and confusion) of expectations placed on universities has become ever more demanding. The ethical and social dilemmas emanating from the potential goals and uses of education and research seem increasingly difficult to resolve. The questions of the appropriate relationship of universities to government and to the commercial world appear irreconcilably contested. Disputes over the quality and effectiveness, the costs and benefits, the privileges and equities of higher education have multiplied.

In the midst of such bewilderment, it is refreshing to find a clear and penetrating intelligence that conscientiously accepts and confronts those problems and discordances of the contemporary academic world, celebrates its enlarged capacities, and refuses withdrawal into the nostalgia that would substitute abstract claims and simplistic nostrums or conventional rhetoric for genuine engagement with profound complexities and the determination to undertake the tasks implied in a constructive sense of the future.

Ours is an age that requires not so much the university founders of the past, distinguished as they were, but re-founders and renewers, participants in a collegial enterprise, definers of institutional purpose, spokesmen for universities and the academic ethos itself. Today's leaders among university presidents are those who look steadily and carefully to issues that, precisely because the issues are neither fashionable nor susceptible to easy solution, require the utmost consistency in analysis and persuasive communication.

Neil Rudenstine has been such a president. To read his thoughtful and beautifully crafted speeches is to hear the voice of a teacher deeply committed to the vocation of opening minds to reflection and insight, listening intensely to his colleagues and entering with them into a continuing process of intellectual dialogue, sharing the convictions and perplexities of the search for understanding. It is the voice of the humanist whose deep engagement with texts and ideas and language is always respectful of nuance and uncertainty, sensitive to the living fabric of history and tradition, generous to other ways of disciplinary study and attentive to the connections among them. It is the voice, too, of the academic citizen for whom the individual freedom of the scholar and student is paramount and for whom, at the same time, the ideal of an academic community has overriding moral power.

President Rudenstine has sustained and strengthened Harvard, preserving and extending its special character and mission, setting and meeting high standards of ambition and accomplishment. At the same time, he has made it his profession to meditate on the large themes of teaching and learning, of the essential values and conditions of academic life, of the nature of its institutions and the changes they must take into account. In doing so, he has fortified not only Harvard, but has served all our universities by laying out so eloquently just why they matter and what matters about them.

The last decade has seen a great growth in resources and programs at Harvard. The campaign that President Rudenstine led has already become legendary for its scope and its success. More important than the remarkable sums raised, however, is the academic purpose that drove the campaign's planning and appeal. President Rudenstine seized the opportunity to see the University whole, to support the initiatives of its different constituent parts and simultaneously to stimulate inquiry into how their intellectual riches might join further toward configurations and collaborations that would cross boundaries and carve paths that could link Harvard's internal neighborhoods to one another and produce new forms of learning and investigation.

At the outset, in his inaugural address, and insistently onward, President Rudenstine set out priorities that would foster the goals of the larger university, of liberal education, of serious scholarship and research, of excellence in professional training. Those priorities have to do in the first instance with honoring and protecting the conditions within which a university can flourish: the uncompromising conditions of academic freedom and untrammeled debate, together with those of civility and tolerance and a willingness to acknowledge the possible limitations to which even the most brilliant and talented minds may be subject.

Beyond these essentials, President Rudenstine's priorities have been focused on expanding and securing access for students of all backgrounds by the provision of financial aid based on a policy of need-blind admissions, on advocating the educational benefits of affirmative action and an increased diversity of the Harvard community, on extending the international role of the University, encouraging interfaculty initiatives, and bringing the fruits of the revolution in information technology to the service of education and research. Under President Rudenstine's leadership, financial aid has been significantly enlarged, new international initiatives created, a series of interfaculty programs established, and information technology and its attendant questions brought to center stage.

New and wide-ranging goals have been set for the sciences. The Radcliffe Institute for Advanced Study, building on the legacy of Radcliffe College, has created a major and promisingly interdisciplinary center within Harvard that could never have been realized without President Rudenstine's patient guidance. Important physical renovations underscore the adaptation of older facilities to new needs, possibilities, and technologies. So, for example, the humanities have been brought together in a new home at the Barker Center; Widener Library is undergoing massive reconstruction, and the Yard dormitories have been renovated.

President Rudenstine's stewardship of Harvard reveals an unfaltering attention to explicating and keeping faith with Harvard's history and special character while pointing to those elements of change that carry with them both risk and opportunity and that need to be debated and carefully assimilated. A reverence for reasoned discussion, combined with a sensibility that gives place to imagination, taste, and feeling; a delight in the individuality fostered by Harvard's environment, combined with the exhortation to high standards of community responsibility; a grace and generosity in giving credit to others, combined with a confidence that the best thinking of all will prevail; a willingness to live with complexity and ambiguity, combined with the sure conviction that there are principles and truths that must be defended in the university's cause; such are some of the characteristics that emerge through the words spoken at so many different times and occasions over the past decade.

Add a touch of pomposity-defying wit, blend in clarity, integrity and modesty, mix in humane sympathy, and season the whole with a profound love of learning and belief in the incalculable value of an always elusive wisdom: there you have a portrait, an unintended self-portrait, as it were, of Neil Rudenstine, a teacher who has taken the University and the purposes of education as his subject and their quality as his presidential mandate. President Rudenstine's service to Harvard and to higher education has been founded in the vision his voice conveys and its realization in the vigorous institutional life of a great university.

— Hanna Holborn Gray
President Emeritus
The University of Chicago

THE ENDURING UNIVERSITY

The Values of Education

Presidential Installation Address, October 18, 1991

WILLIAM JAMES was one of Harvard's great teachers and imaginative scholars; he was also a charming and generous-spirited person. So I was taken aback when I recently read a passage that he wrote to a friend in 1869, when one of Harvard's presidential giants was appointed:

> [The president] was confirmed... yesterday. His great personal defects, tactlessness, meddlesomeness, and disposition to cherish petty grudges seem pretty universally acknowledged; but his ideas seem good and his economic powers first-rate, — so in the absence of any other possible candidate, he went in. It seems queer that [Harvard] should go begging for candidates.[1]

We now know that James was much too gloomy about the appointment of President Charles Eliot, but he was entirely correct on another score: it is nearly impossible to imagine any particular person who can fulfill, even in small measure, the expectations of this office. If I accept the charge that has been given to me today, I do so with great humility, and I do so imagining only too vividly what James would be saying at this moment, if he were nearby on the outskirts of our gathering.

Let me add that I am given heart by the presence of two of Harvard's most distinguished presidents — Presidents Pusey and Bok — who are here today. I also want to welcome elected leaders from Cambridge, Boston, the Commonwealth of Massachusetts, and the nation, as well as representatives from other universities, guests, and friends.

I want to talk this afternoon about some of the ways in which higher education is not only respected, but also seriously criticized in our society today. Those major universities that are committed to several important activities — including undergraduate and graduate education in the arts and sciences, professional education, and advanced research — are seen as indispensable national and even international assets. Yet they are also viewed by many people as highly problematic and often deficient.

Each of us could make a list of the problems (real or perceived) affecting our universities today. Why is tuition so high, and why do universities always seem to need more money? Are universities as scrupulous and accountable as they should be, financially and otherwise? Are undergraduate education and good teaching neglected in favor of graduate education or research? What is the climate on campus for freedom of inquiry and speech, especially speech that may be unpopular or even offensive to other members of the community?

These are just a few of the issues that are creating tensions between educational institutions and our larger society. Some of the issues have been with us for many decades; others have emerged more recently. What makes this moment unusual is that so many problems have come into sharp focus simultaneously. They have attracted national attention, and they are seen — rightly or wrongly — to be more acute than in earlier periods.

We can better understand the present state of our major universities if we take a moment to remember when and how they developed. Their structure is unusual, and in their full breadth and scale they are very different from virtually all other universities in other nations. As early as 1814, Thomas Jefferson wrote to a friend sketching one of his many educational visions. He wanted a comprehensive institution that would study all the liberal as well as the useful arts at all levels — and his list covers three full pages, including ancient and modern languages, history, medicine, architecture, government, gardening, rural economy, optics, statics, hydrostatics, painting, sculpture, and navigation, to name but a few.

Half a century later, Charles William Eliot became president of Harvard. Eliot was not an altogether lovable person, but he had a clear sense of what was needed. He was very determined and wonderfully patient. Since he was president for forty years, he could — whenever he met with exceptional resistance — simply wait a decade or two until his opposition finally vanished from the scene. "The endless controversies," he wrote when he took office, "whether language, philosophy, mathematics, or science supplies the best mental training, whether general education should be chiefly literary or chiefly scientific, have no practical lesson for us today. . . . We would have them all, and at their best."

Eliot — like Jefferson — opted for everything. Having inherited a residential undergraduate college in the Oxbridge tradition, he quickly grafted onto it a graduate school that would produce Ph.D.s in the Germanic tradition. He increased the number of professional schools, expanded enormously the spectrum of academic fields, and hired a faculty capable of undertaking advanced research at the highest level. In undergraduate education, he did away with nearly all of the prescribed curriculum, and introduced the system of "free elective courses" that soon became a model for nearly all other colleges in the United States.

When Eliot was once asked whether a graduate school was really necessary, and whether graduate education and research would not interfere with the quality of undergraduate education, he replied immediately:

[No,] it will strengthen the College. As long as our teachers regard their work as simply giving so many courses for undergraduates, we shall never have first-class teaching here. If they have to teach graduate students as well as undergraduates, they will regard their subjects as infinite, and keep up that constant investigation [or research] which is necessary for first-class teaching.[2]

In short, Eliot and others believed that different educational activities, at different levels, could and should be brought together into a single institution where every function could extend and reinforce the others. Yet, even at this early date, we can begin to sense the risks and potential problems. The attempt to include everything might well make the University seem shapeless, lacking a clear definition and sense of coherence. That very criticism was expressed about Eliot's elective course system.

George Santayana, for example, was professor of philosophy in Eliot's time, and he was no enthusiast of the new system. At one point in Santayana's novel, *The Last Puritan*, an undergraduate complains with a mixture of exasperation and world-weariness: "Let me have that Elective Pamphlet. When all is quiet in the middle of the night, between one dream and another, I will collect my thoughts to see if among the 286 fountains of wisdom I can find [any] at which a gentleman may drink with decency." His final choice: "A half-course on Villon and the troubadours, one on Saracen art in Spain, and one on the military history of Europe in the seventeenth century."

Impeccable intellectual coherence? Brilliant introductory courses brimming with delectable general education? Not precisely. The struggle between letting a thousand curricular flowers bloom, or meticulously cultivating a modest-sized bed of carefully chosen specimens, was already under way nearly a century ago. President Eliot's new university model was obviously strong, and superior to what preceded it. But from the very beginning, there was certainly no unanimity of views.

Many decades later, one of the most perceptive observers of contemporary higher education in America presented a series of lectures about our major universities. He suggested that there may well be "a 'point of no return' after which research, consulting, [and] graduate instruction become so absorbing that faculty efforts can no longer be concentrated on undergraduate education as they once were." As an antidote, he urged universities "to give adequate recognition to the teaching skills as well as the research performance of the faculty."

These remarks, so thoroughly current in tone and substance, were made on the Harvard campus – not in 1990, or 1980, or 1970, but in April 1963 – as part of Clark Kerr's attempt (in his Godkin Lectures) to trace important developments in our universities from the late 1940s to about 1960, a period that he correctly identified as the second great watershed in American higher education.

Kerr went on to say that a few of the great private universities had succeeded in maintaining their high standards of excellence in undergraduate education. But in general, he saw that a considerable shift of the weights and balances had certainly taken place within many institutions.

Not only was Kerr strikingly perceptive at a very early date, but his analysis of the problems facing undergraduate education and teaching continues to be voiced today, often as if the situation were entirely new, rather than the product of developments that were taking place – and being described – decades ago.

Although Kerr's lectures were sometimes critical of these developments, they also celebrated real achievements. Graduate education and research had never been stronger. The number and diversity of students attending university – at all levels – had never been greater. Faculty members at major universities were making more and more fundamental discoveries in physics, the biological sciences, and other fields. Basic and applied research helped to energize the economy as well as to make contributions in areas such as medicine, international affairs, business, law, architecture, and public health.

Equally important, we came closer than ever to realizing the Jeffersonian ideal of a broadly educated citizenry: students who were learning from both the liberal and the useful arts to think more incisively and imaginatively about themselves, and to lead lives that could make a difference to others.

All of this was possible because of an unusual national consensus about the value of education — about the ways in which universities could educate individuals and also contribute to the larger purposes of our society. The total effort was astonishingly ambitious and required an active partnership among the federal government, the states, the private sector, leading foundations, generous individual donors, and the universities themselves.

No one of the partners could have undertaken this enterprise alone. The universities could provide major "assets-in-being": faculties, libraries and laboratories, talented staff and students, and a commitment to high academic quality as well as to significant human values.

They would have to rely, however, on government, foundations, and private sources to help create the necessary (and expensive) new scientific facilities; to support the large research effort by underwriting a full share of the indirect as well as direct costs; and to contribute the necessary scholarship funds to help educate greater numbers of graduate students in addition to undergraduates. Without a joint venture of this kind, committed for the long run, the whole undertaking would have had no chance of succeeding.

The universities certainly had no monopoly on what was accomplished. Many institutions — including small colleges, research institutes, corporate and government laboratories — were all fully involved. But Jefferson's educational vision of the single "big tent," and Eliot's idea of an all-embracing university that could contain the maximum amount of intellectual and human energy in a carefully confined space, created something unique and powerful.

The model has its imperfections, and some of these — as we have seen — were clear almost from the very beginning. They were accentuated further in the period of dynamic growth after the war. Real adjustments are in order today. But it would be a very great mistake to overlook the power of the model itself, or its formidable achievements in the past, or those of this very moment.

✦ ✦ ✦

It is tempting to romanticize the years from the late 1940s to the mid-1960s. By any standard, however, the era was a remarkable one for higher education, and there is no question that a major change began to develop in the late 1960s. The last two decades have been markedly different from the preceding period, essentially because the broad national consensus concerning the value and quality of our universities, including all of their main activities, has weakened.

There has been a loss of confidence and conviction on many fronts. No one cause has been responsible for this shift. The late 1960s produced serious political strains. The sudden shrinkage of the academic job market in the early 1970s led to a dramatic and wrenching loss of federal and foundation financial support for graduate students. Meanwhile, as I suggested earlier, criticism of the universities has intensified, and has focused on a number of issues, including the rising cost of education, the quality of the undergraduate educational experience, the perceived imbalance between teaching and research, the cost of research and the way in which research funds are managed, and the question of free inquiry and free speech. Some recent clashes have proved to be exceptionally damaging.

I do not believe that our universities are at a single turning point of crisis proportions, even though the present moment is more hazardous than it may seem. The greater danger, in my view, is that the recent pattern of controversy and conflict will continue indefinitely, until we reach a point where quality in many of our strongest institutions will have been significantly eroded, essentially because matters were allowed to drift in an almost random way.

Are there realistic steps that we can take to alter the present situation, and begin to make progress? This will not be easy, in part because some of the crucial factors that define the existing situation have little to do with universities themselves. For instance, conditions in our society have obviously changed since the 1950s and 1960s. In 1991, we are less productive as a nation than we were, and the financial resources at our disposal are more constrained. We also have urgent problems to address – in our cities, our public schools, and many other parts of our society. Finally, we are more divided than we were: more buffeted by strongly held opposing views, more complex in our cultural and ethnic diversity, and less certain about how to resolve our differences. There is more contentiousness and stridency in the air, and we have come to accept this as an almost normal part of our daily lives. In one sense, our public debates – so often acrimonious – can be seen as signs of a healthy democracy at work. But from another point of view, the situation is disturbing, because there is often so much less common ground on which we can all stand.

Under such conditions, it will be hard to create a new partnership that addresses the most important needs of higher education, while also concentrating on critical difficulties that confront the nation. Any effective action will take time, immense effort, and some additional resources. Yet we have no reason to remain simply passive. There are some actions that the universities themselves can begin to take. In closing, let me focus on a few of them. Some may be relevant to higher education in general; others are more directly related to Harvard.

First, we must reach out to groups and institutions beyond the university – in our local communities, the private sector, and the government — in order to strengthen relations with them, and to see how we can help address problems in the larger world around us. We need to listen carefully to others, in addition to explaining our own views. Creating a climate for the frank discussion of important problems is a necessary prelude to everything else. We may ultimately agree or disagree with others on any particular question, but that is not so much the issue at stake. If we communicate more directly and forthrightly, there will be a far better chance to create mutual understanding and achieve forms of partnership that can serve the public interest.

Second, we can evaluate our own performance more carefully, to make certain that we are using our resources as effectively as possible. Financial resources are one major concern, but we also need to consider others. How well are we carrying out our central educational purposes? Are we encouraging the development of all our human talent — our staff as well as students and faculty? Are there ways in which teaching and research in professional education should change, given the fact that several professions are now being fundamentally transformed? In the broadest sense, we must be accountable: to ourselves most of all, but also to the world outside.

Third, I believe that we can do a better job in undergraduate education, and I also sense that the faculty and other members of the university community agree. More can be accomplished with the resources we already possess. But at Harvard, our faculty-student ratio is less favorable than that of some other universities with which we compare ourselves. If we want to make progress — especially in our most heavily enrolled departments — we will have to add faculty on a selective basis. That will take time as well as money.

The goal is not to emulate the best small liberal arts colleges, because we cannot do that. We have a different mission, a different scale, a different ambience. Graduate education and research are critical to us — and to the nation. But we can create more opportunities for faculty to be directly involved in small-group teaching of undergraduates. We can also develop more effective structures that will allow us to review and strengthen the substance of our curriculum on a continuing basis. Aspects of undergraduate residential life also need attention, including the reinvigoration of some programs and the renovation of important facilities.

Fourth, we must begin at Harvard to create a University-wide agenda and a stronger University-wide consciousness that extends beyond the confines of any one or two schools or faculties. In academic terms, this will involve the development of inter-School efforts, some of which are already under way: studies of the environment, including our "built environment"; of the field of health care; of the problems of newly emerging democratic societies; of the difficulties facing our public school systems; and of business competitiveness and economic growth in our current "world economy." These topics — as well as others — are important both to the University and to society as a whole. In approaching them, however, we will have to be selective, concentrating our efforts on those few fields in which we can excel, and which can especially benefit from a strong University-wide commitment.

Fifth, special support will be critical for the natural sciences, the applied sciences, and technology. During the next decade, the connections among many scientific fields will certainly increase, and the distinction between basic and applied research will continue to diminish in several areas. More coordination and planning will be needed on our part to help guide these developments. But without substantial help from the government and the private sector, and a much clearer set of understandings and guidelines that can help minimize conflict, universities will simply not be able to make the contributions they are fully capable of making.

There are, we know, other very important subjects that also need our attention at this moment. The social sciences, the humanities, and our programs in the arts are too often forced to operate in very straitened circumstances. Student interest is very high, enrollments are substantial, and yet we lack resources to improve some major programs and facilities. Equally important, research in the humanities, as well as in some social sciences, remains underfunded.

Sixth, the cost of higher education is a subject to which I want to return on future occasions, because I believe the topic is extremely important and not well understood. My message today can only be brief and therefore oversimplified. Clearly, universities must do everything that they reasonably can to control expenses and to moderate fee increases. Discipline of this kind is essential, and Harvard is already taking stringent steps to economize. But even the tightest cost controls have never made it possible for private institutions of the highest quality to be broadly accessible to large numbers of middle-income and low-income students. Historically, generous financial aid has been the only effective means of achieving that goal, and it now allows Harvard – for example – to admit all undergraduates purely on the basis of their accomplishments and personal qualities, without any reference to their financial need. We have never in our history been as accessible as we are today: more than 60 percent of our entire student body receives some level of financial aid – most of which comes from Harvard itself, thanks to the generosity of its alumni and friends.

If we are committed to remaining genuinely accessible and diverse – and I believe strongly that we must be – then maintaining the strength of our financial aid, for graduate students as well as undergraduates, will continue to be one of our most important priorities in the years to come.

Finally, I want to say a few words about the University, not only as an academic institution but as a human institution.

It is no accident that Harvard had its beginning as a residential college, and that we continue to think of ourselves as a single place – a tangible campus, however extended, that embodies an intangible vision of unity and order.

We come here to study or to teach. But we also have a common life, and we form a collegial society outside the classroom as well as inside. As an academic institution, we are dedicated to intellectual free inquiry and free expression; as a human institution, we are committed to the idea of a single community, composed of individuals with a wide diversity of cultural, national, religious, political, and other points of view. It is just this combination of academic and community values that poses a special challenge for us, because it is the source of much of our vitality, and yet it also has the capacity to divide us.

How do we encourage and protect genuine freedom of inquiry and speech, even speech that may be offensive to some, while also encouraging the development of other important values that are essential to the creation of a community — values such as mutual respect, generosity of spirit, civility, and a genuine desire to understand those with whom we may profoundly disagree? The problem of how individuals and groups establish and assert their own identity, without being tempted to repudiate or diminish the identity of others, is one of the deep riddles of our time. It perplexes our world, and even now threatens to break apart nations and peoples, just at the moment when newfound freedoms might well be able to bring them together.

For us, in the University, there can be no compromise concerning either set of values — the academic, or the communal. If we are to resolve this dilemma, I believe we will succeed only because of the institutional tone that we manage to create. We have it in our power, after all, to speak our views perfectly openly, but in ways that are also consistent with the purposes of a university, where the fundamental motive is to learn and to understand, not to abuse.

We can be civil without being simply innocuous. We can be controversial and provocative without necessarily declaring open season on those who disagree with us. The way we talk to one another, and the tone we use in argument or debate, will often be as important as what we actually say.

Events will not always flow smoothly. There will inevitably be some breakage, some tensions and problems. Universities have for centuries pursued an ideal of unity and wholeness, only to find themselves often fragmented. But the ideal is a powerful one. It continues to survive, and we can come closer to realizing it if we think more consciously about how to accept and reconcile both our diversity and our common humanity.

Nearly a century ago, a young writer captured something of this ideal, including its complexity. His world could scarcely have been more different from ours. His style will also seem too romantic for our taste. Yet the passage speaks in its own way to some of the themes I have discussed this afternoon. It was composed not long after President Eliot began creating new separate schools for Harvard, while also pursuing his own vision of a strong unified institution:

> *I floated up into the higher drier air, that I might, for once, see the total body of [the University]. There [it] ... lay far beneath me, like a map in grey and black and silver. All that I had known only as great single things I now saw outspread in apposition, and tiny; tiny symbols, as it were, of themselves, greatly symbolizing their oneness. There they lay, these multitudinous and disparate quadrangles, all their rivalries merged in the making of a great catholic pattern....*
>
> *[The University] was venerable and magical, after all, and enduring.*[3]

1 William James, *Selected Letters of William James*, ed. Elizabeth Hardwick (Boston: David R. Godine, 1980), 82–83.

2 Samuel Eliot Morison, *Three Centuries of Harvard, 1636–1936* (Cambridge: Belknap Press, 1969), 335–336.

3 Max Beerbohm, *Zuleika Dobson* (1888; reprint, London: The Folio Society, 1966), 126–127.

THE UNIVERSITY
AND DIVERSITY

Diversity and Learning at Harvard: A Historical View

Address to the Massachusetts Historical Society
Harvard Club of Boston, November 6, 1996

I WOULD LIKE to share with you some of the background of my present thinking on the subject of diversity in higher education. When I embarked on the research approximately two years ago, I found that there was little identifiable documentation of the history and certainly no historical study of the subject.

My goal was to try to define the case that might be made for college and university admissions programs that took the concept of diversity seriously: programs that made conscious efforts to reach out to identify and enroll selected students from under-represented minority groups — including groups that are usually classified as "racial" or ethnic in nature, such as African Americans, Native Americans, and Hispanic Americans.

I was pragmatic in my quest. You will recall that the Supreme Court had ruled — in the well-known *Bakke* case[1] of 1978 — that there was likely to be only one possible rationale concerning this subject that might be acceptable to the Court. The opinions of the

Court were unusually divided in the *Bakke* case. It was left to Justice Powell to expound the view that conscious efforts to achieve diversity — including racial and ethnic diversity — in university admissions were acceptable, but only when the goal was part of an articulated effort, with a carefully designed process, to enhance the educational benefits — the nature and quality of education itself — in a college or university.

In addition, Justice Powell stated that race and ethnicity could be taken into explicit account in the definition of diversity only if a college's or university's admissions policy and practice could withstand the difficult legal test of "strict scrutiny" by the courts.

Without leading you too far into the intricacies of the *Bakke* case, I hope I have said just enough to suggest which intellectual and historical questions might have intrigued me, and why.

My own thinking, I should add, coincided very much with Justice Powell's: that is, if a university were to make special efforts in outreach and admissions, then those efforts would have to be strongly linked to the university's central purpose: to the central activity of education and learning, and the development of leaders capable of making effective contributions to our society — a democratic, heterogeneous society of considerable complexity.

Since most people in the United States currently associate the concept of diversity with the idea of affirmative action and with the civil rights legislation of the 1960s, I was also interested to see whether there was good evidence for a tradition of diversity that was distinct from affirmative action and that unequivocally predated the civil rights movement.

If one could show that educators, and major thinkers in other fields, had discussed the educational value of diversity long before the politics of the 1960s, it seemed to me that we would have a better chance of shifting the present debate from the charged political and legal arena where it is now lodged back to the educational arena where such matters properly belong.

When I began, however, I had no concrete evidence at hand,

so I simply started out with a hope and a hypothesis. I began with the *Oxford English Dictionary*, looking up the word "diversity" to trace its different meanings over time. There were no dramatic discoveries, but there was one suggestive quotation from John Stuart Mill's *On Liberty*, published in 1859. I also happened to remember — because I had recently read through the annual reports of Harvard's presidents — that Presidents Hill and Felton had both, in the 1850s, discussed the need for Harvard to become a national, even international, university, and I began to wonder what had prompted them to propose that particular kind of expansion or "outreach" at just that time.

In other words, there were some early indicators pointing me toward the mid-nineteenth century, especially the 1850s, and I quickly added to my list of reference books *The Education of Henry Adams*, since Adams graduated from Harvard in 1858.

What was the net result of these initial probes?

First, it quickly became clear that, for President Felton at least, the prospect of a civil war was a precipitating event that led him to think explicitly about ways in which education could be helpful in avoiding regional and national friction, or actual conflict. Felton wanted to promote better understanding across the kinds of geographic, cultural, and social barriers that then existed in parts of the United States. He wrote, in 1860, that he wanted Harvard to have:

> *students from every State and Territory in the Union — without a single exception or secession, [because gathering students together] from different and distant States must tend powerfully to remove prejudices, by bringing [undergraduates] into friendly relations through the humanizing effect of liberal studies pursued in common, in the impressionable season of youth. Such influences are especially needed in the present disastrous condition of public affairs.*[2]

That, in effect, was the early theory of the case: educate young, impressionable students from different parts of the country in one institution, and they will get to know one another, learn to understand one another, and overcome their prejudices through such contact. When they leave college, they will take their new forms of understanding with them back to their local communities. As they mature and become leaders, they will in time create a kind of national network, capable of bridging the great gaps that were so clearly emerging in mid-century American society. In short, student "diversity" – the gathering of different sorts of young people coming from different places, with different prejudices and points of view – could be a potentially powerful force in education and in the public life of the nation. That was the major reason Felton wanted to move Harvard from being a mainly regional institution to being a truly national one.

Was the idea plausible? Was there any evidence to suggest that education might really be enhanced if different sorts of students were in fact brought together in this way? When I looked at the chapter on "Harvard" in *The Education of Henry Adams*, I found Adams acknowledging that he, like most undergraduates in the Class of 1858, was from a well-established New England family. But, as he also wrote, "chance insisted on enlarging [Adams'] education by tossing a trio of Virginians" into the mix – a trio that included "Roony" Lee, the son of Robert E. Lee. Adams and Lee became good friends, although Adams recognized "how thin an edge of friendship separated" him and the Virginians "from mortal enmity" on the brink of the Civil War.

This experience in diversity proved to be important. For the very first time in his life, Adams wrote, he was brought "in contact with new types [of people] and [was] taught . . . their values. He saw the New England type measure itself with another, and he was part of the process." Even though it was already too late for the students in the Harvard Class of 1858 – the Civil War would soon be upon them – Adams remembered throughout his life that this "lesson in education was vital to these young men," and it clearly left a lasting impression on him.

We can see, in the 1850s, the beginnings of a theory of the

educational benefits of diversity — in contrast to the view that students would generally be expected to come from the same geographical region, and more or less the same economic and social backgrounds, and very likely the same religious background. Even though neither President Felton nor Henry Adams actually used the word "diversity," the idea was clearly in the air, and at least two other important writers of the period did in fact use the term — and use it regularly.

John Stuart Mill, for instance, stressed the need for "diversity of opinion" in deliberative institutions and societies that were at least partly democratic in nature. He stressed the value of bringing "human beings in contact with persons who are dissimilar from themselves, and with modes of thought and action unlike those with which they are familiar."

Moreover, diversity in points of view — or modes of action — was not something that one should simply read or hear about; "real contact" with others was essential, because (as Mill said) it is important to hear "arguments" from

> *persons who actually believe them, who defend them in earnest and do their very utmost for them. [One] must know [the arguments] in their most plausible and persuasive form [and] feel the whole force of the difficulty [that one's own arguments must encounter].*[3]

In short, reading about points of view — or about other types of people, or actions and customs different from your own — is one important way of learning. But books do not talk back to you directly, and do not respond to your arguments with the power and conviction of someone who can speak persuasively about what he or she believes and why. Contact, personal encounters, human associations and conversations and dialogue and debate make a difference to the substance and texture of what one learns and how one learns it.

For Mill, as for Felton (and Adams), a critical aspect of education depends on being in the actual presence of people who are "dissimilar" from oneself in significant ways. In colleges and universities, the way to gain the particular educational values that come from various forms of dissimilarity is to have an admissions process that takes diversity explicitly into account as one of its important goals and that brings different kinds of students together in a residential community committed to learning in all its forms — outside the classroom, as well as inside.

Diversity can of course be defined in many ways, and few people tried to be more concrete in their definition than Charles William Eliot, who became president of Harvard just after the Civil War, in 1869.

Much has been written about how Eliot transformed Harvard from a small college into a genuine university, how he ushered in the elective system, and so forth. But relatively little has been written about his ideas concerning student diversity and its importance to the process of education.

His views were complex, and I cannot do justice to them in this brief talk. But Eliot saw diversity — along regional, social, economic, religious, and racial or ethnic lines — as a defining feature of American democracy. And he brought an expanded conception of diversity to Harvard. He envisioned a university that would gather together students from a wide variety of "nations, states, schools, families, sects, [political] parties, and conditions of life." Harvard, he wrote, should welcome children of the "rich and poor" and of the "educated and uneducated," students "from North and South" and "from East and West," students belonging to "every religious communion, from the Roman Catholic to the Jew and the Japanese Buddhist." Bringing them together, he wrote, would allow them to experience "the wholesome influence that comes from observation and contact with" people different from themselves.

Eliot's conception of "race" was different from our own — especially in its emphasis on characteristics that we might today associate more with ethnicity, national origin, and immigrant status. But he specifically identified the "great diversity in the population of the United States as regards racial origin" as a crucial and positive element in American democratic society. He wanted to keep the races — whether Celtic, Teutonic, Mediterranean, Slavic, African, or otherwise — separate from one another, and he had his own Anglo-Saxon preferences. But he was able to entertain and embrace a vision that was considerably larger (and more inclusive) than his purely personal tastes, and he set about — quite consciously — opening Harvard's doors to at least some of the children of new immigrants, to members of religious minorities, and also (although in very small numbers) to African Americans.

Before Eliot's presidency, for instance, there were — as far as we know — zero black graduates of Harvard College. During his presidency, there were eight. They did not come accidentally or unnoticed: they were deliberately recruited, and they had an impact well beyond their numbers. Also, at the beginning of Eliot's presidency, there were just seven Roman Catholics, and three Jews enrolled in the College — out of a total of 563 students. By the end of Eliot's tenure, 9 percent of the student body was Roman Catholic, and 7 percent was Jewish, for a combined total of 16 percent, compared to *less than 2 percent* when Eliot started.

Interestingly, it was one of the African American students, W. E. B. Du Bois, Harvard College Class of 1890, who would later affirm the significance of Eliot's broad vision. Harvard, Du Bois wrote, "was no longer simply a place where rich and learned New England gave the accolade to the social élite. It had broken its shell and reached out to the West and to the South, to yellow students and to black.... [Eliot and others] sought to make Harvard an expression of the United States."

It would be possible to cite testimony from other students if we had time — students such as John Reed, who was an undergraduate in the last years of Eliot's presidency. Reed wrote an interesting set of reflections on his Harvard experience, and he specifically mentioned the fact that he had once abandoned a close Jewish friend, when it became clear that the friend was becoming a social liability.

There was a later reconciliation, but the anecdote demonstrates that the lessons and the benefits of diversity are not always easy to discern, and that they are sometimes painful – even if the pain is subsequently transmuted into something valuable.

As things turned out, Reed came to appreciate and even revel in Harvard's diversity, and he saw the University as a place which brought together "characters, of every race and mind, poets, philosophers, [and] cranks of every twist," offering them all "anything [they] wanted" from the world's vast storehouse of learning.

Eliot himself was certainly no sentimentalist. He knew that diversity can cause friction and turbulence, and can sometimes make the experience of being a student more difficult – and, at times, even alienating. But he insisted on the importance of a more open, diverse, and even disputatious university, where a "collision of views" would promote "thought on great themes," teach "candor" and "moral courage," and cultivate "forbearance and mutual respect." He saw that an inclusive vision of higher education not only would benefit individual students, but was also essential in a heterogeneous society whose citizens simply had to learn to live together if the nation's democratic institutions were to function effectively, and if its ideals were to be fulfilled. He insisted, in other words, on the link between diversity in education and the requirements for citizenship and leadership in a diverse nation such as ours.

+   +   +

If we step back for a moment, we can take stock of the concept – and practice – of diversity at Harvard during the half century that passed between the late 1850s and the end of President Eliot's tenure in 1909.

First, we can see that the definition of diversity steadily expanded throughout this period. The early emphasis was primarily on diversity of ideas or points of view. But the most perceptive thinkers soon realized that those curious things that we call "ideas" are not disembodied phenomena or abstractions. They are complicated bundles of perceptions, intuitions, arguments, opinions, dispositions, convictions, feelings, attitudes, and rhetorical gestures that cohere — and also shift, mutate, and sometimes fail to cohere — in live human beings who constantly express, modify, reconsider, and reformulate what it is they think and feel, or what they *think* it is that they think and feel.

Moreover, these live human beings, in turn, are also not abstract phenomena, floating in a vacuum: they come from some specific place or places and have been affected by the customs, attitudes, and beliefs of their families, and the culture of their points of origin. Each has a local habitation and a name that is partly regional, religious, racial or ethnic, economic, and social in nature.

That is why the effort to define diversity in college admissions almost always involves at least two major factors: first, a complex assessment of every individual as a unique human being; and, second, a thoughtful consideration of all those more general differentiating characteristics that can have a strong bearing on who we are and what we are — characteristics such as those enumerated by President Eliot when he said that Harvard should have students from different nations, states, schools, religious groups, political parties, and conditions of life.

There is no guarantee, of course, that a farm boy from Wisconsin will bring something substantially different to a university, compared with a student from a large high school in the Bronx, or one from a *lycée* in Paris. But it is a perfectly reasonable assumption, as a first approximation, and the assumption can then be tested in detail when admissions officers look carefully at individual applicants and their applications.

Similarly, there's no necessary reason that an African American student from West Virginia should have ideas or perspectives or experiences or aesthetic tastes that are different from those of an Asian American student from Los Angeles, or a white student from Maine. But I think it would be odd if three such students did not turn out to be significantly different from one another in any number of interesting and stimulating ways, capable of expanding one another's horizons – and those of their fellow students.

In other words, it is not at all surprising, looking over the historical record, that educators like Felton and Eliot often talked in terms of broad categories – such as geography, or economic background, religion, or race – when they wanted to identify important indicators of diversity. The categories are in fact extremely effective points of reference, and they have served many colleges and universities very well for at least a century. The critical issue, of course, is that we should not be trapped by these categories, or use them mechanically as a substitute or shortcut for a thoughtful rounded assessment of each individual candidate.

If we care seriously about diversity, therefore, we will want to make sensible use of the relevant categories at our disposal, recognizing their limitations as well as their utility. I want to stress this point, because several recent proposals and judicial rulings – in California and Texas, for instance – have essentially banned the use of some well-established factors (specifically, race, ethnicity, and even gender) in college admissions, while allowing others to remain standing (such as socioeconomic background or regional place of origin). I, myself, believe that it is very difficult to identify a logically consistent set of reasons to justify these particular distinctions; and I also believe that, from an operational point of view, any excellent admissions process would find it essentially impossible to comply with prohibitions of the kind I just described. But these are policy considerations which – however important – deserve a much fuller discussion, on another day.

✦   ✦   ✦

If we look briefly at developments during the major span of our own century, it is clear that the concept of diversity shifted meaning a number of times when applied to college and university admissions. There was no single, simple line of development, but rather a series of changes and reversals.

The most important moment to focus upon – and it was a historical moment of the greatest significance – came in the years following World War II. Several things happened simultaneously: there was a massive expansion of the entire system of American higher education; there was substantially increased access to college on the part of different kinds of people, beginning notably with the GI Bill and moving through to the admission of more minority students, more foreign students, and, of course, the admission of women to previously all-male colleges. In addition, there was the rapid development of standardized testing – through the College Board and the Educational Testing Service – as a way of evaluating and sorting, on a national comparative basis, the huge number of students who were beginning to apply to college. And, finally, there was a major investment (by many, but not all, colleges) in the entire process of outreach and assessment in admissions, because admissions officers were now faced (for really the first time in history) with the complicated task of selecting a very limited number of students from a large and expanding pool of candidates.

Given this situation, it became essential to develop much more explicit admissions criteria and guidelines, because it was no longer possible to enroll most of the people who wanted to matriculate. Not surprisingly, any set of admissions criteria could be, and came to be, openly challenged through discussion, debate, and even litigation.

The challenges have come in many forms, but the most visible – and divisive – have been legal cases in which white students have litigated against particular universities because the universities were said to have admitted African American (or other minority) students who had lower "grade point averages" and lower standardized test scores than the plaintiffs. The *Bakke* case in California, and the recent *Hopwood* case[4] in Texas, are the two most conspicuous of these, but there have been others as well.

In very broad terms, we can see these legal conflicts as bringing to a head the clash between a particular "meritocratic" idea of educational quality – defined largely in terms of statistically measurable academic achievement – and an equally strong idea of education associated with the concept of diversity, including all the different forms of knowledge, the variety of human qualities and talents, and the multitude of perspectives on experience that are obviously not very measurable in statistical terms, but are no less real for that.

Let us suppose, for a moment, that Harvard were to subscribe, in a consistent way, to a statistical "meritocratic" view. What would happen, for example, if we were to take only those students with the very highest test scores and grade point averages, going mathematically from top to bottom, until an entire entering class was filled? The results would almost certainly be very curious. It is not at all clear, for example, how many of the students, chosen in this way, would be very talented in the arts, since certain creative abilities do not correlate at all strongly with SAT scores – or even with high grades in many subjects. It is not clear how many students with a capacity for leadership we would have in such a class – or individuals strongly committed to public service; or how many students who have exceptional and unusual abilities to understand other people, or to penetrate complex human and societal situations; or students who are good at ice hockey, or who are descended from our alumni.

Equally important, it is not clear that we would have assembled a group of students who were sufficiently dissimilar to learn very much from one another: about the varieties of human nature, about how people from different places, different social and economic backgrounds, different ethnic and racial backgrounds, different countries and religions and cultures experience the world, articulate their values, and, indeed, live their lives.

In this respect, it is important to remember that when we *do* admit a class of first-year students to Harvard College, we do not do so "atomistically," looking at each candidate in isolation from all the others. Instead, we try to "compose" a class that, in all its variety, has considerable power to "teach itself," so to speak.

Of course, we want a very high level of academic achievement, measured in more or less traditional ways. But, we also want students to be able to achieve, at college, all those other dimensions of intellectual and human capacity — dimensions that are most likely to emerge in the actual dynamic process of education — through innumerable encounters, associations, and discussions among students as well as with faculty, day in and day out. Educational quality, as we know, has every bit as much to do with realizing potentialities still to be developed — in an environment designed to help such development — as it has to do with measuring prior achievement.

✦   ✦   ✦

Perhaps I am wrong. But, I believe that very few of us — if any — would be very satisfied with a college admissions process that was mathematically driven by test scores and similar statistics; yet, it is just such scores and statistics that are being used as the chief evidence in the legal cases I have mentioned.

These statistical scores and grades are certainly useful, and certainly important to take into account in any sensible admissions process. But, when we try to describe why they are not wholly sufficient, I think we find ourselves mentioning criteria and qualities and characteristics that are mainly associated with the concept of diversity.

That, I believe, is why John Stuart Mill, President Felton, President Eliot, and students such as those I have cited, were driven to the conclusion more than a century ago that the concept of diversity or "dissimilarity," of significant differences among people, was central to any serious theory of education and learning. All of these individuals obviously valued academic excellence. But none of them thought that a narrow view of excellence was robust enough to capture anything like the full range of capabilities that we would want to include and help students to develop in a definition of education. Felton and Eliot and others sensed that their nation, and the world, were multifarious; that the needs and requirements of heterogeneous democratic societies were becoming complex beyond any imagining; and that one of the only effective ways to begin to understand and absorb some substantial part of that multifariousness and complexity was to encounter it directly, and come to know it through actual association, through having direct contact with a considerable variety of people, through diversity.

That recognition is every bit as important now – perhaps more important – as it was a century and a half ago. In closing, let me confess that I find it ironic – and inauspicious – that on a day when we can look back on President Eliot's clear-sighted determination to reach out consciously to enroll students of different immigrant groups and races, the State of California has just passed a resolution prohibiting any consideration of ethnicity, race, or gender in college admissions.

1 *Regents of the University of California v. Bakke*, 438 U.S. 265 (1978).
2 Cornelius C. Felton, *Report of the President to the Board of Overseers, 1859–60*, 6.
3 John Stuart Mill, *On Liberty* (1859; reprint, London: Penguin Books, 1985), 99.
4 *Hopwood v. State of Texas*, 78 F.3d 932 (5th Cir. 1996).

Free Expression in a Diverse Society

Commencement Day Address, June 4, 1992

GATHERED in this Yard, with its great trees and simple buildings, we might well believe that we have the power to create
and sustain the deepest possible human harmonies. For our universities do have this power – especially through their commencement rituals, and through the shared experiences of tens
of thousands of students, faculty, staff, alumni, and friends.

But if we feel a special sense of unity at times like this, we also
realize how rare such moments are, and how few people are fortunate enough to experience them with any frequency. Much of
the world is in considerable disarray, and as we look about, it is
obvious that we have more than enough problems and issues to
occupy us. I would like to talk about one which – for want of a
better term – I will simply call the problem of living together.

✦ ✦ ✦

How, on this increasingly populous and heterogeneous planet of
ours, where geographical boundaries are now so permeable, where
we are no longer insulated from what is happening in countries
far across the world, where ideas as well as people move from

place to place more swiftly than they can be absorbed; how, with so much flux, and so many random acts which no amount of preparation can ever fully anticipate; how shall we find the human capacity and the resources necessary to live peacefully and fruitfully together?

We rub elbows every day with people whose religious and political beliefs differ from our own, people of different nationalities and cultures, people from different racial or ethnic groups who may speak languages we do not know, people who have their own cuisines, their own music, their own modes of dress. And if we do not literally encounter such a range of people every day, we read about them, we hear about them, we watch them on television.

Given this diversity and the increasingly close quarters in which we live, we might conclude that matters could be far worse than they are. But most of the time, I believe, we are inclined to think just the opposite: we ought to be doing much better.

I am frequently asked, for example, why it is that ethnic, racial, and other relations among students seem to be so tense on many campuses throughout the country. Why do students of different races or religions or cultures sometimes choose to eat, or even live, separately from one another? If our students — so capable, so carefully selected, so clearly intended for leadership in the future — cannot live together more harmoniously, taking every opportunity to intermingle and learn from one another when conditions are so favorable, what can we possibly expect from the rest of the world, most of whose people live in conditions that are barely tolerable? The assumption behind these questions is usually clear: that the situation on our campuses has become worse in recent years — or, at the very least, has not improved.

✦   ✦   ✦

There are no simple answers to these questions, nor do we have time here for a long analysis. But I would like to start by framing a hypothesis for your consideration. I ask you to entertain the idea that the situation on our campuses today is at least as good as – and in some respects better than – that which existed at many times in our past. What we see today needs far more subtle interpretation than I can provide in a few minutes. But the divergent and sometimes conflicting student voices on campus are often signs of vital and even necessary controversy, of healthy self-assertion, of difficult but essential human growth, and of jarring but important moments of sudden discovery and self-discovery. They can also bear witness to sobering events that are painful, disturbing, and even repugnant. But it is precisely this complex intermixture of experiences that usually characterizes periods of profound change in life; and I believe that we are indeed in a period of such change.

Let me elaborate. I think there are at least four important characteristics which make the present moment different from – and potentially more healthy or positive than – earlier periods.

First, the diversity we now have is greater than at any previous time, and that means there is a wider range of voices ready to speak out. If we think for a moment of the collegiate world of the 1950s (when I was a student), the differences between then and now are striking.

In many of our institutions, there were scarcely any black students, or Asian Americans, Hispanics, or Native Americans. Women were still excluded from most of the major private universities. Jews were still largely restricted by quota, and Roman Catholics were few in number. Political outliers – whether very conservative or very liberal – were either quiescent or nonexistent. Assertive religious orthodoxy was virtually unknown. Gay and lesbian students were scarcely acknowledged as a reality. Students from foreign countries were present in only very modest numbers. And how many physically impaired students did we enroll, and how much institutional attention did we focus upon their particular needs?

To be sure, campuses were generally more tranquil throughout the period from 1945 until the mid-1960s. But that tranquility was purchased at the cost of not including vast segments of our society. We are immensely more inclusive now. We should not be surprised that we are also — sometimes, at least — rather less tranquil.

My second point is this: our new inclusiveness is neither timid nor tepid. Many students as well as faculty have not been shy about speaking out. And whatever complications this may have added to our lives, the polyphonic results are fundamentally better than something more plainly monotonic. In addition, the freedom we enjoy is manifestly preferable to any artificial consensus that might be created through subtle or more overt forms of censorship. We know that such censorship was not uncommon at many universities through the nineteenth century and into the twentieth, and that the resulting human and intellectual price was very high.

A Harvard audience in particular should remember that barely a century ago, Charles Eliot Norton — a formidable figure from our university's past — was nearly denied tenure here because he was thought to be an agnostic — which in fact he was. And Cardinal Newman's little novel, *Loss and Gain*, quietly records the poignant tale of an Oxford student who was suspended from his university for questioning some of the Thirty-Nine Articles while also expressing an interest in the tenets of Roman Catholicism.

Current critics of the university scene, who see threats of oppression from either the "politically correct" or the "politically incorrect," are rightly concerned about any form of intellectual or other coercion. Such coercion has no place in a university, and we know how damaging its effects can be. Even when there is vigorous debate, there is a worry that some voices will dominate and that others will feel too reticent to speak. There is also the hazard that certain groups will press for decisions that would be unwise or simply wrong. These dangers are real, and critics have not been slow to point them out. Our own goal is clear: we must remain fully committed to creating and maintaining a climate on campus that is genuinely civil and tolerant, while also open to a wide range of views.

Maintaining the actuality of such openness is not always easy, because civility and "tone" cannot be legislated. Nor is there any way to insure that everyone will feel equally at ease in the large forum of a major university: much depends not only on the climate we create but also on differences in individual temperament and disposition – on personal impressions, inclinations, and will. It is all the more important, therefore, that those who are in positions of responsibility evaluate arguments and decide issues on the merits, seeking to do what is best, rather than what may seem most "responsive" at any given moment.

Although some recent critics of universities have correctly identified important issues such as those I have just mentioned, they have, in my view, also tended to overlook much of the full – and crucial – historical record on this topic, and have tended to imply that there were times in the past when a maximum of true freedom of expression and diversity were combined with a maximum of civility and tranquility. I doubt seriously that a careful reading of the record will sustain that view. At the very least, we need – on this subject, above all – far more scholarly and meticulous attention to all the relevant evidence, and a much more informed discussion than we have had to date. Few current subjects offer an easier target for those who are interested in it for ideological or political or polemical reasons. Surely it is time to turn to our most scrupulous observers of institutions and our very best historians of education for clarification and deeper understanding.

Let me expand a little on this second point. What we now have on our campuses, as already suggested, is a plenitude of voices and views that are sometimes – but far from generally – discordant. While I have stressed many of the positive aspects of this situation, I certainly do not underestimate the depth and difficulty of the issues it raises. For example, individuals and groups have sometimes been deliberately provocative and offensive in their statements about other members of the university. Others have used obstructive – if nonviolent – means in an effort to press their points of view. These forms of action are fundamentally different from one another, and each must be evaluated on its own terms.

But we do need to recognize that each has the potential to divide communities quite sharply; and some actions, if they constitute the direct harassment of individuals, obviously infringe upon basic rights. Over time, patterns of behavior that are divisive or clearly disruptive can take a heavy toll, especially in the setting of a residential university. Precisely because universities are intrinsically open and conducive to free expression and debate – and because their decision-making processes are highly consultative as well as subject to constant review and criticism – we all have a special responsibility to use these processes in such a way as to increase understanding and to resolve differences whenever possible. At the very least, we must respect and accept conscientious disagreement by exercising a large measure of mutual patience and forbearance.

While acknowledging the difficulties and possible hazards of our present situation, I do want to return to my fundamental point: we have an exceptional degree of openness and free expression on our campuses, and I doubt whether we have ever had so many articulate voices exploring a broader range of perspectives with so much confidence. To some observers, this variety may seem more like cacophony than polyphony; and we do have our intensely cacophonous moments. But when I listen to the student discussions that take place on campus every day, I hear – far more often than not – something that is remarkably humane, searching, spirited, and "conversational" in nature. And if that is indeed the case, do we not have reason to take some real pride in this fact?

Third, in spite of the complexity that a wide range of voices and views can create, we have been – and must continue to be – unyielding in our determination to uphold the right of free speech for all students, faculty, and invited speakers. There is a powerful university-wide consensus behind this principle on our campus, and that is a great credit to faculty and students alike. There have been hundreds and hundreds of speakers at Harvard this year, expressing an immensely wide range of opinions on countless topics. Not one single speaker has been blocked, not one has been shouted down. There can be no swerving from this steady course.

Fourth, we would be mistaken — as I have already suggested — either to exaggerate the amount of tension or conflict that exists on campus, or to underestimate the full extent of intermingling and real learning that take place among students and faculty. People do succeed in reaching across gaps; deep friendships are formed; moments of exhilaration — as well as discouragement — are shared. Day in and day out, the University works as a lively, interesting, and convivial place where students and scholars live together and learn from one another.

+   +   +

I have asked you to entertain the hypothesis that matters on our campus may well be better today, not worse, in certain important respects. I have cited four main reasons: a far greater inclusiveness than ever before; a much greater willingness on the part of many students and faculty to express their views openly; a strong commitment to the protection of free speech; and a vital community of students and scholars who learn from one another with great vigor, seriousness, and enjoyment. I would now like to offer a few additional observations to keep in mind as we continue to evaluate our present situation.

The first involves some sweeping and therefore certainly debatable generalizations about how human beings tend to behave. I am neither a pessimist nor a deep skeptic. But I do believe that our species — viewed from a broad historical perspective — has generally been tribal and sectarian; quite passionately attached to political, religious, or other convictions, sometimes with violent results; deeply intolerant of groups or castes or races that have been categorized as impure or inferior or apostate; and highly nationalistic in our modern era — even pathologically so through-out much of our twentieth century.

If this analysis is at all correct, then any society or institution which deliberately tries to seek out and embrace diversity is act-ing against the grain of strong human instincts and much human behavior. Such attempts have scarcely ever been made. America, for all its imperfections and contradictions, remains the one bold, idealistic, though yet unfulfilled, living experiment that has con-sciously set itself the task of including people of widely divergent backgrounds from every part of the world.

And our university — as well as others — has recently taken upon itself an even more challenging role: to maintain the values of diversity and free expression, while also attempting to create a humane community in which people respect one another's dif-ferences, and seek to understand and know one another well. Defining this complicated task — this task of living together — is relatively easy. But finding the means to achieve it is far more difficult. Indeed, it is a task that has never, to my knowledge, been tried before on anything like the scale that we are attempting.

Why, then, should any of us ever have thought, even for a moment, that the job would be easy? When the populations of the world have quarreled and fought for millennia in order to protect their religious, ethnic, national, linguistic, and other character-istics or symbols of group identity, why should we expect thou-sands of younger people — even when working with faculty and staff — to create easily or swiftly the kind of community that vir-tually all humanity has tended to resist? Indeed, to see the contin-uing strength of the world's resistance, we need only read about what is taking place in the streets of what was once Yugoslavia, or in regions of the former Soviet Union, or Northern Ireland, or the Middle East, or parts of Africa, or elsewhere.

I do not find it surprising, therefore, that we should find ten-sions between Jewish students and black students on our campus-es, or between white students and Asian Americans, or between different groups within the Hispanic community. Nor do I find it strange that students from the same ethnic or other groups should often seek one another's company at meals, or in their dormitory accommodations.

I would be deeply happy if there were even more intermingling than there is, and I believe strongly that our institutional structures – and the spirit that we seek to create on campus – should foster such intermingling. But if we look closely at our larger American society (and if we are candid with ourselves), we cannot fail to notice that vast segments of our population live, socialize, and even work with people who have racial, religious, or cultural characteristics very similar to their own.

These patterns and boundary lines are created partly – though not entirely – by choice, and they are generally guarded with vigilance. We know the statistics and anecdotal evidence, for example, that demonstrate the powerful obstacles encountered by many minority families when they try to move into "majority" neighborhoods. We also know about the conflicts that arise when the reverse occurs, or when borderlines between different minority groups fall into dispute.

If we are alert to these and similar characteristics or social structures that define – and always have defined – so much of our national life, we should be able to understand more clearly the rhythms and patterns of our students' lives. Indeed, we may well discover that our students manage their affairs rather better than the rest of us. So, while I look forward to a time when there will be less tension and misunderstanding on campus, I would be surprised if that happened very rapidly or painlessly. Our undertaking, by its very nature, brings into close association many different people with different views and perspectives, and this fact alone guarantees that there will be debate, disagreement, argument, and difficulty.

In this respect, it is helpful to reread some of our most thoughtful statesmen on this general subject. Neither Abraham

Lincoln nor Martin Luther King turned away from the kind of challenge we are discussing, but neither promised any simple solutions. And for a frank, unvarnished view of the conception of humankind that underlies some of the thinking behind our Constitution, we can learn a great deal from rereading James Madison's contributions to *The Federalist Papers*.

Madison had very little confidence that the full exercise of freedom in a democratic or republican society would lead to easy agreements or tranquility. Instead, he viewed the human species as highly factional — addicted to forming tightly knit groups that in turn struggle with other groups. This was of course one of the reasons that he favored a complex system of checks and balances in our government, with its careful separation and distribution of powers: he hoped that, through such a structure, the power of particular groups would be blocked or contained by the contending force of other groups. "The latent causes of faction," Madison wrote, "are ... sown in the nature of man."

> *A zeal for different opinions concerning religion, concerning government, and many other points...; an attachment to different leaders ambitiously contending for pre-eminence and power; or to persons of other descriptions whose fortunes have been interesting to the human passions, [all these] have, in turn, divided mankind into parties, inflamed them with mutual animosity, and rendered them much more disposed to vex and oppress each other than to co-operate for their common good.*[1]

We certainly do not have to agree with Madison, at least not entirely. And our government, as well as the spirit of our political and civic life, owes an obviously profound debt to that more optimistic Jeffersonian stream of thought which is part of our national identity. But the tendency to associate with people who have characteristics and values similar to one's own is as typical of America as is our persistent effort to dissolve such distinctions in order to promote intermingling through the vehicle of a national "melting pot." A good deal of "melting" does take place. But we also continue to have our Polish American and Asian American societies; our Columbus Day, Easter Sunday, and St. Patrick's Day parades; and our Latino, Italian American, African American, and Hasidic neighborhoods.

The reality of America's unity or its diversity is far from simple: most efforts to find a single metaphor or succinct phrase to describe our aspirations or our actual national experience capture part of the truth but are inevitably less than adequate. We are a melting pot — but also a nation of free, equal, and unique individuals; a mosaic of different cultures and groups; an assemblage of fifty separate states; a union or single nation "indivisible"; a "rainbow coalition"; an expanding New Frontier or Great Society; a ground where Madison's contentious factions struggle; a land of opportunity for individuals with the desire and will to succeed; a lonely crowd; and an aggregation of separate racial or ethnic communities who live in clannish ways.

Our national search for self-definition is obviously one of the continuing, unresolved dilemmas of America. At what levels of experience do we in fact intermingle and "melt"? Do we try — in substantial measure — to preserve, cherish, and celebrate our different cultural or ethnic customs and traditions? Or do we prefer — with little fanfare — to live our quite separate lives? Or do we manage, in some complex manner, to act in several of these ways, adjusting ourselves to different roles at different times?

The troublesome and threatening factions that Madison feared are — when viewed from a more positive perspective — the familiar and unifying political parties that we join, the religious congregations we belong to, the "single issue" organizations we form, and the extended families and identifiable neighborhoods that we sustain. But whether we assign a more negative or more positive value to our human inclination to create such associations, the gravitational pull of that tendency is clearly very strong. Madison's incisive analysis should remind us, at the very least, that our nation and its complex institutions will almost always contain assertive subgroups or subcultures or "factions." Even if these groupings are often benign, we can scarcely expect that matters will ordinarily proceed smoothly, with little friction or stress.

Before concluding, let me underscore one additional point: our current enterprise in diversity is quite recent in origin. In the nation as a whole, much *legal* discrimination against African Americans ended only in the last three to four decades, and the removal of many *de facto* restrictions on some groups is still far from complete. Most major private universities have been coeducational for only the last twenty-five years, and their inclusion — in any significant numbers — of individuals from a wide variety of political, ethnic, racial, religious, and other groups or persuasions is even more recent.

From the long perspective of human history, we have had scarcely more than a fleeting second of time to undertake a transformation that is unprecedented and that is occurring in a world where many nations and communities are moving in precisely the opposite direction — that is, toward societies which are ever more tightly and narrowly defined in terms of their group characteristics. If Harvard enrolls a student from Saudi Arabia, and if he or she rooms near a student from Israel, should we expect that the two newcomers will immediately understand and trust one another, simply because they have crossed the Atlantic and landed in Weld Hall? Or if an African American student rooms in his first year with a white student, should we assume that each of them will forget all they may have heard or read about one another's race — or about the Civil War and so many other events in our history? They *might* do so, but we should certainly not count on the fact. Examples could be multiplied, including those that involve the attitudes of some men toward women, or some women toward men.

Our experiment is a new one — hardly two or three decades old — and it is taking place in a nation that is itself deeply troubled by unresolved issues concerning race, equity, and educational opportunity. We will need more time to accomplish what we would all like to achieve. Some people will be understandably impatient for more rapid change; others will point out correctly how much has already taken place. My own view is frankly evolutionary. We are unlikely to reach solutions — or, more precisely, resolutions — easily or immediately. Indeed, it is not obvious — in an untried experiment of this kind — what our realistic expectations can be. But we know there are no alternatives that are either more humane, or more in accord with the realities of our world. Our experiment in diversity must be pressed forward with energy and conviction, in a manner that preserves the fundamental strength and fabric of this great but also very human university. We are and must remain a living organism, something essentially different from a mere organization.

+ + +

Let me now conclude by suggesting some of the principles and ideas for action that may be able to guide us as we look to the future.

First, we will need help and strong support in order to maintain an unwavering commitment to the goals we have set ourselves: to sustain the highest possible quality in education and research at Harvard, and to promote — simultaneously — the greatest degree of openness and of inclusiveness within our institution. I have concentrated in this talk on issues of diversity, but I have not done so because of any lack of full commitment to academic and related forms of excellence. Diversity is in itself not an absolute value, and it cannot be dissociated from other values that are fundamental to a university: free inquiry, intensive research and scholarship, integrity of mind and thought, devoted teaching and passionate learning. At bottom, the goals of diversity and quality are deeply interrelated and need to be addressed together.

I have insisted that we must press forward with our experiment in diversity, essentially because I believe that our students must in the future live and function as effective leaders in an increasingly heterogeneous and internationalized world. Diversity is important, therefore, not as an abstract ideal, but as an essential educational goal related to the nature and texture of our actual lives. It enables us to create within the university an environment in which students can encounter – under propitious conditions – some of the most important issues and forms of knowledge critical to their own and to their world's future.

Next, if we are to preserve our commitment both to the highest quality, and to the greatest degree of openness, we must stand utterly firm on the issue of freedom of speech. We will not tolerate the direct harassment of individuals; but free expression in all the many forms that are honored in our society must be protected, and will be protected in this university.

Next, while reaffirming our determination to protect the right of free expression, we must also bear in mind the primary – but not exclusive – purposes of such freedom in a university setting. Our chief concern, after all, is the process of learning and the discovery of important truths. If we care about such learning, then we will want to understand not only abstract ideas, but also the people who articulate different ideas and perspectives. Consequently, the ways in which we talk with one another – the tone of voice we use, the extent to which we listen as well as speak – will often be as important as what we actually say. If we cannot be courteous, civil, respectful, and sympathetic in our behavior – as well as incisive, assertive, and sometimes contentious – then we will surely have failed to realize one of the most important purposes of an education in the liberal arts. If we cannot be fundamentally humane in the use of our intellect and knowledge – and in our relations with other people – then the full, unfettered exercise of all our precious freedoms will yield something immeasurably less rich and enlightening than it should.

Last of all, we will need a more determined commitment from administrators, faculty, and staff – as well as students – to invest time in getting to know one another better, in humanizing our daily lives, and in structuring more carefully the ways that we work together. We will have to learn to anticipate the complicated problems that can come from living together in a diverse university, to manage and respond to difficult issues more effectively, and to understand their implications more fully. We will need more conscious planning and coordination, informed by frank discussion.

Meanwhile, the simple but challenging task of thinking more considerately about our day-to-day human relationships is crucial. In E. M. Forster's novel *Howards End*, two phrases recur as leitmotifs throughout the book. The novel tells of very different kinds of people — from widely divergent backgrounds and social classes — who come into great conflict and then manage to reknit their lives because of the considerable pain they have endured together. The motto that characterizes the episodes of conflict in the novel is the repeated phrase "telegrams and anger": "anger" because the protagonists are given to furious outbursts when they shout but rarely listen; "telegrams" because they tend to vent their fury by firing off intemperate messages into the void.

The novel's other motto has to do with finding ways to bridge the chasms and gaps in our relationships with others. Doing so is far from easy, because the gaps can be enormous. Over and over again, people in the book are asked to take fuller account of the harsh problems that others are facing, to imagine themselves in one another's predicament in order to experience things from a completely different point of view.

For this to happen, however, much more is needed than mere intellect or reason. A special kind of human imagination and a sympathetic disposition toward others are essential. Some courage is also necessary, because imaginative leaps of this kind always involve yielding — if only provisionally — some part of our own ideas and feelings in order to see things as others do.

Forster continually urges his characters to reach out and make that imaginative leap: "Only connect," he tells them. The process will never be entirely smooth or complete. Hard lessons will have to be learned time and again. Disturbing incidents will recur, because our tendency to treat others insensitively is at least as strong as our desire to treat them with understanding and affection. But real learning can nonetheless deepen; free inquiry and free expression can flourish; and the fruits of diversity can be harvested, if those of us in our universities – and in our larger society – can make the essential imaginative leaps that alone will enable us to "connect."

1 James Madison, *The Federalist Papers, No. 10* (1787).

Sustaining an Inclusive Vision

President's Statement to the University Community
April 4, 1996

A S YOU MAY KNOW, a federal appeals court recently issued
a major decision concerning diversity and university admissions. In *Hopwood v. Texas,*[1] the U.S. Court of Appeals for the Fifth
Circuit ruled that the University of Texas may not use race as a
factor in its law school admissions, despite the university's asser-
tion of a compelling interest in fostering student diversity. Although the *Hopwood* decision does not apply directly to Harvard
(or other institutions outside the Fifth Circuit's jurisdiction,
which includes Texas, Mississippi, and Louisiana), I have received
a number of questions about its implications, and I want to offer
a brief comment.

I believe that student diversity contributes powerfully and
directly to the quality of education in colleges and universities.
For more than a century, Harvard has placed a very high value
on the creation of a residential community that brings together
people with a wide range of backgrounds and experiences. The
breadth of views and voices in our university challenges each of us
to think harder, to see the different sides of any issue, to confront

our own assumptions and preconceptions, and to develop the kind of understanding that can come only when we are willing to test our ideas and arguments in the company of people with very different perspectives. It also gives us the chance to come to know, understand, and respect a remarkable variety of men and women whom we might not otherwise have the opportunity to learn from or even to meet.

The educational importance of student diversity has informed our admissions process for many decades, as I suggested in my recent report to the Board of Overseers.[2] In choosing from among a pool of well-qualified applicants far larger than the number of available places, we take great care not to view people simply as the sum of their grades and test scores, however helpful those measures may be. We view applicants as individual human beings with a complex set of talents, qualities, interests, backgrounds, and experiences — all of which bear on their record of achievement and their future promise, as well as their capacity to contribute to the educational experience of their class as a whole.

Race and ethnicity are among the many factors that our admissions officers and faculty members may take into account as part of the selection process. Harvard's policies in this regard antedated the Civil Rights Act of 1964, and the United States Supreme Court's 1978 decision in the *Bakke* case. The federal appeals court in *Hopwood*, taking a position contrary to that of Justice Powell's pivotal opinion in *Bakke*, has now expressed the view that the consideration of race as a factor in the admissions process "is no more rational on its own terms" than considering "the physical size or blood type of applicants." I respectfully and strongly disagree. To my mind, race has historically been, and still remains, a significant factor that influences the process of growing up and living in the United States — one that helps to shape the outlooks, experiences, and opportunities of millions of people.

I do not believe we can solve the persistent dilemma of race or ethnicity in American life simply by stating that we live — or ought to live – in a society where these characteristics have ceased to be significant. Our hope for progress lies in gradually narrowing the real gaps that continue to exist among many people of different races. That can be done only by creating fruitful ways of bringing people together – ideally, by educating them together.

To say that factors such as race and ethnicity may be taken into account in the admissions process does not mean that they should be elevated above all others. It does not imply efforts to achieve specific numerical targets through quotas. It means that a person's race or ethnicity may be considered as a potential "plus" factor among the many considerations that go toward assessing each individual as a whole person: as someone whose "merit" cannot be measured purely in terms of numbers, as someone who has the potential to bring something distinctive and important to Harvard and to society.

Over many decades, this approach has made Harvard stronger both as an academic institution and as a human community. Progress has come slowly yet steadily – not without interruption, not without friction and strain, but with impressive results. Now is a time to reaffirm our commitment to building upon that progress, and to sustaining an inclusive vision of higher education that I believe has been essential to our university and to the nation.

1   *Hopwood v. State of Texas*, 78 F.3d 932 (5th Cir. 1996).
2   Neil L. Rudenstine, *Report of the President to the Board of Overseers, 1993–95.*

Persevering

Martin Luther King, Jr., Day Celebration
Smithsonian Institution, January 18, 1993

D R. MARTIN LUTHER KING wrote his last book, *Where Do We Go from Here: Chaos or Community?*, in 1967 — the year before he was assassinated. Every page shows Dr. King's humane vision: his sense of identification with people of every kind; his belief in the worth of every individual; his commitment to unify, not divide us; his ability to face the most difficult problems in a clear-sighted way, maintaining his determination while recognizing that any particular project might end in defeat or even disaster.

Many of the ideas that Dr. King expressed in the last year of his life speak to us even more forcefully now than before. I want to draw on a few of these ideas, as I discuss some of the difficulties faced by our country's educational system.

✦ ✦ ✦

By 1967, Dr. King had come to believe that achieving social justice — overcoming racism, ensuring equality of opportunity in all spheres — would depend a great deal on addressing the problems of America's cities.

Early in *Where Do We Go from Here?*, Dr. King mentioned the massive investment needed to address those problems. "The real cost lies ahead," he wrote – and he cited predictions that, without such an investment, the nation would face "further deterioration of the cities, increased antagonism between races and continued disorders in the streets."

A quarter century later, those words describe the state of many American cities all too well. And many of our urban schools, despite the efforts of teachers and other dedicated people, are in a discouraging state of disarray – in some cases, near collapse. Overcrowding is epidemic. Buildings are literally crumbling. In the City of New York alone, a recent report estimated that $24 billion is needed to repair the city's 1,053 school buildings – and to build enough space for the 300,000 *additional* students who will enter the system before the year 2000.

This situation is calamitous for everyone. But it takes a disproportionately harsh toll on the urban poor, including millions of minority students and their families. Another recent report, concerning a different urban school system, concluded that public education is failing completely under the double burden of poverty and racial isolation.

Consider the profile of a typical inner-city fifth-grade class described in a second report. Of twenty-three students, *five* were born to teenaged mothers; *eight* live in housing officially classified as inadequate; *nine* of the twenty-three have parents who are out of work; *fifteen* live with single parents; *fifteen* live below the poverty line.

The problems suggested by this profile – the joblessness, the housing, the family situations – affect and in many respects overshadow the problems of substandard school buildings, or the level of financial investment in the educational process itself.

In such an environment, schools can succeed only if they somehow overcome formidable odds. Dr. King saw all of this developing twenty-five years ago, and the urban situation he described has generally become worse, not better.

✦   ✦   ✦

Of course, not all the problems facing our system of education are caused by inner-city poverty or racial attitudes. Many are the result of broader cultural and other patterns in our society, and they have had an effect on virtually all young people, regardless of their background.

We know, for instance, that vast numbers of our students never learn to read or write or calculate beyond the fourth- or fifth-grade level, and even many high school graduates never advance beyond the eighth-grade level.

We also know that our students, nationwide, continue to do poorly on well-designed tests given to students from many different countries — especially in mathematics and science. We know that SAT verbal scores have fallen since 1967, and that science proficiency has declined among our seventeen-year-olds.

We know that fewer than half of the students who enroll in full-time four-year college programs directly out of high school manage to complete the requirements for a bachelor's degree within six years. And, according to a recent survey, only about one in three freshmen spends six hours or more per week on homework — a figure that puts studying roughly on a par with watching TV, and well behind such activities as exercise or sports, working at paid jobs, and socializing with friends.

By all sorts of measures, we are performing far below standard. Large numbers of our young people are now, in effect, educationally handicapped.

✦   ✦   ✦

This analysis leads me to another of Dr. King's basic convictions: many of our nation's most pressing problems affect all of us, and they ought to unite us in common cause. If we want to improve the conditions for education in our country — and certainly if we want to improve relations among people of different races and cultures — we can do so only if we work together collaboratively, recognizing our differences while remembering our very deep common bonds.

In *Where Do We Go from Here?*, Dr. King describes the long civil rights march across Mississippi in 1966 — the march on which James Meredith was shot. After the shooting, some leaders argued that whites should be discouraged from participating further in the march. Some felt that whites had begun to exercise disproportionate influence over the civil rights movement and that blacks needed to regroup among themselves, so they could retain control over their own most important affairs.

Dr. King yielded to no one in his determination to create a stronger sense of group identity and maintain leadership among blacks. But when it came to dealing with the largest issues facing America, he believed that neither blacks nor whites — nor any other group — could hope to succeed alone. Real progress would require something more complicated than separatism, on the one hand, or a simple melting away of important individual or group differences, on the other.

Summing up the debate on the Mississippi march, he wrote:

> [T]he answer ... was not to give up, not to conclude that blacks must work [only] with blacks in order for Negroes to gain a sense of their own meaning. The answer was only to be found in persistent trying, perpetual experimentation, persevering togetherness.
>
> Like life, racial understanding is not something that we find but something that we must create.... [T]he ability of Negroes and whites to work together, to understand each other, will not be found ready made; it must be created by the fact of contact.[1]

These words offer no easy remedies. Dr. King describes the dilemma, and he relies finally on his own strong faith, declaring that the only answer to racial or ethnic conflict will be found in "persistent trying, perpetual experimentation, persevering togetherness." Progress, as he says, will have to be "created" with great effort from the hard "fact of contact."

His choice of words — persistent... perpetual... persevering... trying... experimentation... creation... contact... — suggests that there will be no obvious end to this process, and that we must press forward even if there are moments when we seem to be losing ground. Indeed, as we look around the world today, "the fact of contact" among people of different races and cultures appears to be generating at least as much conflict as understanding. For every act of liberation we have witnessed in the last few years, every stride toward freedom, every increase in the measure of human dignity, we can find a contrasting example of violent — even barbarous — religious, ethnic, nationalist, or racial strife. Many people in our world — perhaps a great majority — appear to have no special interest in learning to live with others who are different from themselves; often, it seems, they would rather be rid of them.

In America, and not least in our schools and colleges, many of the signs are also deeply troubling. We hear and read about more acts of racial harassment and more instances of hateful speech. According to one study, attitudes on racial issues have recently tended to "harden" — to become less tolerant, not more — as many students pass through college. A large proportion of students now regard race relations on their campuses as "generally bad." And we know that on some campuses there have been severe racial crises in the last few years — serious enough to bring entire institutions to a standstill.

✦   ✦   ✦

Surveying the landscape of 1967, Martin Luther King might well have lost heart or drifted into cynicism. Instead, he reaffirmed his principles and framed proposals for change. As we think about our problems today, especially in the field of education, we should ask how to answer Dr. King's question for ourselves: Where do we go from here? Are there steps we can take to address the problems that confront us? What realistic alternatives are open?

First, although no single, all-encompassing solution is likely to emerge — at least not soon — we must still keep in mind that the problems of the schools cannot be separated from those of our families, our communities, our cities, and our towns, or from the state of our national economy. This is no less true in 1993 than in 1967: without the kind of major investment in our cities and in our more general human environment that Dr. King called for in his last book, we will inevitably face staggering problems as we try to improve the schools themselves.

An added difficulty, of course, is that our nation's available resources at this moment are so much scarcer now than twenty-five years ago. We also have less confidence in our ability to produce long-term structural changes, changes that will actually create healthy economic conditions, better opportunities for employment, and decent housing and neighborhoods where people have some genuine sense of ownership and pride. Yet until some significant renewal of this kind takes place, many of our public schools and whole districts will continue to function under immense pressure, pressure that intensifies as we ask the schools to provide more of the services, and to solve more of the problems, that are fundamentally the responsibility of whole communities and the larger society.

In the meantime, what other actions can we take? Let me suggest two.

First, the last decade has shown that the country as a whole has a strong and continuing interest in the predicament of our public schools. There has been more experimentation, more investment of private funds, and more volunteer time committed to the problems of the schools than anyone might have dared to imagine fifteen or twenty years ago.

But while we have to continue to experiment and be receptive to new ideas, the time clearly has come to take stock, and to pay much more attention to those programs and approaches that have begun to yield good results. For example, if the effort to rebuild the school system of an entire state shows evidence of success — as in Kentucky, or South Carolina — then we must study such situations in detail, to see which elements are critical and are making a difference.

In other words, this is the moment to identify and capture not every latest new idea, but the best ideas that are being tested and carefully evaluated. We need to adopt a more systematic and long-term approach, investing in programs that are working, trying to understand the ways in which lasting results can be achieved, and building as much as possible on what we have already begun to learn. And we need to support good programs over a period of many years, so that they have time to develop and reach maturity.

Second, at the level of the individual school or district, we have to help teachers, principals, and superintendents perform an almost impossible balancing act.

To begin with, there is the day-to-day work with students who often do not want to be in school at all. Many teachers rise to the challenge. But the work is draining and exhausting, with relatively few visible triumphs and only modest material rewards. Nothing less than excellent leadership from principals and super-intendents can help to motivate and strengthen the work of teachers and students, creating schools that are communities rather than simply facilities.

Then there is the even harder — and perhaps the most impor-tant — challenge. Our greatest educational problem is not that our schoolchildren fail to master basic skills, skills that are often the product of memorization and routine. Whatever shortcomings we may have on that score, they are far overshadowed by the fact that we are not managing to teach our students how to analyze new situations and problems, how to use facts as evidence in order to produce logical and persuasive arguments, how to take different points of view into account rather than simply express-ing personal opinions without ever examining them.

All the tests show that the point at which our students fail is just that point where they must write — not simply a sentence or two, but a coherent paragraph or essay — or where they have to think through a "word problem" in mathematics. These are the moments when active learning and the real use of the mind begin. Yet it is just at these moments that so many of our students falter.

We need to find more effective ways of teaching — using much more interesting and stimulating curricular materials, using real books, but also drawing on the help that interactive technology can offer. Our communities and schools need to convey the message that academic achievement is absolutely vital: it certainly is not the only priority, but it must be the highest priority of any school. We have to begin with the premise that even our youngest children are already very skillful as well as talented, and they have managed to master extremely complicated processes — such as speaking and understanding a language — even before they arrive at school.

If we do that — if we take our children and their abilities very seriously from the earliest stage — there will be a far greater chance that they, in turn, will begin to take themselves seriously and to strive for real achievement. Unless they know that we have confidence in them and are willing to devote time and attention to them, it will be very hard for them to have the kind of confidence in themselves that is absolutely critical.

This will not happen easily. Students and their teachers face situations every day that are discouraging enough to demolish months of patient work and progress. But I see no other way, except to move ahead with the assumptions and attitudes that I have just tried to describe. In this effort, colleges and universities can help, by building cooperative programs with schools and communities. Corporations and foundations — as well as others — must continue the work they are already doing. Everyone will have to be prepared for setbacks, and for a very long voyage. But unless we stay the course and aim high — and find ways to help our students to aim equally high — there will be no real progress.

1 Martin Luther King, Jr., *Where Do We Go from Here: Chaos or Community?* (New York: Harper & Row, 1967), 28.

University Debate and
Freedom of Speech

An Open Statement to the Harvard Community
November 14, 1991

During the past few days, there have been reports of controversial incidents related to the issue of sexual orientation. I would like to state as clearly as possible my own views on the broad range of concerns raised by these incidents:

First, actions that are intimidating and are directed at specific individuals are repugnant and intolerable. The recent incident (as reported in the *Crimson*) involving the defacement of the door of a student's room with a homophobic epithet – or similar vandalism or attacks directed at any member of the University – are not only a violation of University regulations; they are cowardly and contemptible.

Second, actions that are clearly in the realm of freedom of expression and speech, that offer opinions or statements in a more general way, must be protected, even if they are offensive to some members of the community. If we find certain statements offensive, then we can respond in ways that are appropriate to a university. Some people may simply choose to ignore such views. Others may wish to debate them, offer counter-opinions, or reply with parody, wit, or ridicule. To attempt to censor such speech, however, would be totally inappropriate.

Finally, debate on controversial issues is inevitable and essential. I would hope, however, that all members of the community will continue to bear in mind the fundamental purposes of the University: that we are here to evaluate ideas and ask new questions, but that our basic goal should be to do so in a way that actually advances the cause of learning, of new knowledge, and of understanding.

It is not difficult to caricature, parody, or in a general way disparage the views of others. Indeed, sometimes — as brilliant satirists have shown us — this can be very healthy, even necessary, and can sharpen our vision of what is true. There is no question of our remaining open to a variety of forms of expression and debate. At the same time, we are also likely to serve one another best if we remember that — as members of a single university community — civil discourse, thoughtful arguments based on informed views, genuine scholarship, and careful as well as imaginative expression are at the very heart of our work as students, teachers, scholars, and staff members.

It will not always be obvious how to reconcile the twin goals of guarding genuinely free expression while also attempting to build a community free of intimidation and harassment, based on a respect for individuals as well as a desire to learn from others. We will always have the problem of resolving difficult cases that are ambiguous or unclear.

There is no simple solution to these dilemmas or to the tensions inherent in them. But a university by its nature should be prepared to address such complexity, to live with it, and to deal with it in ways that are constructive and humane. That will happen only if individuals and groups who disagree with one another are willing to discuss their differences candidly in the hope of achieving deeper mutual understanding and a shared sense of being members of a university that has powerful common values and goals.

Access and Affordability:
A Commitment to Need-Based
Financial Aid

Excerpts from Testimony to the National Commission on the Cost of Higher Education, November 7, 1997

ALLOW ME TO TRY to address, directly, the question that led to the convening of this Commission: how do we ensure that college education remains accessible and affordable to students from across the economic spectrum?

I want to talk about Harvard's approach, not because it represents some sort of platonic ideal, or a model that is workable for all institutions of higher education — but because it is one model, and one that illustrates a systematic effort to address a serious problem.

Let me begin with the number that all too often serves as not just the beginning, but the end, of discussions about college access. What might be called our comprehensive fee — the total of tuition, room, board, and other charges — is now around $30,000 a year. It is not quite the highest in the nation, but it is still very steep. Yet, based on our estimates, it is still only about two-thirds of what it actually costs to provide our students with an undergraduate education in a residential setting. The remaining third is underwritten largely by endowment and annual gifts. In this sense, all of our undergraduates – even those who pay the full comprehensive fee – receive a significant subsidy or implicit scholarship.

As a private college and university committed to a very broad set of programs in education and research, Harvard has for many decades had high fees which, if viewed in isolation, would place a Harvard education well beyond the reach of the great majority of students and families in the United States. But there is, of course, more to the story. Back in 1854, Harvard's President Walker summarized the problem and the solution very succinctly: "There is no objection," he said, "which weighs so heavily against an education in Cambridge as the expense; and the only practicable way of reducing it would seem to be by the institution of scholarships."

As this suggests, Harvard's approach to college access has long been rooted in a simple insight: given that it is inherently expensive to provide an excellent residential college education, and given that a great many families are not able to afford the full price, financial aid based on need is the most direct, effective, cost-effective, and economically practicable way to reduce the net cost of college for many students – while also maintaining a steady flow of tuition revenue from those students whose families can afford to pay the total sum.

The modern version of this philosophy has been with us for several decades now. We have made it a cardinal principle that students should be considered for admission without regard to their financial need. We want our doors to be open to the most able and promising students – rich, poor, or in between.

That's only half the principle. The other half – the one that converts ideal into reality – is that students who are admitted, and who choose to come to Harvard, are provided with a package of financial aid that is sufficient to enable them to attend.

We advertise the nature of this program widely, and we recruit students vigorously. As a result, we are able to attract a wide range of applicants from literally all income groups, and from an enormous variety of backgrounds. The number of applicants to our first-year class has grown, over the past five or six years, from 12,000 to more than 16,500 — essentially ten applicants for every place in the class — and over three-quarters of the students who are offered admission choose to enroll.

Our commitment to need-based aid is expensive. Two-thirds of our undergraduates receive some form of financial aid, and they will together receive some $80 million in aid this year — in the form of scholarships, loans, and work-study jobs. More than half of that aid — $42 million — takes the form of scholarships; and nearly nine out of every ten of those scholarship dollars come from our institutional funds.

Almost half of all our undergraduates qualify for scholarship grants, averaging $14,000. Added to that are a loan and a job that cover another $6,500. That combined total — around $20,500 — is roughly two-thirds of our full comprehensive fee. In other words, for about half of our students, the average amount remaining to be paid, on a current basis, for a year at Harvard College is roughly $9,500.

I want to emphasize that the figures I've given are averages: some students receive over $20,500; others receive less, depending on their own level of need. And the aid reaches students from a very broad band of family incomes. Our scholarship students include, for example, some 375 students whose family incomes are less than $20,000 a year, as well as some 250 whose family incomes are greater than $120,000 a year; the others fall between.

Over time, as our comprehensive fee has steadily increased, we have tried to make sure that the families of our scholarship students not be asked to bear an increasing share of the students' budgets. In 1980–81, for instance, the typical parental contribution for students on scholarship was 26 percent of the total student budget. Seventeen years later, the figure is still 26 percent.

Meanwhile, the portion of the total student budget covered by scholarship funds has grown, on average, from 43 percent to 49 percent.

We have also tried, by investing heavily in need-based scholarships, to avoid leaving our students with huge debts when they graduate. In our most recent graduating class, almost half our seniors managed to leave Harvard without any outstanding student loan debt at all. And only 8 percent of all our seniors graduated with debt burdens of more than $20,000.

In fact, as the real value of federal scholarship grants has eroded in recent years, and as the balance of federal aid has shifted strongly in the direction of loans, colleges and universities have reached deeper into their own funds to provide scholarship aid. At Harvard, while tuitions have continued to rise faster than inflation, our own undergraduate scholarship budget has risen at a significantly faster rate than tuitions: more than twice as fast, when measured in constant 1997 dollars over the last decade.

Having said all this, I do not at all underestimate the severe problems and real anxieties faced by many students and families struggling to pay for college. And I do not propose that strong need-based aid is the be-all and end-all of an effective approach. We need to keep up the effort to moderate the growth of tuition and fees, as we have been doing. At Harvard, we have lowered the rate of tuition growth each of the last five years. The increase from last year to this — 4.1 percent — was the lowest in percentage terms since 1969. Our intention is to continue this trend, although it will require even more intensive efforts to raise endowment and other sources of revenue, to budget systematically, to control our expense growth, and to make sensible cuts and economies that do not compromise the fundamental quality of our academic programs. It will also require some help from the national economy.

All in all, however, we need to be realistic in our expectations. Whatever the exact percentage increase in next year's tuition and fees, the full price of attending Harvard will still be high – higher than a great many students and families can reach on their own. We will be left to do what I believe it is absolutely essential for us to do: reaffirm and redouble our commitment to a program of need-blind admissions and strong need-based student aid.

Some Essential Institutional Values

Divinity School Convocation Address
September 23, 1992

IN THIS 175th anniversary year of the Divinity School, there is a wonderful coincidence between the commemorative events and the present state of the school we are celebrating. One of Great Britain's more notable but also dyspeptic public figures was once asked what he thought of the established Church, and he said in reply something that might, alas, also apply to a good many schools of divinity: "The great point about the Church," he stated, is that "if you leave *it* alone, it will leave *you* alone." But in Harvard's case, happily, we have a divinity school that, in the most collegial way possible, does not leave us alone. It has clear purpose. It has its own voice. It has a presence — as well as the will to make that presence an active part of the University as a whole. As we celebrate this 175th anniversary, we can above all celebrate this very moment in the life of the School.

While I have been asked to offer an address, I am obviously not equipped by training or by natural genius to speak with the tongues of either theologians or members of the ministry. We must all settle, therefore, for something modest. Recognizing my ignorance, I have nonetheless decided to throw caution to the wind, and *not* speak to you on a subject (such as higher education, or even the present state of literature and the arts) about which I might possibly know as much as my audience.

I want to focus on a few questions or dilemmas that are very much on my mind, and that I believe the members of the Divinity School are in a better position to elucidate than I. Defining the questions is difficult, and can often lead to misunderstanding, but I shall attempt to share some of my thoughts.

Well before the political conventions of this summer, I had begun to wonder about the meaning of the term "values," partly in response to the questions of a close friend who has for the past two years been studying the issue of values in relationship to universities: Which values are most important to a university? Which values are *essential* to such institutions? If we believe in certain institutional values, how do we go about the process of defining, articulating, teaching, and adhering to them?

As I have groped for clarity and definition in this area, I have felt the need to know how (if at all) we should distinguish among the three terms "values," "morals," and "ethics." It seems to me that many people have begun to use them almost interchangeably, and that gives me pause.

"Morals" and "ethics" are obviously very close to one another, but there are important contexts where one term is clearly more appropriate than the other: for example, we speak intelligently about "professional ethics" or "practical ethics," but it is not at all clear that we could so intelligibly talk about "professional morals" or "practical morals."

But whatever differences there may be between the two terms "morals" and "ethics," it is nonetheless clear that both of them are deeply rooted in conceptions of conduct, action, and choice: human behavior that is measured against established standards or codes in a way that leads toward the making of judgments. A given action may be morally or ethically "right" or "wrong" — or not altogether one or the other. But however complicated our judgments or our standards, we will find it very difficult to make any sense of the words "morals" and "ethics" without ultimately turning to considerations of conduct and the judgments that we bring to bear upon conduct.

Values are obviously something rather different. They are intertwined with ideas of estimating and judging, but their relationship to conduct, action, and choice is much more oblique. One of the interesting points about the term "values" is that it is not easy to discover when it began to be used to convey anything like its present set of meanings. I found the *Oxford English Dictionary* only moderately useful on this subject. For most of its history, the word seems to have been used in the singular more than the plural, and its meaning has been closely associated with the tangible or convertible. The value of something was estimable in fairly precise ways: it could be weighed, or measured, or bargained about. "Value" and "values" were not floating out there as amorphous, cloud-like, and elusive quiddities – full of significance, but marvelously ambiguous; clear to the initiated, but often puzzling to those who are more naïve or perhaps simply humble.

My purpose is not to suggest that values, as we now use the word, are not extremely important. I only want to stress that the term itself (including its history), and the qualities or activities or objects that we refer to when we use the term, are in very serious need of renewed discussion, clarification, and more careful analysis than they are now receiving. As I try to participate in this process, I will share with you some untested intuitions and impressions, in the expectation that they will soon be corrected and wither in the face of superior analyses.

First, it seems plausible to me that the meaning of the word "values" has broadened, becoming more inclusive, as a result of at least two important developments that are characteristic of contemporary society. The first is the gradual but steady recognition that the concept of value or worth – of the actions, objects, or ways of living which are judged to be admirable or valuable because they have an internal consistency, coherence, and integrity of their own — has become more complex as our consciousness of the world's variety and its pluralist nature has increased.

In effect, we are all anthropologists now. We know far more about the species of humankind in all its innumerable cultural manifestations, and we have come more and more to understand and appreciate the achievements (in art, in cosmology, in religion and other spheres) of people who are very different from one another. It is not surprising, under these conditions, that we should see a greater multiplicity of "values" — varieties of worth — in our universe, and that the word itself is increasingly useful because it allows us to acknowledge (and to some degree manage) this multiplicity. In addition, to the extent that there has been any recent shift away from the term "morals" to "values" (or even to "ethics"), that change may well reflect the increasing difficulty or discomfort which many people encounter when they attempt to make judgments in this sphere. There was a time when people talked quite frequently — if only somewhat loosely — about "the work ethic." Many are now much more likely to talk about the "value" of work — or, perhaps more revealingly, the value of leisure, or even leisure values. We talk very naturally about aesthetic values, community values, and cultural values: the list could be lengthened considerably. We also talk, without apparent strain, about *moral* values, and that in itself implies that we make a natural distinction between morals and values. In short, using the word "values" is one way that we can legitimately, but also ambiguously, indicate respect for aspects of human life and conduct without having to rely on categories that relate to choice and judgment — to the language of morals.

My second general impression about "values" relates closely to the first. Even before this summer's [1992] Democratic and Republican conventions, it was becoming clear that the term was entering more and more into the realm of political — as well as more general public – discourse. As this occurred, the word was not surprisingly being used to signal differences as well as commonalities, to highlight distinctions and preferences rather than multiplicity and inclusiveness. This is perhaps a predictable antiphonal development to the movement I described earlier. As our concepts of worth and value expand, becoming more complex and inclusive, we should not be startled to find a simultaneous effort within our society (and within ourselves) to discover and isolate that special set of values which are most definitively "ours." We seek, in some sense, our own identifying and distinguishing special qualities. This process can produce greater stridency, a tendency on the part of many individuals and groups to seek firmer and perhaps narrower definitions of identity – or, as we might say in religious terms, more fundamental or "fundamentalist" conceptions of belief and behavior. Under such circumstances, different sets of values can quickly begin to collide quite visibly – whether the issue is abortion, or the nature of the family, or questions related to the environment, or the treatment of people from ethnic, racial, or religious communities that are different from one's own.

Political discourse can reflect such developments and collisions in many ways. The approach of the moment does seem to be one that tries to find language – the language of values – which is sufficiently general and ambiguous to have a quite wide appeal, but sufficiently decodable to reassure particular groups and individuals. Those in the political arena who have recently tried to move from this strategy to one that uses the language of morals and moral judgments more openly – on questions such as "nontraditional" families, sexual orientation, or abortion – have found themselves more isolated (even repudiated) than they appear to have expected.

My last general observation on the topic of values can be stated more briefly. It is no secret that, over the course of the last two to three decades, we have suffered a widespread loss of public confidence in many of the central institutions of our society: government, businesses, many religious institutions, the media, and educational institutions, to name only a few. It is not my intention to try to explain this shift, but rather to focus on one of its by-products: the fact that, increasingly, our society has a less and less distinct view of the legitimate distinctions we can and should make about the appropriate role and mission of different kinds of institutions. Of course we maintain, at some level, a reasonable sense of how governments differ from corporations, or corporations from churches, or churches from universities. But there has been more blurring of the lines: less clarity about real differences, and some tendency to press many institutions to play a broader and more inclusive public, if not political, role.

In my view, aspects of this development have been very healthy. That major institutions should not be so specialized and so self-enclosed that they are isolated from the general affairs of life is something that most of us would affirm with conviction. But I suspect that the hazards in the direction of more self-enclosure are, at this moment, relatively minimal, as compared to the ambiguities and potential problems that can result from the opposite tendency.

There was a time, for instance, when the purposes of a college or university could be stated fairly succinctly — in terms of academic and personal education, as well as research and the creation of new knowledge. Major universities have, in addition, always been connected to the larger society in more direct ways: by preparing people for the professions, by doing applied as well as basic research to help solve pressing problems, and by providing advice and technical assistance on a wide range of matters.

But the number and range of interactions between the university and the wider world have increased enormously over the years, and so has the expectation that the university should be more directly involved in a growing number of external activities and relationships. What we might call the explicit public role of the university is part of our agenda in a new way. This is partly because we ourselves are more conscious of this aspect of our mission, and partly because society itself sees us more and more through this lens: viewing us, perhaps increasingly, in ways that it views other institutions (whether we think in terms of government regulation, or "consumer" attitudes, or the desire for certain "products").

This brings us full circle to my initial question of values in the context of the university and its purposes. At least some of the current tendency to blur distinctions among institutions might be mitigated if those of us in the university attempted to articulate our primary "functions" more precisely — the activities we simply must engage in, and the activities in which we have a special capacity to excel. In addition, we must try to be clearer about the essential conditions — the shared understandings, as well as guarantees and protections concerning matters such as free inquiry and free expression — that are necessary if we are to carry out our purposes. In the process, we will inevitably be defining our central values, and discovering those points of tension where our own core values may have the potential to conflict with one another.

The effort is not to "solve" these issues, but to clarify them, so that we can think and act more intelligibly, more in concert, with a clearer sense of what we are and what we aspire to be. This is critical, not only for ourselves, but for our continuing conversation with other institutions, groups, and individuals in our society — indeed, throughout the world. I know of no school that is better situated than yours to help us think through these difficult matters, and I look forward to further conversations in the months and years ahead.

THE ARTS AND HUMANITIES

The Challenging Nature
of the Humanities

Commencement Day Address
June 4, 1998

I WANT TO OFFER some thoughts on the challenging nature of the humanities, on their strong links to other fields of learning, and on why they are essential, not only to any serious definition of education, but also to the health of society as a whole.

The humanities — together with the arts — are obviously not very tidy. They include all the known religions and philosophies, as well as languages, literatures, histories, and cultures, with their varieties of music, theater, dance, and visual arts. The kind of knowledge they offer us is not susceptible to elegant proofs, such as we find in mathematics; or to parsimonious theories together with verifiable data; or anything as neat as an econometric model or a rational-choice decision-making tree; or even much in the way of game theory.

Instead, the humanities and the arts thrive on the pattern, texture, and flux of experience, where very little is provable or predictable. They are less abstract in what they consider to be knowledge than either the sciences or the social sciences. They prefer the audible, tangible, visual, and palpable. When we are reading *Anna Karenina* or *Dubliners*; when we are watching *Othello* or *Riders to the Sea*; when we are wrestling with Thucydides, or reciting Keats, Yeats, or Seamus Heaney, we know that we are about as close to the vital signs of human experience as any representation is likely to take us.

Obviously, there are exceptions. The humanities and arts have their own special forms of abstraction – in philosophy and music, for example. And we know only too well that history, art history, literary history, and theory can all become as vivisectional and obscurantist as we care to make them.

Nonetheless, there is nearly always in humanistic and artistic fields a strong pull that ultimately leads us back to an original source – a particular novel, painting, poem, or string quartet; or a great philosophical, historical, or religious text that can dramatize and reimagine life in ways that expand our vision and deepen our sense of what is possible, delightful, terrible, or impenetrable: in short, something that can enlighten us, move us, and genuinely educate us.

What does it mean to learn – or to gain knowledge – in this way?

The purpose is not so much closure along a single line of inquiry, as we might find in the sciences. The search, instead, is for illuminations that are hard-won because they can be discovered only in the very midst of life, with all its vicissitudes. If we are fortunate and alert, we may gradually learn how to see more clearly the nature and possible meaning of situations and events; to be better attuned to the nuances, inflections, and character of other human beings; to weigh values with more precision; to judge on the basis of increasingly fine distinctions; and perhaps to become more effective, generous, and wise in our actions.

As we think about these special characteristics of the humanities, however, we also soon discover that it is extremely difficult to draw a convincing or firm line between these particular fields and those of the social and natural sciences. It is not possible, for instance, to read very far into major humanistic texts – such as the works of Aristotle, or Plato's *Republic* – without being thrust into questions about political theory and practice; the role of law in human societies; civic as compared to moral obligations; physics as well as metaphysics; economics, cosmology, and even the nature of plants and animals. Great humanistic texts, in other words, lead us very quickly into other realms of knowledge; and conversely, great scientific work, if we really want to understand it, will lead us straight back into the domain of the humanities and the arts.

The great Harvard evolutionary biologist Ernst Mayr has recently reminded us of this point, suggesting – for example – that the biological sciences depend upon constructing and interpreting important concepts that bring them into close touch with major humanistic ideas, as well as with several fields in the social sciences. Biologists need to define and try to explain, for instance, complex processes such as development, cognition, and evolution, as well as communication, learning, "territoriality," and even altruism. All of these concepts connect many forms of animal life with human life – and they all lie as much in the sphere of the humanities as of the natural or social sciences. In fact, without significant contributions from the humanities, the hard task of clarifying, examining, and refining the meaning of these concepts cannot be carried out persuasively. Precisely the same point holds, of course, for concepts closely associated with the sciences themselves: "cause and effect," "determined behavior," and even time, space, or dimension.

The traffic must move in both directions. The humanities are essential to science and social science; at the same time, science and social science have obviously had a significant impact on humanistic thinking, especially since the seventeenth century, and nowhere more dramatically than in the case of Charles Darwin. His ideas, as we know, had a profound effect on established religious beliefs, on metaphysics and philosophy of mind, and (by extension) on all the factors that we take into account whenever we think about the various perceptions, drives, motives, and values — as well as the powers of reason, imagination, and memory — that make up our idea of the Self, what it means to have a Self, or to be a Self. In short, although all knowledge may not constitute a unity, there is a very strong case to be made for its "interconnectedness," a different — but far from trivial — matter.

This interconnectedness means that the humanities cannot, in effect, be successfully subjected to any paradigm of knowledge imported from either science or social science — any more than the reverse would be acceptable. When it comes to central questions about the nature and meaning of human life, neither the humanities, the sciences, nor the social sciences can be sovereign.

These essential linkages among these broad fields — the ways that they need each other and must work together — are strikingly apparent in Harvard's interfaculty program called "Mind, Brain, and Behavior," which cuts across nearly all the schools and departments of the University, bringing the insights of neuroscientists and biologists into direct contact with those of cognitive psychologists and of scholars in law, business, government, religion, literature, philosophy, and other fields.

Recent developments in magnetic resonance imaging and rapid advances in other technologies now allow scientists to observe and map neural activity in the brain with amazing accuracy, explaining much about how neurons transmit their signals and how the signals pass from one cell to another. But neuroscience cannot, on its own, explain how chemical signals somehow turn into human emotions, thoughts, and feelings — or how they lead to self-conscious action and behavior, in all their complexity. Above all, neuroscience cannot, on its own, provide an understanding of the concept of "mind" with its "mental functions" — functions that are obviously distinct from the chemistry, physics, and biology that make up that apparatus which we call "the brain."

The realm of the mind is, in fact, exactly the place where the humanities and the arts become crucial and indispensable. We cannot demonstrate exactly what a "mind" is because we can neither observe it nor account for it in strictly scientific terms. But we know that only a "mind" has consciousness, which in turn allows us to have a sense of Self, with its continuous identity and history, its capacity to think and arrive at conclusions, to make free choices, and to develop *culturally* — long after the time when the brain has ceased, in any significant way, to evolve *biologically.*

It is also in this region of the mind — of consciousness, of reflection in the light of experience, of choice and deliberate action — that "values" are created. Whenever we reach a decision, or make a reasoned judgment, we do not express a mere preference: we create a value. And the humanities and arts are those fields which are most deeply and continuously engaged with probing, dramatizing, and clarifying values.

To do this, they must draw not only on specific fields of knowledge but also on human experience: on encounters with the actual flux of life, where the mind attempts to make sense of what it is perceiving, of what meaning and value a particular incident or situation may have.

Henry James, in his great essay "The Art of Fiction," captured in a very few words what it means to learn from — and to write from — experience that has been sifted and evaluated until it begins to take on meanings:

What kind of experience is intended, and where does it begin and end? Experience is never limited, and it is never complete; it is an immense sensibility, a kind of huge spider-web of the finest silken threads suspended in the chamber of consciousness, and catching every airborne particle in its tissue. It is the very atmosphere of the mind; and when the mind is imaginative… it takes to itself the faintest hints of life, it converts the very pulses of the air into reve-lations.[1]

When we talk about the humanities and the arts, among the things we surely have in mind are the enlarged capacities or powers that these fields can help us to develop, and that can make it possible for us to interpret experience with greater insight. For James, the important capacities were a constantly cultivated and finely tuned sensibility; a heightened consciousness, always on the alert; and an imaginative mind with its own "atmosphere" — its own accumulated store of impressions and perceptions that have been filtered, named, and somehow organized so that new encounters with even small particles of experience can be registered so precisely that they yield "revelations" of significant meaning, so long as we are awake enough to see them and "convert" them.

Whether we believe that this is how an imaginative and powerful mind actually works is not so much the point. What *does* matter is that the passage can hardly help but illuminate something important about the quality of our interior life, as we experience it; about how consciousness can be tuned and even mobilized; about how we can learn enough to be prepared for revelations, however small or large, when they come. In short, the passage compels us to envisage the mind — and how it works — in new ways.

In closing, I want to touch very briefly on one more critical role of the humanities: that is, the fundamental contribution that the humanities can and must make to the health of democratic societies and to international cooperation in the world today.

If the humanities and the arts are the realm where experience is encountered directly and dramatized, as well as filtered and evaluated, and where values are clarified and modified under the pressures of existence, we should remember that they are also the spheres in which different values can collide or clash: sometimes amicably, sometimes acrimoniously, and often tragically.

We do not have to describe particular examples in order to remember the nationalistic, religious, racial, ethnic, and social conflicts of this century — some of which have now been quieted, while others rage even as we speak. Here, the humanities can help, not so much by stressing the importance of strong convictions and commitments as by reminding us of our limitations and fallibility. They can help us to cultivate a respect for the more modest but vital values of tolerance, restraint, compromise, and a readiness to entertain the possibility that we may often be wrong.

The late Isaiah Berlin, in his wonderful book *The Crooked Timber of Humanity*, held out the hope that these inevitable clashes and collisions of value "even if they cannot be avoided, can be softened."

> *The first public obligation is to avoid extremes of suffering. Revolutions, wars, assassinations, extreme measures may in desperate situations be required. But history teaches us that their consequences are seldom what is anticipated; there is no guarantee, not even, at times, a high enough probability, that such acts will lead to improvement.... So we must engage in what are called trade-offs — rules, values, principles must yield to each other in varying degrees in specific situations.... The best that can be done, as a general rule, is to maintain a precarious equilibrium that will prevent the occurrence of desperate situations, of intolerable choices — that is the first requirement for a decent society....*[2]

Isaiah Berlin was a humanist first, and a philosopher second: he understood that important values are given meaning and expression by the force of strong convictions. But he also knew that strong convictions, if carried forward with unmitigated ferocity, can also destroy human values.

There is, alas, no easy way to inject such wisdom into the world at large. But it is just such wisdom, grounded in a respect for human rights and human values, that the humanities and arts can offer. This wisdom may or may not prevail, but without great and humane minds to articulate such a vision, we will have no chance at all of achieving our deepest purposes.

1   Henry James, "The Art of Fiction," in *Partial Portraits* (1888; reprint, Ann Arbor: University of Michigan Press, 1970), 388.
2   Isaiah Berlin, *The Crooked Timber of Humanity* (New York: Vintage Books, 1992), 17–18.

A Perpetual Visual Motion Machine

The 100th Anniversary of the Fogg Museum
November 3, 1995

T HE GIFT that made the Fogg Museum a reality came without any warning or expectation. It floated down upon Harvard, in 1891, as a bequest from Mrs. Elizabeth Perkins Fogg.

Neither Mrs. Fogg nor her late husband had any direct affilia-
tion with Harvard. The benefactor provided $200,000 to con-
struct a building "for the collection and exhibition of works of
art of every description, and for education and enlightenment of
the people."

Nothing more elaborate than that. No restrictions on the deed
of gift. No hint as to how this ambitious goal should be achieved.
And certainly no limits placed on the aspirations of either the
Museum or the multitudinous people who might come to seek
enlightenment.

Surprisingly, the $200,000 actually proved enough to engage
the services of one of America's best-known architects – Richard
Morris Hunt – and to pay the full costs of Mr. Hunt's rectangular
beaux arts marble neoclassical boxlike edifice, which, to judge
from old photographs, looked uncomfortably compact, and in-
flexibly travertine.

Indeed, within a very few years, our first director – Edward Forbes – complained that the new museum was "a building with a lecture hall in which you could not hear, a gallery in which you could not see, working rooms in which you could not work, and a roof that leaked" – helpful neither to the Museum's collection of paintings and photographs, nor (worse yet) to its water-soluble plaster casts.

No matter. The collections grew, works of every conceivable description arrived, and the "people" – as Mrs. Fogg had hoped – were apparently educated and enlightened. Then, in 1924, Harvard undertook a massive fund-raising campaign. The University's goal was to raise the unprecedented sum of $10 million. Of that total, $1 million was designated for the Fogg: Mr. Hunt's marble mausoleum was slated for discreet demolition, and a new Italianate structure was designed to take the place of the existing Roman rectangle.

The $1 million was promptly raised. A new and pleasant palazzo appeared on Quincy Street and was widely applauded. The Fogg as we know it now – more or less – settled in comfortably for the next several centuries.

We are familiar with much of the history that has unfolded since that time: the stream of gifts of stunning objects; the development of the library and conservation center; the continued growth of the Art Department – from our one lone Norton Professor of a century ago; and most of all, the constant attention to Mrs. Fogg's original vision of education in all its forms, through the presentation and use of the collections – in the galleries, in special exhibitions, in relation to teaching and advanced research and students' independent work, and so much else.

All of which is to say that the Fogg is in some respects not strictly a museum at all. It is a vivacious university center: a center for the mind and heart and eye; for intellect, taste, and imagination; for students, faculty, conservators, librarians, professionals, amateurs, visitors, and pilgrims of every kind. It is a nerve center that energizes and helps to organize many of the ways that we encounter and reflect about art in a great university devoted to learning, and also to life.

Let me say a few words about how some of this learning actually takes place — and how it can affect our lives.

I have tried to remember a few of my own first visits to the Fogg, and what I learned from them. They began thirty-five years ago, when I arrived at Harvard as a graduate student in English literature. My first impression was that our Quincy Street palazzo was not quite like any museum that I had seen before: no splendid long gilded galleries, no grand staircase or any other obvious flourish of architectural rhetoric — and certainly not the cool lucidity of an indoor-outdoor *casa moderna*.

I entered by the front door and began to wander, without a compass, not quite knowing where one ought to begin, or which was the right direction to turn. I was surprised but pleased to discover that the Fogg was constructed like a film by Godard, where every room or corridor or stairwell seemed as much a middle as a beginning — and where there was fortunately no end at all, but something more like a perpetual visual motion machine.

At the top of my first set of stairs, turning the corner, I encountered that striking blessed damozel painted by Dante Gabriel Rossetti: not like the portrait of any woman I had ever seen; quite stunning to a neophyte like myself, and so quintessentially pre-Raphaelite that if I had never again seen another similar work, the style would have left its permanent imprint on my admittedly impressionable imagination.

At the time, of course, I had never heard of Rossetti except as a poet; so much the better, because the painting struck me like a kind of projectile from out of the blue: an unidentifiable flying object that had neither name nor label nor provenance to commend it. It came free of pre-established expectations, or any bothersome baggage of prior knowledge, on my part. Fortunate: because I know that if someone had told me, before my visit, to seek out a large oil painting by a Victorian English artist whose first name was Dante, I am certain that I would not have gone near the picture – then, or probably throughout my entire graduate student career.

Thus the Fogg began to teach me in its own labyrinthine ways. One day, I stumbled unaware upon the late Botticelli *Crucifixion* – another completely foreign object to me: strange, involuted, animated, contorted, yet full of mysterious grace. Was this the same Botticelli whom I thought I knew – the Botticelli of whom Peter Ustinov once said that if he were alive today, he would be working for *Vogue* magazine? Apparently it was – the very same Botticelli. My learning, and even my enlightenment, proceeded apace.

I won't go on, except to say that I happened upon object after object – or rather the objects seemed to happen upon me. My factual knowledge was slender – most of the dates, and some of the names, came later. But what I brought away from these early excursions into the Fogg and mist were all those new images, and the experience of suddenly encountering them, revisiting them, reflecting on them, and somehow drawing nourishment, energy, and even confidence from them. Because any great achievement of the imagination, realized in art, nourishes our sources of hope and confidence, and gives substance to our conviction that human beings are capable of extraordinary acts – acts of aspiration and creation.

Melodic Transgressions

Introduction of John Harbison '60
Arts First Medalist
May 6, 2000

W HEN I WAS a first-year undergraduate at Princeton in 1952, the course I most wanted to sign up for was a famous canonical hit called "Ren and Ref" ("Renaissance and Reformation"). It was taught by Professor E. H. Harbison, John's father, who was known to be not only a fine historian and teacher, but also, in his private life, a composer and musician.

Later, that course took on a greater and intriguing symbolic meaning for me, and came to represent the unresolved dichotomy of Princeton – at least the Princeton of my own era: the fascination with, and indulgence in, stylized excess, juxtaposed with an equally powerful need for Presbyterian or Calvinistic self-purgation and constant moral scrupulousness. In the Renaissance part of Professor Harbison's course, we encountered all those dubious, extravagant, amorous, venal, and aesthetic Medicean and Borgiaesque cardinals and popes, who were then followed so swiftly by Savonarola's sackcloth; by the Reformation's Luther, Zwingli, and Calvin – people who generally disliked large outdoor parties and who reinvented the concept of "Arts Last."

Any institution that had the puritan Jonathan Edwards as one of its earliest presidents, Woodrow Wilson as its greatest recent public figure, and F. Scott Fitzgerald as its most famous unshakable literary icon was bound – at least in the 1950s – to have some form of deep psychic angst at its core. To jazz or not to jazz? That was at least *one* of the abiding dilemmas. And Professor Harbison, reigning over "Ren and Ref," seemed to me to embody and nearly to resolve, in an especially gracious way, the university's heritage of threatening antinomies: he was witty, but serious and demanding as a teacher; kind and even indulgent, but full of a certain sobriety; a slightly self-effacing historian in public and, apparently, an imaginative, expressive musician in private.

I do not want at all to suggest that John Harbison, who has generously agreed to share this weekend with us, had somehow (when he was growing up) to deal with the entire symbolic burden of Princeton's rich but also dichotomous history. It is true that he and I were both there when the shadows of Woodrow Wilson, who had died only a little more than three decades earlier, and Fitzgerald, who had died barely a decade earlier, were very much in evidence. Nevertheless, John was already discovering alchemical ways to transmute Princeton's paradoxes into something rich and strange, without having to re-enact for himself a dialectical drama of stark choice between extremes – a sort of *Harbison Agonistes* – and without simply seeking some easy but incoherent amalgam of the great variety of musical and other traditions that he realized might be accessible to him.

By the time John was twelve, he had formed his own jazz group; he had been listening to radio broadcasts from the Metropolitan Opera every week; he was playing some Beethoven on the piano, coming in touch with New York musical comedy, and talking with Roger Sessions (who was then teaching at Princeton) about twentieth-century music.

His most significant musical exemplars were evident early in his life: Bach, especially the cantatas; Stravinsky; Thelonious Monk and other jazz greats such as Coltrane; figures from American popular music (Gershwin, Lorenz Hart, Irving Berlin, Hammerstein); and opera, spanning at least Mozart and Verdi to Debussy's *Pelléas* and beyond.

In other words, from the beginning John did not so much struggle with, but rather absorbed and began to take as "given," several traditions — several musical canons that he made his own, essentially because he was so strongly drawn to them, and riveted by them.

This is not to say that the going was always easy. At Harvard, in the face of an austere historical approach to the study of "classical" music (if one can use that term), John discovered that the then Music Department's conception of history stopped somewhere in the nineteenth century, and he had to make a special case for wanting to press further. Later, when he returned to Princeton to study composition, he ran into a different kind of orthodoxy, based on twelve-tone and atonal modernist traditions. John held out for a wider range that could include transgressions that were melodic in nature. This left him rather on the periphery of things at Princeton, and he still remembers the day when one of his classmates turned to him and said: "You're really just a tune man, aren't you?"

John *isn't* "just a tune man" any more than he is "just" anything else. He has his modernist severities, moments of jazzmania, of melodic arias and other arresting complexities. Most of all, he has the capacity to manage, with extraordinary ease of transition, the shifts and moves from one set of stylistic allusions to another in a way that is unsurpassed among contemporary composers.

All of these talents are nowhere more in evidence than in John's most recent major work, his opera *The Great Gatsby*, which premiered at the Metropolitan this past winter. Quite apart from its boldness and its insistence that the music (not the "plot," so to speak) must carry the work, John clearly gathered up in this work a very great deal from his decades of immersion in so many different kinds of art: returning to Fitzgerald, and *Gatsby*, with all their own internal contradictions and burdens; to jazz and swing and popular music; to the stringencies of modernist recitative, and the constraints of modernist arias. John, of course, concentrated in literature — not music — through most of his undergraduate time at Harvard; so it is not surprising that he should have used a quintessential American text, a Jazz Age text, and really a Princeton text, as the grounding for this major public entry into opera.

But if John's *Gatsby* gathers together and intertwines a great deal of the past, it also obviously looks outward in a new way to an open future. Over the course of his career, John has composed string quartets, symphonies, other operas, and a cantata, among much else. Like all formidable composers, he keeps coming back for yet another act, in an age that is less than hospitable to contemporary music. It takes not only talent and commitment, but no little courage and poise, to carry forward in this way. Happily, the world has often recognized John's capacities. He has been a Guggenheim Fellow and a MacArthur Fellow; in 1980, he won the Kennedy Center Friedheim Award for his *Piano Concerto*; and in 1987, he won the Pulitzer Prize for *The Flight into Egypt*. He has been composer-in-residence at any number of places, from CalArts to Aspen to the American Academy in Rome. In short, in his invariably modest, reflective, impassioned, but also intellectually disinterested way, he has, in effect, done it all. Harvard and Arts First are honored to have him here among us.

Testing the Limits

Remarks at the Opening of the Ellsworth Kelly Exhibition
Sackler Museum, March 4, 1999

I WOULD LIKE to make a few remarks, from a purely personal point of view, about Ellsworth Kelly's work.

I am not certain that I know any art that is more demanding or more difficult than Ellsworth's — notwithstanding the fact that it is so often radiant, so full of invitation, and seems (sometimes) to be so disarmingly accessible.

But when we consider the infinite repertoire of worldly and otherworldly objects that one might draw or paint or sculpt; the range of techniques one might use; the kinds of gesture and illusion one might create — when we think of this entire array of capacities that has been available to artists throughout much of history — then Ellsworth's work seems like a marvelously radical and continuing exercise in self-denial. So much of his art depends on everything that he has *eliminated* from the work, including any of the ordinary traces of the artist as a presence who clearly "creates" either as interventionist, compositor, image-maker, or magician.

The journey that I feel I am asked to take with Ellsworth is in one sense a journey of deliberate renunciation and deprivation —

93

granted that what we ultimately discover more than compensates for all that he has sacrificed. For me, at least, the rewards of his art reflect the enormous achievement of a visual sensibility and intelligence that have been purified to the point where every nuance and inflection, in each new piece, every shade and tone and value, matters absolutely. Every move that might all too easily lapse into something familiar or merely imperfect, or into an imitation of previous moves — all that has been avoided. As a result, we are forced to try to "see," with each new revelation, what we are actually looking at: what a particular new juxtaposition of shapes and colors, or the silent presence of a new solitary object, seems to indicate; what seems to have shifted since the previous chapter of Ellsworth's work; what readjustment of nearly indiscernible weights and balances has occurred, demanding that we respond — testing the limits of our capacity — to the differences we sense, or the meanings that have suddenly been discovered.

T. S. Eliot once remarked that we can only get the better of words for those things we no longer want to say. For Ellsworth (as for Eliot) the constant effort is to find "objective correlatives" for those new perceptions that one's intuition and sensibility have somehow grasped, but that one is still struggling to articulate and clarify in art, using whatever equipment — whether words, or shapes and colors — one has available.

Ellsworth, we celebrate all that you have given us over many years — for helping us to see what we had missed, or what had simply never existed before you brought it into being. Most of all, we toast your presence among us, your friendship, and your unwillingness to tolerate — whether in work or in life — anything less than what has been purified, perfected, and only then "presented."

Firmly Grounded Ideas

Commencement Day Address
June 8, 2000

W E ARE VERY PRIVILEGED to have with us today Seamus Heaney and Amartya Sen, both Nobel Laureates, both long associated with Harvard University, and both committed to the central values embodied in a great university such as ours.

Their presence here gives us the chance to reflect on the ways in which both of them — each in his own field — have explored ideas about the nature of a good society and of a fulfilling life. As we do so, we will, I think, discover some important common threads that link their experiences, their concerns, and their commitments.

Seamus Heaney and Amartya Sen were each born in lands — Ireland and India — that have, during the last century, been torn by colonial strife, as well as by religious and political conflict. Both have lived international lives, remaining strongly attached to their homelands while also cultivating the kind of considered disinterestedness that comes from caring — but not caring so totally as to allow themselves to become imprisoned by the local circumstances into which they were born.

As a result, both Seamus and Amartya have continuously sought to expand their vision, to seek more inclusive as well as firmly grounded ideas concerning the essential elements of a healthy and just society. Both have clearly chosen not to be exiles — and certainly not expatriates. Instead, they have become purposeful wanderers and explorers, with deep roots at home, yet roots that have allowed them to flourish abroad, precisely because they have taken nourishment from their relation to what is local and indigenous, while testing that heritage and its values against their experience of the wider world in which they have lived and journeyed.

Seamus Heaney's poetry has, inevitably, had to come to terms with the religious and political conflict in Northern Ireland, where he spent the first decades of his life. He has had to decide — under great pressure — how far to become engaged politically, or whether to leave his native city, Belfast. He has had to judge the moral weight that such choices might exert on the character of his life and the spirit level of his verse. As a result, the complexity of the act of choosing, the importance of having the freedom to choose, and the need to understand the implications of one's choices have all had their bearing on the substance and the texture of his poetry.

Meanwhile, Amartya Sen's view of economics has, from the beginning, been grounded in moral philosophy and political theory, in problems of justice, of human and societal development, and of moral choice. He has worked to show how certain fundamental freedoms and rights — including such things as the right to an education and to basic health care — are essential for individual fulfillment and for the functioning of a healthy society.

Therefore, I think of both Seamus Heaney and Amartya Sen primarily as humanists, very much kin to one another and always preoccupied with those questions with which the humanities, arts, and social sciences have traditionally been engaged: how — and even where — to live; how to define one's obligations and responsibilities, not only to society but to oneself; how to exercise one's freedoms and rights wisely; how to enable societies to be productive and also just; and finally, how to use words — whether in poetry or in prose — precisely, faithfully, and lyrically so that we do not sow even more confusion than already exists in the world, either through the willful distortion and crude simplification of language and meanings, or through any careless disregard for the intellectual and imaginative stringency necessary to the task of articulating truths.

If Heaney and Sen often pose similar questions, they also resemble one another in cherishing many of the same values — above all, the value of freedom. Neither of them views freedom as a promise of something without boundaries, something purely liberating.

Instead, they would characterize it as the opportunity to define one's own commitments among possible glimpsed alternatives. Freedom allows us to choose, not the boundless, but the ways in which we ourselves wish to be bounded, pursuing whatever we believe might nurture greater hope and more communal trust.

To arrive at moments or points along the way when values and purposes that are positive seem capable of holding sway over forces that are corrosive or destructive; to have the capacity to activate those energies and aspirations which can help us give more satisfying shape to our lives and to our societies: these have been fundamental motives behind the quests that Seamus Heaney and Amartya Sen have both undertaken. And, clearly, neither quest would have been even conceivable if the kind of freedom I mentioned a few moments ago had not been cultivated by them and available to them.

If we step back to consider some significant movements or developments that have been especially significant in the twentieth century — and that also relate in important ways to Seamus and Amartya — then at least two major patterns, I believe, stand out.

First, there has been the unprecedented scale of mass warfare, including the subjugation, displacement, and forced exile of so many millions of people. These events have had several causes, but high among them have been one or another kind of expansionist ideology: some motivated by beguiling utopian visions of seemingly ideal societies that might be created, others based on distorted conceptions of transcendent national, racial, or religious power.

After a century of such experience, the climate of much world opinion has shifted in very important ways. The illusory romanticism or pride that tempted many to dream of unbounded *Lebensraum* or the promise of brave new worlds has actually been diminished. The cost of such illusions is now seen, in large measure, as being simply too high, and the level of present disenchantment is simply too great.

As our contemporary inheritance, we now live with a special form of difficult realism — but a realism that can also accommodate certain forms of equally difficult idealism: both grounded in a recognition of the fact that the use of force in human affairs must be far more limited than in earlier eras, and that utopian visions must be continuously resisted.

The second of the two twentieth-century movements or developments I would highlight has been the steady, growing conviction — affecting more countries and regions, as well as individuals — that freedom is a fundamental human value that must not be alienated.

During the past hundred years, dozens of colonies have ceased to be ruled by foreign states. Even in the last decade or so, we have seen the former Soviet Union crumble; apartheid in South Africa fall; several authoritarian regimes in Latin America vanish; and steady, however inadequate, steps toward peace in the Middle East, Ireland, and elsewhere.

We know, however, that such freedom certainly does not come easily, that it is hard to sustain, and that it is always vulnerable to forces waiting to undermine it. Nevertheless, by any measure, the balance sheet concerning the extent of freedom in the world today, as compared with a century ago, unquestionably shows a vast increase.

In the context of the two twentieth-century patterns that I have just mentioned, Seamus Heaney and Amartya Sen seem to me to be emblematic figures — "relics and types" of important aspects of the past century's experience.

Both, as I suggested earlier, have been schooled as witnesses to conflict and war — the often unyielding ferocity and exiguousness that have so wounded so much of our recent history. Both Seamus and Amartya have, as their intuitive heritage, that kind of unenchanted realism which also contains within itself the sources of, and resources for, sustained hope and well-tempered idealism. Both have resisted, therefore, the pressure to overpromise or to overprescribe, although both have also helped us to see and celebrate humane values and possible ways of leading satisfying lives that have shape and form, and that sometimes may shine forth.

They offer us not blueprints or designs, and certainly not illusory visions, but fruitful, reasoned, imaginative, and tested ways to conceive of how a good society might be animated and ordered; how an individual wanderer and explorer, devoted to poetry or to economics — or indeed to any deep vocation — might find a proper habitation and a name over the course of a lifetime, a lifetime committed to the kinds of freedom which offer scope and room, but that are also lovingly bounded; even how a university such as Harvard, devoted to its own vocation, might be continuously energized in its pursuits, because our books do indeed stand open and our gates unbarred.

In closing, I want to leave you with some lines spoken by Seamus Heaney in 1995, on the occasion of his receiving the Nobel Prize in Literature:

> *As writers and readers, as sinners and citizens, we have developed a realism and an aesthetic sense that make us wary of crediting the positive note.... Only the very stupid or the very deprived can any longer help knowing that the documents of civilization have been*

written in blood and tears. . . . And when this intellectual predisposi-
tion coexists with the actualities of Ulster and Israel and Bosnia
and Rwanda and a host of other wounded spots on the face of the
earth, the inclination is not only not to credit human nature with
much constructive potential but not to credit anything too positive
in the work of art.

Which is why for years I was bowed to the desk like some monk
. . . in an attempt to bear his portion of the weight of the world, know-
ing himself incapable of heroic virtue or redemptive effect. . . . Then
finally and happily, and not in obedience to the dolorous circum-
stances of my native place but in despite of them, I straightened up.
I began a few years ago to try to make space in my reckoning and
imagining for the marvellous as well as for the murderous.[1]

Seamus then went on to suggest the "need on the one hand for a
truth-telling that will be hard and retributive, and on the other
hand the need not to harden the mind to a point where it denies
its own yearnings for sweetness and trust."

This invitation to allow our own yearnings and trust to
emerge and take hold, this accommodation for the miraculous as
well as the murderous, has marked the lives and works of our two
speakers. And so we celebrate them — as we do this university —
for being so committed (in Seamus' words) to "freedom like this":
freedom that we are able to enjoy together, in the sunlit shine of
a lucky Commencement day such as this one.

---

1 Seamus Heaney, *Crediting Poetry: The Nobel Lecture* (New York: Farrar, Straus &
Giroux, 1996), 28–31.

A Continuing Conversation

Dedication of the Barker Center
September 12, 1997

W E ARE HERE to toast the transformation of the original Harvard Union – Major Higginson's vision of a college association housed in a handsome building – into a new union: a bright center for the humanities, bearing the names of Robert and Elizabeth Barker. From the beginning, one of our main purposes has been to make certain that the original conception – the notion of a gathering place for individuals and groups – would not be lost but could actually be renewed and strengthened; that faculty and students, as well as departments and programs and humanistic fields of knowledge, would be brought together in a way that would make the daily exchange of ideas and views natural and easy; and that these conversations would inevitably yield insights that can help us understand human beings, human cultures, and human nature more clearly and more comprehensively.

We have no very convenient, concise definition of "the humanities." Part of what we mean is captured in the Latin phrase *literae humaniores*, "humane letters": those books and texts, especially the ancient classical texts in literature, history, and philosophy that have not only taught us so much about the world and ourselves, but are also great works of art in their uses of language, in their energy and suppleness as well as in their largeness of vision. We feel this immediately if we break in, for example, on one of Plato's dialogues, at almost any point:

> *Socrates: Is not rhetoric, taken generally, a universal art of enchant-*
> *ing the mind by arguments; which is practised not only in courts*
> *and public assemblies, but in private houses also, having to do with*
> *matters great as well as small?… And … what are plaintiff and*
> *defendant doing in a law-court — are they not contending [against*
> *one another]?*
>
> *Phædrus: Exactly so.*
>
> *Soc.   About the just and unjust — that is the matter in dispute?*
>
> *Phædr.   Yes.*
>
> *Soc.   And a professor of the art [of rhetoric] will make the same*
> *thing appear to the same persons to be at one time just, at another*
> *time, if he is so inclined, to be unjust?*
>
> *Phædr.   Exactly.*
>
> *Soc.   And when he speaks in the assembly he will make the same*
> *things seem good to the city at one time and at another time, the*
> *reverse of good?*
>
> *Phædr.   That is true.*[1]

We have essentially all the crucial elements of the humanities here: an intriguing two-person drama; an interesting unfolding philosophical argument; a purposeful but playful questioner (in this case Socrates himself) who is both serious and witty; a convenient agreeable companion (surely the original model for all succeeding generations of "yes-men"); an artful passage that uses persuasive rhetoric to convince us that artful speech and persuasive rhetoric are likely to be deceptive — they are forms of enchantment, capable of misleading juries, political assemblies, and plain ordinary people into believing that the very same things which seem true one day can be made to appear completely false on the following day.

In the space of a few paragraphs, the law, politics, rhetoric, argumentation, and all their practitioners — essentially all human beings, speakers and listeners alike — come intriguingly close to being viewed as rather suspect: when they are not willfully misrepresenting things and deceiving others, they are themselves in the process of being misled. In fact, both processes occur simultaneously, almost all the time, since a very large part of life is spent talking and listening, writing and responding, trying to persuade and being persuaded. Meanwhile, Socrates alone seems to stand somewhere outside this fiendish little circle of reciprocal enchantment that binds and blinds everyone else. Although (as we discover a little later in the dialogue) Socrates (or Plato) does provide a possible way out for us, it is a way that is itself, of course, also open to further questioning and reply, debate and re-debate.

There are no clear morals to be drawn from this lively text, or from most other great humanistic texts. Once the process of serious inquiry into matters such as the nature of truth, of rhetoric, of justice, and of politics has begun — once we allow and in fact encourage debate on these and other subjects — there is no obvious point where the discussion can be stopped. And there is no way to be certain about the directions and turns it will take, especially as more and more people (with a growing number of views) begin to participate.

Out of all this talk, what William James used to call "gossiping about the universe," out of this conversation in philosophy, the arts, history, and social or cultural studies emerge just those ideas that enable us — every now and then — to make slightly better sense of some part of human experience. At the same time, the whole enterprise is also a risky one. It can bewilder and perplex. It raises questions and challenges on every side and provides few if any definitive answers. It can wander and go astray. And its practitioners sometimes press forward so strenuously that they can come to be viewed not simply as inquisitive, brilliant, eccentric, interesting, or annoying; they can also be seen as disturbing, threatening, or even potentially dangerous.

After all, Socrates himself was sentenced to death at a time of political crisis in Greece — having been charged with misleading and subverting the minds of Athenian youth. Almost 2,500 years later, in a relatively minor and amusing but still revealing incident, the British Board of Film censors decided to ban Jean Cocteau's strange yet beautiful surrealist film, *The Seashell and the Clergyman*. The year was 1929, and the board explained its decision by stating that "this film is so cryptic as to be almost meaningless. If there is a meaning, it is doubtless objectionable."

Socrates and surrealist films are worlds (and even millennia) apart from one another. But they are, in their different ways, interesting cases, because the charges in each situation had to do with how we explore and create and present meanings — whether through philosophical inquiry, formal rhetoric, everyday conversation, or the cinema and other kinds of fiction or art. The charges also concerned (to a greater or lesser extent) whether the meanings being created were false and improper, and therefore disruptive of important moral and civic values; or whether it was possible to judge the meanings at all — and by what standards, and from whose point of view, especially if the presentation was so complicated or obscure that it was seen to be "almost meaningless," whatever the phrase "almost meaningless" might possibly mean.

✦   ✦   ✦

"We couldn't get along in life," states Thomas Nagel in an introductory volume about the nature of philosophy,

> without taking the ideas of time, … knowledge, language, right and wrong for granted most of the time; but in philosophy we investi-

gate those things themselves. The aim is to push our understanding of the world and ourselves a bit deeper. Obviously, it isn't easy. The more basic the ideas you are trying to investigate, the fewer tools you have to work with. There isn't much you can assume or take for granted. So philosophy is a somewhat dizzying activity, and few of its results go unchallenged for long.[2]

If philosophy is a "somewhat dizzying" and complicated activity, we know that many other fields in the humanities and arts have also become more complicated – more philosophical and dizzying, so to speak – during the past three to four decades. Common assumptions and first premises have been reexamined at a deep level – in (for example) history, anthropology, art history, linguistics, literary studies, and the actual practice of the creative arts.

National public debates have often taken center stage and have been characterized, in cartoonlike fashion, as "culture wars": battles concerning which texts should be part of the curricular Canon, or which aspects of Western civilization (or other civilizations) should be studied, and how. These issues, in themselves, are not new, but the much greater scope and intensity of recent disputes are what have made our own era seem different from many earlier times.

One of Jane Austen's heroines declared, nearly two centuries ago: "But history, real solemn history, I cannot be interested in.... The quarrels of popes and kings, with wars and pestilence, in every page; the men all so good for nothing, and hardly any women at all."[3] Lately – and beneficially – "real solemn history" (along with other fields in the humanities) has obviously widened its lens and focused more systematically not only on "popes and kings" (or prime ministers, presidents, and conquistadors) but also on the ordinary lives of ordinary people and their *mentalités*; on neglected ideas and ideologies; on the lives and roles of women in different societies; on new forms of economic and social analysis; on the experience and culture of African Americans, Native Americans, and other peoples in many parts of the globe.

Meanwhile, historians and others have also asked themselves —
perhaps more incessantly than before — what is the evidence for
this or that claim? In fact, what *constitutes* evidence, and what are we
overlooking or leaving out — without even knowing it? Is the latest
historical magnum opus simply one individual's version or "construction" of what he or she prefers to think might possibly have
happened — among all the countless other things that must also
have been happening — in what we choose to call "the past"? Or
does the opus seem to be in touch with what might be "reality" —
something actual that is genuinely "out there"? How do we know?
Who decides?

Far be it from me to try to answer such questions. But let me
at least offer some of my own tentative thoughts about where we
have recently come from in the humanities, and what may be
possible in the future.

First, I do take it as a given that the humanities will always be
destined to exist in a state approximating perpetual flux. Of
course, there will be oscillations: times when there is more of a
rough consensus (but certainly never a complete one) about many
fundamental matters in a particular society, and other times when
there is a great deal of sharp disagreement. But as long as the
humanities remain committed to an open, continuing conversation and inquiry into human values and human affairs — involving
countless participants — they will remain essentially, by definition,
dynamic and subject to surprise as well as to change.

If we have any doubts on this score, and want a useful reference
point outside (but not so very distant from) our own historical
period, we simply have to remember the great chasms that opened
— and the powerful shaking of the foundations that occurred — in
nearly all fields of learning, including (prominently) the humanities, throughout much of the nineteenth and early twentieth centuries.

Any number of examples will come quickly to all our minds:
the revolutionary effects produced by Darwin and the concept of

evolution; the great transformations and schisms in religion that *preceded* (as well as succeeded) Darwin's work; the introduction and full establishment in universities of "modern" humanistic studies, from the 1880s through the turn of the century. These studies included English literature, art history, and the "modern" languages and literatures (among them French, German, Italian, and Slavic), as well as the development and legitimatization of the social sciences as academic disciplines. And this entire sea change led, of course, to the idea, born at Harvard, of a curriculum based largely on an "elective system," allowing students to choose from a rapidly growing number of courses taught by an increasing number of faculty, from a variety of points of view, incorporating a wider and wider range of texts and other materials.

The elective system shattered the previously existing order of prescribed courses and canonical classical texts to make room for a vaster and more complicated multiverse of knowledge. And the resulting cascade of new subjects and specialties produced a feeling on many sides that the world was no longer quite so coherent and comprehensible a place. Toward the end of his masterpiece, *The Education of Henry Adams*, Adams found that he could look to the future with little more than deep uncertainty and perplexity:

> *The child born in 1900 would, then, be born into a new world which would not be a unity but a multiple. Adams tried to imagine it, and an education that would fit it. He found himself in a land where no one had ever penetrated before....*[4]

If Adams, writing around 1900, could not imagine an education that could "fit" his increasingly complicated world, we should not be surprised if – after an additional century of unprecedented growth in complexity – we too are experiencing some real turbulence, and are not always entirely certain about how to prepare or "fit" the child born not in 1900, but in the year 2000.

My second point about the humanities is a simple one: many

of the discussions and debates of the past few decades — even at their most disputatious — have significantly broadened and deepened our ideas about human nature and experience in extraordinary ways. We know much more about the human past — and present; about the values, the ways of life, and the art of people in a far greater number of societies; and about individuals and groups whose very existence, and whose contributions, were often overlooked and certainly underestimated.

Such a great shift in knowledge and interpretive capacity — such a change in our collective sensibility and our potential for greater understanding — represents a major achievement and simply could not have been realized without real struggle, debate, and disagreement. "One of the greatest pains to human nature," Walter Bagehot once remarked, "is the pain of a new idea." If we have experienced a reasonable amount of pain recently, we have also enjoyed the harvest of many new insights and important new ideas.

Next, while I am certain that our current debates will continue, I also have the impression that the tenor and substance of many conversations in the humanities and related social sciences are beginning to change. The best work of the past twenty to thirty years is already well established. We have now reached a point where we can make much better judgments about the value of what has been achieved to date. We can also assess — far more clearly — which ideas or methods or approaches may have been unnecessarily displaced in these last few decades and should therefore be restored. We can begin to consider which courses, curricula, and research might prove to be most fruitful in the *next* few decades.

To have a place or "home," therefore, where precisely these conversations can be pursued — at just this moment — is nothing less than a stroke of the greatest possible good fortune. In this sense, the creation and opening of the Barker Center for the humanities could not be more timely or propitious.

The Center will bring together under one large roof, in a wonderful space, many of the most recently established programs and departments in the humanities, the somewhat less recent programs, and the elder programs. It will be a kind of forum for students as well as faculty. It represents a significant and imaginative development for Harvard itself, but it is also — so far as I know — unique among major universities in its scope and breadth and inclusiveness. In short, the moment is ripe; the participants are engaged; and the new Center provides us with an unparalleled opportunity to venture forth confidently and creatively.

In closing, I want to read and say a few words about a modest poetic text. It is one of Keats' less-known sonnets, written after he had spent an evening at the home of the poet Leigh Hunt. The conversation had touched on *Lycidas*, Milton's elegy on the death of a young friend, as well as on Petrarch's sonnets to Laura: sonnets born of pain as well as love — and where Laura is inevitably associated in Keats' mind with his own poetic aspirations and with the laurel itself (the fresh green wreath awarded to "laureates"). As the poem begins, Keats has just ventured out into the cold and darkness of a November night:

> Keen, fitful gusts are whisp'ring here and there
> 　　Among the bushes half leafless, and dry;
> 　　The stars look very cold about the sky,
> And I have many miles on foot to fare.
> Yet feel I little of the cool bleak air,
> 　　Or of the dead leaves rustling drearily,
> 　　Or of those silver lamps that burn on high,
> Or of the distance from home's pleasant lair:
> For I am brimfull of the friendliness
> 　　That in a little cottage I have found;
> Of fair-hair'd Milton's eloquent distress,
> 　　And all his love for gentle Lycid drown'd;
> Of lovely Laura in her light green dress,
> 　　And faithful Petrarch gloriously crown'd.[5]

The sonnet is, of course, about many things. It helps to bring the humanities and arts back to a human and personal scale, where friendships and discussion, personal ambition and aspiration, suffering and loss, poetry and imagination all matter.

The sonnet also keeps beautifully in balance the uncertainties, risks, and even dangers of any important humane venture — whether in art, in inquiry and knowledge, or in life: it keeps these difficulties in balance with the possible satisfactions and rich rewards of great achievement.

Nearly everywhere in the poem — in nearly every line or image and inflection — we can find the energies stimulated by companionship, eloquence, love, faithfulness, and conversation. And there are also the remembered pain and distress of early death (as in *Lycidas*), or the pervasive sense of winter's approach and its quickening dark encroachment — with its cold, its rustling dead leaves, and all its inevitable intimations of mortality.

The sonnet creates a microdrama — the humanities and arts in miniature — full of apprehension but also of hope and momentary good cheer. And at the heart of the poem, of course, is a celebration of the restorative power of a dwelling place: of a home where the gathering of people stimulates good talk and aspiration; where ideas — however different from one another — can be humanized, enriched, and perhaps occasionally even reconciled.

Of course, no large center for the humanities can expect to be the small Hampstead cottage of Keats' sonnet. But the Barker Center will, in its own way, enable us to begin new, fruitful, and timely conversations, so that there may well be many more times when each of us, like Keats, may feel

> *... little of the cool bleak air,*
> *Or of the dead leaves, rustling drearily,*
> *Or of those silver lamps that burn on high,*
> *Or of the distance from home's pleasant lair:*
> *For I am brimfull of the friendliness*

> *That in a little cottage I have found;*
> *Of fair-hair'd Milton's eloquent distress,*
> *And all his love for gentle Lycid drown'd;*
> *Of lovely Laura in her light green dress,*
> *And faithful Petrarch gloriously crown'd.*

Meanwhile, let us dedicate and celebrate the Barker Center, "gloriously crown'd."

1 Plato, *Phædrus* 261a–261d, in *The Dialogues of Plato*, 3rd. ed., trans. Benjamin Jowett (New York: Oxford University Press, 1892), 1: 468–469.

2 Thomas Nagel, *What Does It All Mean? A Very Short Introduction to Philosophy* (New York: Oxford University Press, 1987), 5.

3 Catherine Moreland in Jane Austen's *Northanger Abbey* (1817).

4 Henry Adams, *The Education of Henry Adams: An Autobiography* (Boston: Houghton Mifflin, 1918), 457.

5 John Keats, "Keen, fitful gusts are whisp'ring here and there," *Poems* (London: C. & J. Ollier, 1817), 87.

SCIENCE AND TECHNOLOGY

New Technologies and Their Promise
for Higher Education

Address to the First Harvard University Conference on the Internet and Society
May 29, 1996

I WANT TO TALK today about the Internet and higher education. What changes are taking place in universities as a result of this recent advance in information technology? Are the changes significant, and are they likely to be long-lasting (as I believe they are)? If so, why?

The questions are obviously important, in part because our conclusions will determine whether Harvard and other institutions should make very large financial investments in the next five to ten years, at a time when flexible resources are clearly constrained.

But more important than the financial issues are those of educational substance. Any deep transformation in communications — in our ability to gain access to data, information, and ultimately knowledge, and in processes that can help us to discover, invent, teach, and learn — holds the potential to have profound effects on higher education. So as we assess the new information technology – the Internet – we have to make the right bet, because the stakes are high.

When I refer to the Internet, I mean to use the term as shorthand for a cluster of technologies that includes networked personal computers, hypertext and hypermedia, the World Wide Web, and other adjuncts.

This cluster has, during the past few years, already begun to have a dramatic impact on the ways that many students and faculty are approaching the whole activity of teaching and learning. In the context of Harvard and at least some other universities, these changes are more dynamic and pervasive than any previous breakthrough in information technology during this century – including the introduction of the personal computer itself. The effects are visible in nearly every part of our own campus, as well as elsewhere in higher education.

From one point of view, the Internet marks just one more point on a long continuum of inventions – one that has unfolded over the course of the last century and a half – from the telegraph and cablegram, through the telephone, radio, recorded sound, film, television, early calculating machines, and then the earliest computers.

But we know that certain events along a continuum can represent much more than another simple step in a natural, gradual progression. There are moments of real transformation, and the rapid emergence of the Internet is one of them.

✦   ✦   ✦

Many inventions (such as radio, film, and television) have of course had a massive effect on society – on how people spend their time, entertain themselves, and even gain information. But, in spite of many predictions, these particular inventions have had little effect on formal, serious, advanced education. Why should the Internet be any different? Is there any evidence – or a reasoned explanation – for betting on the Internet, when so many earlier inventions have fallen short of expectations?

Let me mention a few facts.

In our Faculty of Arts and Sciences, as well as nearly all of our nine professional schools, teachers and students are on-line, with easy access to the network. E-mail is commonplace. Activity on the Net is heavy at nearly all times of day and night, with the only major slowdown occurring between 3:00 a.m. and 6:00 a.m.

In 1992, we began a retrospective conversion of the catalogue for Harvard's entire library system – the largest university library system in the world – at a projected cost of $22 million. By next year, full catalogue entries for the approximately thirteen million volumes in our ninety-two libraries will be on-line and searchable in any number of ways. In addition, there are, of course, more and more actual texts, images, and other materials on the Net.

The rate of change and growth is exceptionally fast. A year ago, the Arts and Sciences Web site (which includes many subsites) experienced about 150,000 "hits" in the single month of March. This March, just one year later, the number of "hits" had increased from 150,000 to 2.3 million. There is no sign of a slowdown.

In 1995, the volume of e-mail traffic on the Arts and Sciences network was about 80,000 transactions per day. Twelve months later, the number had grown by about 170 percent, to about 215,000 per day – or about 6.5 million per month.

These figures, let me stress, are only for Arts and Sciences. They do not include our Schools of Business, Design, Dentistry, Divinity, Education, Government, Law, Medicine, and Public Health – or our central administration and various other units.

So if I am asked whether something very unusual – something qualitatively and quantitatively different – is under way, the answer is a clear "yes." And we are only at the beginning.

✦   ✦   ✦

In purely economic terms, we expect to spend something in the range of $75 million to $100 million over the next two to three years on academic-related information technology – above and beyond the substantial investments already made since the early 1990s.

The last time universities experienced such far-reaching change in information processing, along with exponential expenditure growth, was during the last quarter of the nineteenth century and the first quarter of the twentieth. It was then that the huge information systems that we call university research libraries reached their point of "takeoff" in accelerated development.

At Harvard, the moment of takeoff came during the 1870s and 1880s. When that moment arrived, universities were forced to confront many problems — including that of information overload — similar to several of the "electronic" problems we now face.

In 1876, for instance, Harvard's President Charles Eliot reported that the main library building had become completely inadequate to accommodate the sharp rise in acquisitions. Books, he said, "are piled upon the floors.... Alcoves are blocked up.... Thousands of [volumes] ... have been placed in temporary positions." He later noted that large numbers of books were being stored haphazardly: "42,000 volumes scattered among twenty-nine [locations] ... in sixteen different buildings."

The real challenges, however, were not those of space and money. They were organizational and conceptual. How should books be arranged for optimal use? What kind of cataloguing system could be invented to allow rapid access to the huge number of volumes that were now being acquired? How could convenient linkages be created among books and articles in different but related fields? How should library books be integrated into the University's programs of instruction — especially if the library owned only one or two copies of a book which fifty or sixty students were asked to read for class discussion?

Finally, what was to prevent students (and even faculty) from disappearing into the stacks for days on end, pursuing a subject from book to book, shelf to shelf, unable to discriminate easily among the unlimited number of volumes, or to absorb more than a small fraction of the information available on a given topic? And what could possibly prevent less industrious students from simply browsing their lives away in sweet procrastination?

Some of these fears were not completely new. Anxieties had been building for some time. As early as the eighteenth century, Diderot remarked that "a time will come when it will be almost as difficult to learn anything from books as from the direct study of the whole of the universe.... The printing press, which never rests, [will fill] huge buildings with books [in which readers] will not do very much reading.... The world of learning – our world – will drown in books."

Meanwhile, a treatise on public health, published in Germany in 1795, warned that excessive reading induced "a susceptibility to colds, headaches, weakening of the eyes, heat rashes, gout, arthritis, asthma, apoplexy, pulmonary disease, indigestion, nervous disorders, migraines, epilepsy, hypochondria, and melancholy."

People were warned not to read immediately after eating, and to read only when standing up, for the sake of good digestion. Fresh air, frequent walks, and washing one's face periodically in cold water were also prescribed for habitual solitary readers. Most of all, it was feared that excessive reading would make people socially dysfunctional, would take the place of direct human contact, and could well lead to a society composed of certified misfits.

Historical parallels are never exact, but the story of university research libraries, and of the habit of solitary reading, has some obvious relevance to modern information technology – especially to the Internet's ability to give individuals unbounded access to a new universe of information that they do not yet know how to manage at all well.

There is also the serious problem of the very mixed quality of the information available. How do we sort it? How do we gain maximum return on the time and energy invested in searching?

Given this situation, it is not surprising that many people are now asking some of the same questions that were raised in the early days of research libraries – and expressing some of the same fears. The Internet is in fact not easy to navigate; much of its available information is trivial; it appears to be hazardous to the health of at least some people; and it also has the capacity to distract many people from following what others regard as more serious pursuits.

Some of these concerns can be alleviated by recalling the story of our research libraries and their evolution. Other concerns — such as the worry that the Internet may turn out to be no more educationally useful than radio or television — need to be answered differently.

✦   ✦   ✦

Why is the Internet likely to succeed as a vehicle for real education, when so many other inventions have faltered? Why isn't it simply one more in a long train of distractions? Doesn't it, ultimately, take students and faculty further and further away from books, from the hard work of sustained study and thought, and from direct human contact with other students and faculty?

Let me suggest some of the main reasons why I believe that the Internet is fundamentally different from those earlier electronic inventions, and why I believe it is already having — and will continue to have — such a major effect on higher education.

To begin with, there is the steadily mounting evidence of dramatic change and intensity of use, as I mentioned just a few moments ago. All of this is certainly not a mirage.

More fundamentally, there is in fact a very close fit — a critical interlock — between the structures and processes of the Internet, and the main structures and processes of university teaching and learning. That same fit simply did not (and does not) exist with radio, film, or television. This point is in many respects a remarkably simple one, but — in the field of education, at least — it makes absolutely all the difference.

If I say there is a critical interlock or fit here, I mean nothing more complicated than the plain fact that students can carry forward their work on the Internet in ways that are similar to — and tightly intertwined with — the traditional ways that they study and learn in libraries, classrooms, lecture halls, seminars, informal discussion groups, and laboratories, and in the writing and editing of papers or reports.

Some of these activities are more cumbersome and less successful when transplanted to the Internet environment. Others are substantially improved. In most cases, however, the new technology acts primarily as a powerful supplement to — and reinforcement of — the major methods that faculty and students have discovered, over the course of a very long period of time, to be unusually effective forms of teaching and learning in higher education.

Specific examples can be helpful here, so that we can see more clearly how the capacities and processes of the Internet relate so closely to the university's traditional forms of education.

For instance, the Internet can provide access to essentially unlimited sources of information not conveniently obtainable through other means. Let us assume for the moment that most of the technical and other problems of the Internet will in time be solved: that there will be, as there are now in the research library system, efficient ways of helping users to find what they want; that there will be procedures for information quality control, and for creating more effective linkages among different bodies of knowledge in different media.

At that point, the Internet and its successor technologies will have the essential features of a massive library system, where people can roam through the electronic equivalent of book stacks, with assistance from the electronic equivalent of reference librarians. In short, one major reason the characteristics of the Internet are so compatible with those of universities is that some of the Internet's most significant capabilities resemble, and dovetail with, the capabilities of university research libraries. Just as the research library is an extremely powerful instrument for learning, so too is the Internet — and for much the same reasons.

In fact, the library and the Internet are being viewed increasingly as a versatile unified system, providing an enormous variety of materials, in different formats — so that data, texts, images, and other forms of information can be readily accessed by students and faculty alike. Indeed, we are already well along this path.

✦   ✦   ✦

If we now shift for a minute from libraries to the formal curriculum, we can see that the Internet has another set of highly relevant capabilities: it can provide unusually rich course materials on-line.

For instance, traditional text-based Business School "cases" are already being transformed. I recently reviewed one of the new generation of multimedia cases, which focuses on a small sock-manufacturing plant in China — an Australian-managed plant plagued by serious production and delivery problems, and losing money much faster than it could make either toes or heels.

The materials for this case began with a video tour of the plant, close-up moving pictures of the workers operating their machines — or not operating them — followed by interviews with several managers at different levels in the company's hierarchy. Detailed production and supply data, financial spreadsheets, and a company report — all of these and more were obtainable in the electronic course-pack.

What one saw, of course, was that the interviews with different people revealed totally different perspectives on the plant's problems, and the data were anything but conclusive. The company's official report, meanwhile, served only to complicate the picture further. Students who were taking this course had to analyze not just a text and statistics, but also the whole range of attitudes, expressions, and behavior — recorded on video — of the different executives, as well as the workers.

How many of the plant's problems were basically cultural — since the key Australian manager spoke no Chinese, and had to communicate with the workers through interpreters? How many problems were the result of a more general human systems failure, given the fact that the plant was embedded in a larger surrounding bureaucracy? How much of the difficulty stemmed from internal inefficiency, bad organization, and managerial blundering?

What is so effective about cases presented in this way is that far more of the entire human and social — as well as operational and financial — situation can be revealed, and this requires students to deal with a vivid dramatization that is much closer to the complicated reality of an actual company functioning in a particular culture. Suddenly, the case becomes three-dimensional or multidimensional. The viewer has to bring to bear all the skills of a careful observer of human nature, along with those of an operations analyst, a financial analyst, and a scholar of organizational behavior.

In short, the Internet turns out to be an exceptionally fine tool for the creation of densely woven, multilayered, and highly demanding new course materials that are in several respects superior to traditional case studies. Once again, an important component of university learning, the course and its texts, can now be reinforced — in this instance, considerably enhanced — by the introduction of Internet technology.

✦   ✦   ✦

Another point of compatibility between the processes of the Internet and those of the university concerns the basic activity of communication. We know that the constant exchange of ideas and opinions among students — as well as faculty — is one of the oldest and most important forms of education. People learn by talking with one another, in classrooms, laboratories, dining halls, seminars, and dormitories. They test propositions, they argue and debate, they challenge one another, and they sometimes even discover common solutions to difficult problems.

The Internet allows this process of dialogue — of conversational learning — to be transferred easily and flexibly into electronic form. Communication can be carried on at all hours, across distances, with people who are on-campus or off-campus. Student study groups can work together on-line; faculty members can hold electronic office hours, in addition to their "real" office hours; and teaching fellows can make themselves available for after-class electronic discussions.

In all these ways, the Internet works to create a significant new forum — a limitless number of electronic rooms and spaces — where one of the most fundamental educational processes — energetic discussion and debate — can be carried on continuously.

It is also worth noting that recent experience suggests that student participation levels tend to rise in the electronic forum. Students who are consistently reticent in actual classrooms are more likely to speak out, regularly and confidently, on the network.

No one should believe that electronic communication can be — or should be — a substitute for direct human contact. But the electronic process has some features that do permit an actual extension of the scope, continuity, and even the quality of certain forms of interaction, even though communication over the network lacks other absolutely essential aspects of "real" conversations in the presence of "real" people.

✦   ✦   ✦

Finally, the Internet may well be having — it is not altogether easy to tell — a subtle but significant effect on the relationships among students, faculty members, and the subject or materials that are being studied in a course.

Let me oversimplify for a moment. The direction of movement in teaching and learning has, for more than a century, been shifting away from a previously established model that viewed the faculty member (or an authoritative text, or a canon of texts) as the dominant presence — as the transmitter — with the student as a kind of receiver.

Since at least the 1870s, the emerging theories of education have stressed the role of the student as an active agent, an energetic learner: someone who asks questions, searches for information, discusses ideas with others, and generally moves ahead as an investigator, discoverer, or adventurous scholar-in-the-making.

In this model, the faculty role, more and more, is to draw students out, to steer but not explicitly control the discussion unless it becomes necessary to do so. The faculty also organizes the structure of the curriculum, individual courses, and class assignments. But the course materials are not likely to be treated as authoritative texts that offer definitive solutions. They are intended to be approached critically, and they are usually arranged in a point-counterpoint way.

This arrangement inevitably suggests that many or even most of the important questions in a course are still open and unresolved, waiting to be discussed and addressed and answered. Faculty play an absolutely vital role in this process, stimulating students to ask the right questions, to search in rigorous and imaginative ways for answers, and to connect their thoughts to a larger set of principles and ideas. But a very large part of the positive charge comes from the students themselves.

We do not have to agree fully with this theory of education in order to see that it has in fact produced very potent results in colleges and universities. We can also see why the structure and basic processes of the Internet technology appear to be so closely linked to — so compatible with — the approach to education that I have just been describing.

The Internet essentially *requires* that the user be an engaged agent, searching for information and then managing or manipulating whatever is found — solving problems, buttressing arguments with evidence, and exploring new, unknown terrain. Students are invited to trace linkages from one source to another. They can easily share ideas with others on e-mail. They ask for comments and criticisms. Their posture or attitude, seated in front of the computer, is to make something happen. And they generally act or pursue, rather than merely react and absorb.

So, if we step back and look at the full picture that I've tried to sketch, we can, I think, start to understand why the Internet and its successor technologies will not only have a profound effect on society in general — as radio, film, and television previously did — but why it has so quickly and dramatically begun to transform significant aspects of higher education, in a way that previous inventions simply did not.

As I have tried to suggest, the cluster of technologies that we call the Internet has very distinctive powers — a unique ability to complement, to reinforce, and to enhance many of our most powerful traditional approaches to university teaching and learning. We will still need our libraries, our seminars and tutorials, our faculty, books, laboratories, and residential environments. But the new technologies will strengthen much of what already exists, and also extend our capacities.

The Internet is new, it is different, and there is always reason for caution when things are changing so quickly. We need to find the right pace in order to achieve the best possible results for education — and those results will require an intense focus on the substance of what the new technology can deliver, as much as on the process.

It takes time and money to create superior course materials. It also takes considerable faculty expertise — technical as well as scholarly. It will take time before the Internet is easily navigable, and before it holds a large enough store of rich material to rival our greatest research libraries.

But these things will happen, and as they do, education will be enriched. Meanwhile, I believe that universities have a special responsibility to exert real leadership in this sphere: not necessarily in the development of the technology itself, but in the imaginative and thoughtful uses of the best technology for the purposes of better teaching and learning.

We must be prepared to do now — over the course of the next ten to twenty years — what our predecessors achieved during the late nineteenth century, when they made a conscious decision to create unrivaled university research libraries, new curricula, and new teaching methods. It can be done, and now is the time to begin.

+ + +

Is there a cautionary note on which to end? Certainly. Good data, new information, and excellent vehicles for communication are all critical to virtually everything that we do, in universities and in life. But they do not in themselves constitute the essential stuff of education.

All the information in the world will be of no avail unless we can use it intelligently and wisely. In the end, education is a fundamentally human process. It is a matter of values and significant action, not simply information or even knowledge. The Internet will not tell us what to do about individuals and societies that cannot afford to be on the Net. It will not tell us how to pay attention to those who are left out of the race – or who appear to have already lost the race. It will not show us – any more than our libraries full of books will show us – how to create a humane and just society. For this, we need – as we have always needed – human minds, human values, and human determination.

As we think in this conference about the implications of the Internet, not just for education but for the larger society, let us not forget what we mean by a "society": what it is that we want to have an effect on – and what kind of an effect we want to have. It is how we address these questions – of purposes, of aspirations, of the consequences of our choices on real human lives, all lives – that will finally determine the effectiveness of our new technologies for education, and for people and communities around the world.

The Fruits of Science and Serendipity

Commencement Day Address
June 8, 1995

FIFTY YEARS AGO, as World War II was coming to an end, Harvard graduates and their families gathered in this Yard for Commencement. Victory had been declared in Europe, but we were still at war in the Pacific. The Commencement audience was much smaller than usual, and so the gathering was held in the Sever Quadrangle. President Conant explained that more than 25,000 Harvard graduates and students were still in uniform. The Harvard Commencement of 1945, he told the audience, was a purely local gathering because of national restrictions on wartime travel. The usual daylong activities of Commencement were condensed into two hours.

And yet the day, while in some ways solemn, was essentially one of affirmation and hope. One of the honorary degree recipients – and the principal speaker – was Sir Alexander Fleming, the renowned British bacteriologist. It was Fleming, in 1928, who had discovered penicillin. And it was penicillin that had saved thousands and thousands of lives during the war: a war in which so many Harvard students, faculty, and alumni served with great courage and distinction – and in which so many gave their lives.

But on Commencement Day fifty years ago, Fleming did not speak about conflict and destruction. He spoke instead about the importance to society of scientific discovery. He talked in an unassuming and personal way about the role of chance — of serendipity — in research, as well as in his own life.

+ + +

As a young man, Fleming had spent five years as a shipping clerk. He couldn't afford the medical education he wanted. Then fortune intervened: a relative left him a legacy that was enough to launch him in his medical studies. He earned his degree, served in World War I, and went on to a career in biological research, studying bacteria.

Within a decade, fortune intervened again, this time as Fleming was working in his laboratory. "I did not ask for a spore of *penicillium notatum* to drop on my culture [plate]," he said. "When I saw certain changes I had not the slightest suspicion that I was at the beginning of something extraordinary.... That same mould might have dropped on [any one] of my culture plates, and there would have been no visible change to direct special attention to it.... However, somehow or other, everything [fit] in.... There was an appearance which called for investigation — with the result that now, after various ups and downs, we have penicillin."

Why did Fleming tell this story on that particular Harvard Commencement day? He said he wanted to offer some advice to young researchers in pursuit of new knowledge. "Never," he said, "never neglect an extraordinary appearance or happening. It may be a false alarm and lead to nothing. But it may, on the other hand, be the clue provided by fate to lead you to some important advance."

We can now see, from our own vantage point, that there was also another significance to Fleming's remarks: he was already helping to shift our focus from the war that was ending to the peace that was about to begin. His own experience reminded everyone that research and discovery could lead to dramatic and unpredictable advances for society, and for all individuals.

✦   ✦   ✦

In fact, our own nation began to invest heavily in basic and applied research during the war years, and increased that investment afterward. Our major universities were seen as senior partners in this enterprise — and not only in research, but in the training of graduate and professional students in many different fields. We need to remember (and it can hardly be stressed enough) that advanced education — providing the constant stream of physicians and health professionals, educators, architects, business leaders, religious leaders, lawyers, government officials, and other public servants — such advanced education depends most of all on a creative faculty engaged in significant research and discovery at major universities.

Without such a faculty, and without support for its research, neither Harvard nor any other university can carry out its fundamental mission, or achieve its own goals and those of society. Research and advanced education are inescapably linked to one another. Neither can flourish without the other.

I want to stress this point because we have reached what may be a critical turning point in our nation's commitment to the creation of important new knowledge and understanding. Decisions now being made in Washington will have a profound effect on the future of research and education in this country. The stakes are very high. And the issue is not receiving the urgent and widespread attention it deserves — because this is certainly the most hazardous moment with respect to federal support for higher education in this country during the postwar period.

In the fifty years since Alexander Fleming spoke at Harvard, it is no exaggeration to say, basic research at universities has done much to transform our world.

We should remember, for example, the discovery of the

structure of DNA — in 1953 — which has increased our understanding of almost every aspect of our biological nature, which began the revolution in genetics, and which led to the creation of the entire new industry of biotechnology.

We should consider the computer revolution — the ways in which it has changed how we learn, how we transmit and access information, how we solve problems that were previously insoluble.

Think about microwaves, plastics, optical fibers, laser disks, superconductors, weather and communications satellites, and many other devices and new materials that have become so much a part of our daily lives that we hardly even notice them any more.

Or the advances in understanding cancer, heart disease, and other illnesses — including mental illnesses. Think how much has been accomplished, but how much more work there is still to be done.

How we travel, how we communicate, what we eat, what we do with our free time, how we protect our environment, how we make a living — all these aspects of our lives have increasingly come to depend in essential ways on the discoveries that flow from our basic and applied research.

The driving force behind this steady advance — as I suggested — has been the cooperation, for a full half century and more, between our universities and the federal government. This joint enterprise has been based on a simple premise that was spelled out in a famous report whose fiftieth anniversary we are also marking this year. The report was titled *Science: The Endless Frontier*. Its author was Vannevar Bush — who also received a Harvard honorary degree, in 1941, when he was the principal speaker at our Commencement.

"Progress in the war against disease depends upon a flow of new scientific knowledge," Bush wrote in 1945. "New products, new industries, and more jobs require continuous additions to knowledge ... and the application of that knowledge to practical purposes. Science ... provides no panacea for individual, social, and economic ills," he continued. But "without scientific progress, no amount of achievement in other directions can insure our health, prosperity, and security as a nation in the modern world."

These words are no less true today than fifty years ago. But our national mood, and certainly our sense of perspective, have changed. We are more skeptical about institutions and what they can achieve. As a society, we have much less patience for long-term investments and long-range solutions. In fact, we have less patience for many things that require it. It is true, in addition, that the financial resources at our disposal are more constrained, and we face difficult choices about how to spend these resources. In such a climate, basic research, which has no broad or obvious constituency in our national politics, finds itself very seriously at risk.

A scientist spends weeks, months, even years studying the genetic makeup of baker's yeast. It sounds completely irrelevant and might at first seem to be an easy target for ridicule. Later, we find out that the results of this work will help pave the way for a breakthrough in understanding the basis of colon cancer.

A team of physicists studies how protons shift energy levels inside the nuclei of atoms — not something that most of us worry about very much in our daily lives. But years later, the work leads to magnetic resonance imaging — M R I — an astonishingly precise tool that allows us to picture and to study normal and abnormal structures inside the human body. With other imaging devices, we can now watch parts of the brain and other organs in action; and we can begin to diagnose many diseases in ways that we could hardly have imagined before.

This is only the smallest handful of possible examples, illustrating what has been accomplished in the last half century, thanks to our national conviction that discovery and increased understanding will constantly lead to real and tangible benefits, of many kinds, for all of us. Now, at a time when our ability to solve increasingly complicated problems — in the economy, in international affairs, in health, in ethnic relations, in technology — depends so much on intelligent leadership, on people who can both analyze and act, on research that can illuminate patterns in behavior or the deepest puzzles in nature: at such a time we cannot afford to give up on the basic commitments and investments that have been so much a source of our collective human and economic strength.

The question many people are asking is whether we can afford to make such investments in research and education. This is now – and always – an essential question to keep before us. But the other question we must ask as we look to the future of our society as a whole is whether we can afford *not* to make such investments.

We dare not underestimate the dangers, even if they are not immediately apparent. If, for instance, the enterprise of basic science is seriously damaged at the National Institutes of Health, the National Science Foundation, and other agencies, we may not see or feel the most profound effects either today or tomorrow. After all, it has taken fully forty years since the discovery of the structure of DNA to begin to realize what it will finally yield in terms of medical, social, and economic benefits. We may well persuade ourselves into thinking that today's budget cuts will really have no profound impact. But that would be a very great mistake. The total impact will be felt later – in a decade, or even two. And then, it will be too late to turn back the clock, and it will cost a very great deal more to rebuild something that now needs only to be kept in good repair.

Many people in the Congress and the Executive Branch understand this. Many have been working hard, helping to follow the thoughtful, careful approach that is needed – and they have done so courageously, and with some real effect. The effort is bipartisan, and continuous. But our many leaders in Congress need to know that all the rest of us care, and that we too want to help. They cannot, in the current national climate, manage this entire formidable job on their own.

With them, we should remember another of Alexander Fleming's remarks fifty years ago. "The unprepared mind," he said, "cannot see the outstretched hand of opportunity." Curiosity alone does not produce new knowledge. Fortuity alone does not produce new knowledge. Rather, significant new knowledge depends on the rigorous work and imagination of prepared minds. It depends on excellent education. It depends on a climate of free inquiry, in which individuals have the flexibility and support that they need to follow their deepest insights and intuitions, in discovering new knowledge about human nature and the natural world.

✦   ✦   ✦

In closing, let us remember, too, that Alexander Fleming almost did not make it to medical school. A small legacy from a relative happened to come his way. Without that financial help, we might well never have heard of Fleming, and we might never have had the benefit of his own well-prepared mind.

In the years since World War II – though we sometimes forget this fact – higher education in America has become far more accessible than ever before. Our society's conviction about the importance of educational opportunity – as expressed in our public policy and in the constant generosity of so many individuals – has steadily opened doors to women and men of talent and energy from all backgrounds and walks of life, even when their financial means have been very modest. The commitment to provide financial aid to students in need – the commitment to openness and inclusiveness in our colleges and universities – has been one of the defining achievements of American society in the last fifty years.

For example, the Harvard class of 1945 included the first Harvard graduates who were supported by scholarships under the GI Bill of Rights, one of the great steps forward in expanding access to American higher education. In the following decades, we have seen even broader efforts to open the doors of our colleges and universities. Here, as in the case of scientific research, the key to progress has been a powerful partnership between educational institutions and the government – as well as generous private donors and, of course, our students and their families.

Here, too, we have arrived at a major crossroads. There are proposals in Washington that would turn back the clock in significant ways. There are deeply troubling signs that an immensely productive investment in financial aid and access to education is in increasing danger.

For instance, the idea of beginning to charge interest on student loans from the moment a student enrolls in college would — if adopted — add very substantially to student debt, for graduate students as well as for undergraduates. The proposals to freeze or cut campus-based aid programs such as work-study, or to freeze the Pell Grant program, are no less disturbing.

We must not let these and similar reversals take place. President Conant told us why, when he spoke here fifty years ago. Broad access to education, he said, "is the great instrument created by American democracy to secure the foundations of a republic of free [people]." He remembered the many Harvard alumni who had given their lives to secure that freedom. And he pledged that we would honor their sacrifice — that we would work even harder, in times of peace, to serve society by continuing to advance knowledge and by keeping the doors of educational opportunity open to everyone.

We must not, at this important moment, turn our backs on that pledge — for *all* of our sakes, and for the health of the nation. We have made good on our shared commitment to education, year after year, decade after decade, for these past fifty years. Let us not begin to falter now.

Our Pursuit of Science and Health

Dinner Remarks at the School of Public Health "Healthier World" Conference
October 14, 1994

ANY SCHOOL that cares seriously about the public and its welfare, that sets out to improve the general health of all peoples, and that concentrates on prevention rather than on convalescence must be inherently optimistic, very smart, quick off the mark, and the very opposite of value-neutral. That's the kind of school – if I only were bright enough to be admitted – that I would like to join. But if I cannot be a true participant, I am delighted at least to be an interloper.

I read carefully through the program of presentations and discussions. It does sound, I admit, wonderfully upbeat. John Spengler's talk, as I remember, is entitled, "Every Breath You Take: Toxins in the Air." Then Tim Ford will entertain you with "Water, Water Everywhere: Is There a Drop to Drink?" Then Walter Willett: "Red Flags on the Menu: Finding Your Way through the Nutritional Maze." Later, Mary Wilson will say something about the health hazards of travel – namely, that we humans seem to be extremely attractive food for every conceivable kind of parasite in every part of the globe.

All of this, I know, will be stimulating, illuminating, and intellectually exciting — as well as important. But, I am glad that my own remarks at this dinner, held in the darkened and no doubt polluted air of downtown Boston, a city surrounded by undrinkable harbor waters that must be inhabited by invisible parasitical marvels beyond our most fertile imagining — I am quite glad that this dinner is happening now, before you learn later that it may be a colossal mistake for you to breathe, travel, eat, or even sit next to one another.

This particular ordering of events — dinner tonight, warnings of nutritional disaster tomorrow — should be taken, therefore, as testimony to our humility, wisdom, and relish of festivity, as well as our pursuit of science and public health. Because while we care deeply about the environment and its effects on human beings, we also do recognize that we cannot control everything during every one of our waking moments. Let us, therefore, be mildly irresponsible gourmets and moderate imbibers this evening, oblivious to the invisible noxious environmental gremlins that are certainly everywhere in our midst at this very moment.

✦   ✦   ✦

Many of the problems — and potential solutions — that you will be hearing about are new. But they also represent something of the School's continuity and its historical mission. For instance, in 1936, at Harvard's 300th anniversary, this school had a major symposium called "The Environment and Its Effect upon Man." What were the topics? They included a panel on "Airborne Infection"; another on "Industrial Fatigue" — I'm not sure whether we've actually cured that problem, or whether we've simply resigned ourselves to living with it; then there was "Toxic Dust or Fumes"; and then something quite ominous and fancy called "Toxic Organic Vapors and Gases," which apparently infiltrated themselves everywhere at that time.

Yes, there is real continuity and some similarity in the topics and concerns of the School, in spite of the obvious differences in nomenclature over the past sixty years. Is there also a significant change, beyond the nomenclature? I believe so. An important emphasis — not the only one, but a strong one — in some of the titles of tomorrow's presentations, introduces the active agent "you" as well as the external objective, environmental objects around you. The focus, in other words, is not simply on the environment but also on what individuals can do through knowledge, awareness, habit, exercise, attention to nutrition, personal choice — through our *behavior*, in other words — to improve our own health and that of the larger population. We are clearly seeking ways to help purify the world outside ourselves. Yet, equally, we are trying to discover what we ourselves can do — through our behavior — to make life more healthy, productive, and satisfying.

This sense of vitality and activity — of emphasizing the active and purposeful individual and our ability to alter conditions in the world, not simply be victimized by them — pervades the spirit of the School of Public Health and its many activities. Let me offer just a few more — somewhat different — examples:

Within the last year, teams of researchers from the School of Public Health have conducted fact-finding missions to Bosnia, Iraq, Haiti, and other trouble-spots, to study and document the different ways in which political upheaval takes a toll on the health of innocent people.

Next, the School is sponsoring a pilot program in a Baltimore public school, for students in grades four through eight: it is called "Eat Well and Keep Moving." The hope, of course, is to teach young children about nutrition, exercise, and healthy habits that can last them a lifetime.

Finally, there is a new initiative, using the media — especially television dramas — to try to have an impact on teenage gangs and violence. The initiative is aptly called "Squash It": when individual teenagers or gangs dare one another to fight, the cool thing to do is for someone to say, "Squash it" — to interrupt the dynamics, call the situation to a halt, and allow the young people to disengage "honorably" by agreeing to follow a new set of rules. This program is in its early stages, but it is a promising new start.

And so I am pleased that we are gathered together this evening to celebrate this school and its programs, its commitments, and its care. As the very opposite of value-neutral it points us — and leads us — in the very directions that we ought, as a University, to follow in our various pursuits, including those of science and of health.

This Astonishing
Technological Phenomenon

Address to the Third Harvard University Conference on the Internet and Society
May 31, 2000

AS WE BEGIN this conference on the future of the Internet
and society, we can be reasonably sure that whatever we predict is almost guaranteed to be wrong, probably by quite a wide
margin. Even if, by chance, some of our ideas are right, few of us, if
any, will have the wit to know it. Winston Churchill once said
about Stanley Baldwin that he "occasionally stumbles on the
truth, but he always picks himself up and hurries on as if nothing
happened." In thinking about the Internet, we shall do well if we
can see our way to making sensible choices – and understanding
at least some of their implications – to guide us over the course of
the next two to four years.

Let me begin by saying that my own view is that the Internet,
with all of its related technologies, has introduced the most profound and far-reaching technological revolution since the nineteenth and very early twentieth centuries, when there was a
dramatic transformation in fundamental modes of communica-

tion, in access to immense quantities of new information in new as well as old formats, and in more rapid means of travel in a more open, internationalized world. Throughout the nineteenth century, there were major shifts in the means of production, and in the structure of business enterprise and the patterns of commerce — and, with respect to universities, dramatic changes in teaching, learning, research, and the very structure of fields of knowledge.

The major inventions, discoveries, and innovations that led to this set of transformations more than a century ago are on the whole very well known. They included wired-cable, then telephonic, and then radio communications; new sources of energy that powered railroads, steamships, automobiles, airplanes, and the machinery used in the production of manufactured goods; the design of modern factory systems, which led to new conceptions and patterns of work, of management, and of productivity; and — in the world of universities, information, and learning — the invention of inexpensive large-scale book publishing, using wood-pulp paper and inexpensive binding, which soon led to the creation of massive research libraries with infinitely more information freely available to students, faculty, and others than ever before. At about the same time, modern scientific experimental laboratories began to be created for research and teaching in colleges.

These last two innovations, the creation of major research libraries and modern scientific laboratories, transformed the nature of study and learning. In fact, they changed the whole experience of, and the approach to, education. For the first time, students could be asked to do library and laboratory research on their own, to write more complicated and extensive papers. There was a much greater emphasis on teaching students to learn how to be apprentice scholars, to work more actively as explorers, rather than passively as the "receivers" of established knowledge. All of these changes created massive shifts in how universities functioned.

Nearly all the transformations that I have just described were accompanied by hymns of praise extolling the marvels to be wrought by the new technologies, as well as by predictions of the mass disaster we would all suffer at the hands of the new machinery. As it turned out, the human race absorbed and adjusted to everything that took place, although it might be difficult to create a thoughtful balance sheet — a calculus of credits and debits — to evaluate the net effect on society of all that happened in that era.

We know that many of the adjustments were certainly not easy. Untold numbers of people, in various forms of cottage industries and handicrafts, were put out of work. Even apparently simple things, such as learning how to travel by railroad, took more time than we might think. Many passengers tended, for example, to look out of their windows at close range, watching objects flash by rapidly, because they had previously looked out of their much slower horse-drawn carriages in exactly this near-range way. The result for large numbers of people on trains was a kind of perpetual vertigo — dizziness accompanied by uncheerful nausea. Finally, passengers began to develop and use what has since been called "panoramic" vision, a concentration on the middle and far distance, where objects and the horizon remain relatively stable and caused only modest — if any — metabolic mutations.

It is worth remembering some of the ways in which the new information and other technologies affected people's lives, and their sense of coherence — or incoherence — a century ago, because it provides at least some perspective on the present moment. As we think about the next quarter century or half century in relation to our own set of new technologies, we can be certain that there will be some adverse changes, but we may take some heart from the fact that other eras have confronted similar problems, and yet we have, it seems, apparently survived.

In higher education, I would venture to bet that as a result of the new technologies, there will, in the next few decades, be many more institutions — and more different kinds of institutions — devoted to education and training. Some will be more virtual than not. Some will reach entire populations of students, at different age levels, that are mainly beyond the reach of our present education system.

In addition, the ability to deliver vital medical information, for example, about new treatments for disease, or better knowledge about serious problems in public health, or in business and law, and many other fields — that ability carries the potential to affect in positive ways the well-being of people and societies everywhere, and to do so more rapidly and less expensively than is now conceivable.

I am inclined to believe that, at least for most undergraduates and first-degree graduate or professional school students, a residential education that is founded on the ability of human beings to educate one another, through constant association — in a multitude of activities, in class and out of class — will continue to be the most powerful, stimulating, and profound available. The new information technologies can reinforce and extend — powerfully — what can be achieved in such campus-based education and research. For instance, over one thousand of our undergraduate courses already have sophisticated Web sites, with many kinds of information on them that is often unavailable in other forms. E-mail questions pass back and forth at all hours. On-line class discussion groups take place before and after face-to-face classes — and so on.

The uses of the new technologies are already affecting — profoundly — how we teach on campus, how we do research, and how we learn.

At the same time, it is hard to imagine a truly excellent education in all the liberal arts and sciences that would be fundamentally carried out "on-line." How much real science, experimental science, could one expect to do "virtually"? Can one really do — at least in a research university — major historical work without an extraordinary library that has rare printed materials, as well as millions of manuscript pages (and other items) that are vital to the scholar and advanced student but are not likely to be digitized at any point in the foreseeable future?

And how do we help to inculcate important communal as well as individual values – including the benefits of a diverse student body and faculty – if we do not have students and faculty present on campus, in an actual living and working residential community where people must learn to come to terms with one another's differences as well as their similarities? How do we sustain and build an educational community where one can, in microcosm, try to achieve a greater measure of tolerance and understanding among many different kinds of people – something that the world at large will have to achieve if we are finally to manage our human affairs in ways that are peaceable, respectful, and decent?

There is, in short, simply too much of education that involves human growth and development, human interaction, and the stimulus of human debate, discussion, questioning, probing, and collaboration; there is too much that depends on the development of human relations that are real and that cannot be compensated for electronically. Given that fact, I believe that campus-based residential education is here to stay, because of its unrivaled excellence and also because it can do certain vital things that on-line or distance learning simply cannot do.

I am certain that the new technologies will have profound, long-term effects in higher education: they will lead to a greater differentiation of institutional types; they will be especially powerful in mid-career distance learning and in reaching whole populations who have essentially no access to education right now; and they will reinforce and extend the capacity and quality of the very best in undergraduate residential education, rather than replacing the on-campus experience.

For all the other ways in which these technologies will alter our lives, I leave to our other conference speakers. I thank you all for coming – and thank you for contributing so much to our collective effort to understand this quite astonishing technological phenomenon that now lives among us and with us.

THE PROFESSIONS,
COMMUNITIES,
AND PUBLIC SERVICE

The Changing Professions

From Part III of the President's Report to the Board of Overseers

1991–93

NEARLY ALL the major professions in the United States — and the organizations associated with them — are in a state of unusual flux. Businesses face a difficult and uncertain economy, an altered international situation, and an era of widespread fundamental restructuring. The health care system is under severe strain and is undergoing large-scale comprehensive reform. Much the same can be said of our troubled public schools. Many institutions of government throughout the world are perceived even by those within them as being in need of serious rehabilitation; and global political developments have made the study and practice of public affairs even more complex than before.

Meanwhile, the legal profession faces a far more complicated international as well as national agenda: increased litigation and regulation, persistent questions concerning human and civil rights, the effort to help frame constitutions and systems of justice in emerging democratic societies, and a domestic criminal justice system under severe strain. The religious landscape has been dramatically transformed during the past quarter century, in our own country and beyond. Some established faiths have waned, while new sects and congregations have burgeoned; various fundamentalist movements have obviously emerged with great force; and questions about the relationship between religion and politics or government have arisen with great intensity in many quarters of the globe. Finally, in architecture and its associated design fields, there have also been profound changes – partly because of the continued internationalization of these professions, partly because of changes in the economy, and partly because of the need to address important social problems, such as preserving our built as well as our natural environment.

These developments in the professions (and in the major systems and institutions that are part of professional life) have an inevitable, far-reaching impact on education. If the professions change in more than superficial or transitory ways, then education for the professions must also change. A fundamental reexamination of many of our basic programs is already well under way at Harvard. Given the variety of Harvard's professional schools – business, design, divinity, education, government, law, medicine and dentistry, and public health – we obviously cannot expect to find a single new educational model or conception that will apply equally well to all or even most of them. Yet a number of common approaches and similar emphases have emerged in the course of our planning process.

✦   ✦   ✦

Among the most prominent common themes and directions emerging from the plans of our professional schools are these:

First, nearly every School is reviewing, or has recently finished reviewing, the design of its first-degree program – and, in some cases, its more advanced training programs as well. The Medical School has led the way: it began to phase in its watershed New Pathway program for the M.D. degree in the mid-1980s, and full implementation is near. The School of Public Health has just reorganized its basic curriculum around five interdisciplinary topics closely linked to its main research agenda; meanwhile, a special fund has been created in the School to support experiments with promising new teaching methods. The Business School is in the midst of a full-scale review of its M.B.A. program, and specific recommendations are expected soon. The Graduate School of Design is reexamining the curriculum for its master's programs, aiming to provide all students with the opportunity for an integrated introduction to the major design fields, including architecture, landscape architecture, urban design, and planning.

These are only a few leading examples of the "reconstruction" now under way in Harvard's professional schools. Comparisons are difficult, but it is hard to remember a time in recent history when curricular reform in professional education at Harvard has been so pervasive, so fundamental, and so potentially significant in its consequences.

Second, the Schools' plans reflect a growing emphasis on the mission of training for leadership in public service. The professional schools have always been motivated to educate students to become leaders who will, in the fullest sense, be useful to society. At present, however, there is an even stronger emphasis on the importance of leadership and on the mission of public service – an emphasis that is not so much ideological as genuinely civic in nature.

There is, as I suggested earlier, a greater concern to help restore the vitality of large-scale systems and organizations that have been weakened in the past quarter century. There is a special concern for the not-for-profit sector of society: schools, government, social service organizations, and cultural institutions and activities. And there is a marked tendency to take into account more profoundly the difficult questions of ethics and values that are intrinsic to all professional practice today.

In other words, many of our professional schools are defining not a new mission, but a different emphasis in the way they are approaching their traditional mission. There is a more conscious awareness that the world is troubled, that the foundations of society seem less stable, that interdependencies are greater, and that our need to be responsive must also be greater. Such concerns — underscoring a determined yet unromantic commitment to serve society — echo through the planning documents of many Schools.

Third, virtually every School has identified the reexamination of teaching methods as a major point of focus in the years to come. For it is teaching, in many different settings, that must bring together fundamental or abstract knowledge, the fruits of current research, and something of the experience of "live" practice and decision making.

Equally important, teaching needs to be structured in a way that involves students as active participants in the process of inquiry. From this point of view, the best teaching should be seen as an embryonic form of research. It should be designed to confront students with the need to test ideas and hypotheses against facts and experience, to find new ways to approach difficult problems, and to search for and analyze relevant evidence. It should, in other words, help students to develop habits of mind that can sustain them throughout a lifetime of facing unpredictable challenges and dilemmas that require continuous learning.

In short, as we move forward in professional education, we will continue to emphasize education for leadership — with a concern for the development of values, qualities, and capacities that leadership requires. Consistent with the University's goal of remaining an international as well as a national institution, we will preserve a strong interest in virtually all aspects of international education. And we will continue our commitment to more effective teaching and learning, with a strong emphasis on small-group classes and seminars; a greater reliance on "cases," problems, or issues that can focus attention on complex situations requiring active inquiry and debate; a recognition of the need to exploit the benefits of modern technologies in the classroom as well as in research; and an increased interest in student internships, fieldwork, or similar activities to help ensure that we do a proper job of connecting practice with formal academic study. In School after School we find that investments in additional faculty — however modest the numbers — are closely linked to investments in better teaching. Finally, we must recognize the benefits to be gained from integrating fields of knowledge, and from encouraging collaboration across different parts of the University in order to make more effective use of the resources we already possess.

A Mind As It Reasons

Introduction of Stanford Law School Dean Kathleen Sullivan
at the Radcliffe Institute Inaugural Lecture Series
April 28, 2000

WHEN KATHLEEN SULLIVAN was an undergraduate at Cornell in the early 1970s, she concentrated in literary studies and was especially captured — as she herself has said — by the moral dilemmas that she found so strikingly portrayed in fiction.

It was just then that the political drama of Watergate was unfolding, and Dean Sullivan began "to see law as a practical arena [in which] to find solutions to moral and ethical problems."

Perhaps not surprisingly, Dean Sullivan (following a sojourn at Oxford as a Marshall Scholar) was ultimately drawn to the field of American constitutional law: the field in which questions of value; of rights and obligations; of freedoms, potential restrictions, public goods, and private as well as public responsibilities come dramatically into play — more continuously, more perplexingly, more subtly, and more significantly than in any other legal field.

Dean Sullivan studied at the Harvard Law School, where she worked with Professor Laurence Tribe — not only as a student, but also as a colleague — on a well-known Supreme Court case in which they defended the right of the Hare Krishna sect to proselytize at the Minnesota State Fair.

The records of the case do not disclose why members of the Krishna sect ever thought the Minnesota State Fair might be a fertile sphere for missionary zeal. But thanks to their unconventional evangelical foray, the team of Tribe & Sullivan was created — and later went on to tackle several other major cases involving the defense of privacy rights, of free speech issues raised in the so-called "Titicut Follies" twenty-four-year litigation marathon, and of the right of newly arrived poor mothers in California to receive AFDC benefits at the same level as long-term California residents.

Kathleen Sullivan began teaching at Harvard Law School in 1984 and remained at Harvard until 1993, when she was lost — inexplicably — to Stanford, where she became Dean of the Law School in 1999. She has written about a wide range of constitutional issues and has won any number of awards and honors, including the most prestigious award for excellence in teaching that the Harvard Law School bestows.

For me, the pleasure in reading Dean Sullivan's work is a very distinct one, because her writing manages to fuse the forms of persuasion that flow from conviction and commitment with those that are the result of such deft and skilled analysis that the activity of the mind as it reasons, and the almost indiscernible interpolation of evidence, are carried forward without any sense of rhetorical or argumentative "forcing," without any more pressure than the minimum required.

If we want to think carefully, for example, about the difference between judges who tend to view the law and the Constitution in terms of a set of rules, as contrasted to a set of standards, then there just is no better reading than Dean Sullivan's 1992 *Harvard Law Review* article on that subject. It is an article that explores why a Supreme Court which included Justices Rehnquist, Scalia, Thomas, O'Connor, Kennedy, and Souter did not turn out to be as "conservative" as many people — including Presidents Reagan and Bush — had expected.

This is not the time or the place to try to summarize Dean Sullivan's hundred pages of text and footnotes, except to say that the essay examines quite beautifully how some (not all) individual justices on the Supreme Court began in the 1980s to use historical precedent in quite different ways, on different occasions — depending on the circumstance and the larger context of specific cases. They became, in other words, more engaged with the particularities of each dilemma or situation and (to some extent) less inclined to invoke more general rules in reaching conclusions. The article also elaborates on how the Court must — within limits — function as a collective, deliberative body, thereby creating for itself a sense of responsibility for, and consciousness of, a more comprehensive and heterogeneous range of views than an analysis of the past practice and views of each individual justice would have led us to predict.

In short, as we read this article, we come to see and feel the developing changes in position or stance, in perspective and amplitude, in the very conception of how law should be interpreted and applied, on the part of several justices: we can trace the kinds of moves and shifts that often occur in any small group whose number of members is highly limited, because at least some of the members soon come to see themselves (and their views) less in fixed or absolute terms, than as parts of a whole in which their own roles are defined (to some extent) in relationship to the roles adopted by their colleagues.

In reading Dean Sullivan's article, we experience and understand the subtlety and nuance of all the changes I have just mentioned, because of the skillful analysis and the lucid prose that guide us at every stage in this unfolding mini-drama. Beyond that, we also begin to sense — gradually — the presence of a larger design in the work, because the entire piece is in fact motivated by a deep conviction concerning the essential integrity of the Court as an institution that somehow discovers and follows a kind of invisible internal compass – that achieves and adjusts its own equilibrium, responding to the necessities of the Constitution as an enduring document, to historical precedents that act as a partial guide, and to the living society in which the law must function with credence and effectiveness. Because the equilibrium of the Court is always subject to constant shifts and changes, predicting how the Court may resolve any particular case becomes very difficult. But this "openness" tends in itself to increase rather than decrease confidence in the responsiveness as well as the strength of the system.

Confidence or trust in significant institutions is not noticeably in great abundance at the present time. It is a rare thing to encounter writing that offers us some considerable measure of persuasive reassurance about the nature of our Supreme Court and the workings of our constitutional legal system. The achievement is all the more impressive because the reassurance is born not from sentiment or any mere simplicity but from the articulateness and clarity of a complex mind in elegant motion.

Leading Medical Education

Daniel C. Tosteson Medical Education Center Dinner
June 12, 1997

W E ARE ASSEMBLED, friends, colleagues, and family members all, to mark the conclusion of a historic Harvard deanship: Daniel C. Tosteson will leave his post in eighteen days, having held it — held it aloft — for 7,382 days, or approximately twenty years.

Longevity alone would make Dan Tosteson's deanship remarkable. His is a profession where many may seem to be called, but few are actually chosen, and even fewer survive, and far fewer yet can be said to thrive.

Yet our dean has thrived, and indeed triumphed, in a way that will not easily be rivaled, much less surpassed.

I have been asked to speak particularly about Dan as an educator — as someone powerfully committed to the education of students at all levels, of physicians, of patients, and of human institutions, such as this university.

It is the institutional dimension — a dimension that really embraces all the others — that I want to focus upon: partly because that is where Dan Tosteson has made one of his most visible, profound, and lasting contributions; and partly because almost all the odds are magnificently stacked against anyone who sets out to transform the curriculum, the pedagogy, the form and process, and consequently the content or substance of university learning. Now it is certainly true that professors of medicine — and medical school departments, organized as they are around intensive research — are known far and wide for their astonishing flexibility, malleability, and willingness to change at the snap of a decanal finger or two. Nonetheless, it is also the case that, until recently, scarcely any medical school has actually changed in a significant way its fundamental process of education.

Harvard has done so, and it has done so because of the vision, insight, relentlessness, persuasive power, and decisiveness of Daniel Tosteson. We should remember that, although academic, departmental, and other structures look like tiny boxes on an organizational chart, they are really made of concrete and steel, buttressed by adamantine marble. And the University as a whole — as well as the profession of medicine — often seems even more implacable than the departments. Caught between these twin forces, both exerting pressure from opposite directions, any dean is bound to feel at least some mild discomfort and constraint. It takes an ingenious person, skilled in prestidigitation, to turn so procrustean a predicament into something providentially creative.

Ogden Nash once wrote: "The turtle lives 'twixt plated decks / Which practically conceal its sex. / I think it clever of the turtle / In such a fix to be so fertile."[1]

Dan has been, between his plated decks, the soul of fertility itself, in the sphere of medical education. Let me mention the main reasons.

First, he recognized the rapid rate of change in scientific knowledge.

Second, he realized that full-scale mastery was beyond anyone, and that much of what one mastered would soon be obsolete in any event.

Third, he saw that the spirit of active learning, of inquiry and discovery, of learning how to learn — to frame the right questions, look for relevant evidence, frame hypotheses and test them, and arrive at conclusions based on less-than-full knowledge – that all of these were the constituents of real education. Of course, content was important, but content would change, and the habits and skill of active inquiry, research, and learning were needed for a lifetime. Next, he saw that the value of problem solving was critical: cases, small groups, tutorials, questions and answers, teamwork – not only in the classroom, but also in physicians' work.

All of this led, of course, to the creation of a powerful model in medical education – the New Pathway program that is now being emulated by many medical schools across the nation. The purpose of the new program is to help foster the kind of sensitivity in medical practice that Dan himself has described:

> *Each medical encounter is unique in a personal, social and biologic sense. Each patient and physician is an individual person reminded by the episode that brings them together that "brass, nor stone, nor earth, nor boundless sea, but sad mortality o'ersways their power." Each patient lives in a specific social context. Each patient is the expression of a genome that has never existed before. All these aspects of uniqueness impose on both physician and patient the need to learn about the always new situation, to find the plan of action that is most likely to improve the health of that particular patient at that particular time. In this way of thinking, a doctor is a teacher helping the patient to learn about possibilities for living in a healthier way.*[2]

Learning is the connective tissue everywhere, throughout the whole process – student, teacher, physician, patient: all seeking to understand, to solve dilemmas, and to keep inquiring for the sake of health and the ability to lead satisfying and productive lives.

In concluding, I would like to read a poem concerning the human spirit's unwillingness to accept limits in the quest to do the impossible – or nearly impossible. The poem has to do with taking the risk of planting a peach tree much farther north than peach trees should be planted, in the hope that it might withstand all the forces marshaled against it, and bloom. It must hold out against the coldest, most formidable deep-winter weather — which is where the poem begins:

> *We sit indoors and talk of the cold outside.*
> *And every gust that gathers strength and heaves*
> *Is a threat to the house. But the house has long been tried.*
> *We think of the tree. If it never again has leaves,*
> *We'll know, we say, that this was the night it died.*
> *It is very far north, we admit, to have brought the peach.*
> *What comes over a man, is it soul or mind —*
> *That to no limits and bounds he can stay confined?*
> *You would say his ambition was to extend the reach*
> *Clear to the Arctic of every living kind.*
> *Why is his nature forever so hard to teach*
> *That though there is no fixed line between wrong and right,*
> *There are roughly zones whose laws must be obeyed?*
> *There is nothing much we can do for the tree tonight,*
> *But we can't help feeling more than a little betrayed*
> *That the northwest wind should rise to such a height*
> *Just when the cold went down so many below.*
> *The tree has no leaves and may never have them again.*
> *We must wait till some months hence in the spring to know.*
> *But if it is destined never again to grow,*
> *It can blame this limitless trait in the hearts of men.*[3]

We can recognize Dan Tosteson here — sturdy against the elements, settling for nothing less than the best — pathways or peach trees, whatever the challenge, it will be met and overcome.

---

1 Ogden Nash, "The Turtle," in *The Selected Verse of Ogden Nash* (New York: Modern Library, 1946), 90.

2 Daniel C. Tosteson, "Learning in Medicine," *New England Journal of Medicine* 301 (1979): 690.

3 Robert Frost, "There Are Roughly Zones," in *The Poetry of Robert Frost* (New York: Henry Holt and Company, 1979), 305.

Landscape Architecture at Harvard

Remarks at the Centennial Celebration
of the Department of Landscape Architecture
Graduate School of Design, April 8, 2000

H ARVARD WAS the first university to offer a four-year course leading to a degree in landscape architecture. That began during the forty-year reign of our greatest president — Charles William Eliot, who held sway over the University from 1869 until 1909.

It was under Eliot that so much of the configuration of Harvard — as landscape, architecture, and incipient urban design — began to take shape: partly planned, partly through sheer accident, and partly by way of recognizing opportunities as they presented themselves.

I mention this partly because it was Eliot's own interests, as well as those of his son and grandson, that helped to spur the growth of all the studies in art, architecture, landscape design, and planning which ultimately resulted in Harvard's School of Design.

In addition, however, Eliot also had a quite clear sense that this particular university would not take the form of a unified, coherent campus — an academic parkland — but would inevitably be compelled to interdigitate with the city growing up around it. He also decided not to adopt a single architectural norm, but moved from Georgian to muted Victorian as he filled out the Yard; then to high-pitched Victorian Gothic at Memorial Hall; then to the idiom of H. H. Richardson at Sever and Austin Halls; and then to sophisticated versions of neo-Georgian buildings designed by McKim, Mead, and White.

Harvard would be various and peculiarly textured, with quadrangles and the Yard to serve as refuges, but elsewhere with sharp juxtapositions and abrupt adjacencies, with street crossings and a mid-center square, and with all the stylistic discordances that we know and love so well. Where else could one stand, rotate, and take in (from a single point) the atonalities, not quite orchestrated, of Sert's Science Center, Memorial Hall, Busch Hall, Yamasaki's William James Hall, the Swedenborg Chapel, Gund Hall, the Sackler Museum and — looking up Quincy Street — the Fogg, Le Corbusier's Carpenter Center, Robinson Hall, and heaven knows what else?

It is interesting that if you compare the prose written about Princeton's campus and that about Harvard's, you see immediately in the syntax, and the length of sentences, not to mention the diction, how Princeton beckons writers to create sinuous, curvilinear, lengthening lines that always seem to yearn for long vistas and romantic crescendos before they come to a close. By contrast, Harvard's passages very occasionally begin to open out in a similar way, only to come very soon to quite sudden, mundane endings, because there simply are no sweeping vistas to sustain very much deep purple prose.

Does Princeton succeed visually, in space and time, as one satisfying version of landscape architecture? Does Harvard succeed, on its own terms, as one (or more) versions, or do we have to move to a much more abstract level of conceptual understanding before we can begin to make sense of it? If movement, crowds, energy, streets, stores, automobiles, visual variety — with some sense of order in the movement from one kind of precinct to another — if all of that matters, then the landscaped architectures and urban non-design of Harvard does seem to be very appealing to students and even adults. It apparently makes up in vitality what it lacks in a certain kind of stylistic unity or apparent coherence. Or else it represents a different sort of coherence, where we can consider and evaluate the built and natural environment only in relation to the particular styles of life of a particular set of converging communities in a complex series of collegiate, commercial, residential, and other spaces.

I raise all these questions and issues partly for selfish reasons. As Harvard now tries to create a few remaining important structures or architectural landscape environments on this side of the river, it has been a major challenge to decide what might constitute successful designs for them. One project is a possible museum of modern art on the river, downstream from here; the other is an international studies center, just around the corner, consisting of two buildings — one on each side of the street.

Neither of these projects is so idiosyncratic as to require unfettered genius for a solution. But each raises quite central questions about the interrelationships between urban design, architecture, landscape, and streetscape, environmental concerns, and the kinds of human communities (including the program of activities) that we hope to foster in each place.

Thankfully, members of this School's faculty are helping us, so I have absolutely no doubt about the ultimate outcome, assuming that we will receive permits allowing us to build anything at all. But I have been led by this entire process to believe not only that the field of landscape architecture is very much alive and well at Harvard, but also that it is faced with exceptionally complex problems at the present time, problems that force us to think about the nature of the field itself — its edges, its center, its fundamentals, and its extensions.

Fortunately, the duties of Harvard's President do not require him to define the nature of academic fields, quite apart from their possible applications in practice. It is more than enough for me to try to assess results in terms of talent and quality of performance. With respect to those criteria, I want to take this opportunity to say that I — and the University — take enormous pride in the distinguished present, and the equally distinguished past, of landscape architecture at Harvard.

It is no exaggeration to say that Harvard's faculty (and graduates) invented and reinvented the field; that thanks in large part to you, there is now a far deeper understanding of the many disciplines that the field comprises; that whether we are talking about plants, about grasses, about gardens, or different forms of natural landscape, or architecture, design, urban planning, regional planning, environmental planning, and any number of other considerations, this department and School have the capacity to analyze, to imagine, to create, to preserve, to restore, and to intervene at a level of excellence that no analogous department or School has realized.

Servant of the Public Good

Remarks about Alan Greenspan
Honorary Degrees Dinner, June 9, 1999

BORN in New York City, educated at NYU, our last honorand
dabbled for a brief few years as the head of his own financial
consulting firm. Then, weary of the burdens of private office, he
moved into the much more profitable public sector to become
chairman of the President's Council of Economic Advisers. Shortly afterward, he became chairman of the National Commission
on Social Security Reform, and then on to any number of advisory, chairmanly, boardly, and commissionly positions, until in
1987 he became chairman of the Federal Reserve.

In a miraculous display of tripartisanship, three separate presidents, from two more-or-less identifiable political parties, have
kept him continuously tethered to what has by now become his
own federally reserved chair.

His achievement has been more than impressive and has con-
founded all the received ignorance of his chosen academic field.
What is the secret of Dr. Greenspan's success? It surely has something to do with his prose style. He has (as he himself has phrased
it) "learned how to mumble with great incoherence." Or, as he

said on another occasion, "If I seem unduly clear to you, you must have misunderstood what I said."

Since my own field is English literature, I recently took the liberty of examining just one page of Dr. Greenspan's prose. In twenty-odd lines I found approximately forty examples of conditionals, qualifiers, and other artful miasmics including everything from "if... but... nevertheless... however... yet... despite... whether or not... while one might... although it is true" to "most... not all... partly... probably... perhaps..." and "as best I can tell... it seems... appears... implies... suggests... I suspect... it would be unwise."

These paragraphs, moreover, tend to be studded with intermittent conclusions, assuring us, for example, that a particular question (and I quote) "will be answered" not by the chairman himself, "but only with the inexorable passage of time." In this deconstructed age of ours, it is a distinct pleasure to have someone at our economic helm who is so much in tune with the literary theory of our era, and wears his linguistic indeterminacy so lightly upon his sleeve.

Nevertheless, Dr. Greenspan's homespun prose, like Penelope's daily knitting and unknitting, really does matter. In his speeches and articles, he raises all the hard questions, the substantive issues, and the entire range of pertinent considerations, and he does so with scrupulousness and finesse, as if weighing the finest and most transparent of virtually weightless particles, in order to see where the balances will finally quiver themselves to rest, at their precise point of equipoise. What we apprehend, in other words, is the faculty of informed, experienced, seismically sensitive, and marvelously sure judgment in action — judgment so fine that it has earned him the confidence and respect of millions around the world.

Celebrating Courage and Commitment

Nieman Fellows Reunion Remarks
John F. Kennedy Library, April 29, 2000

LONG AGO, when the Nieman bequest fell out of the sky, without any warning, onto the otherwise tidy desk of President James Conant, his reaction approximated something that might be described as intensely unqualified ambivalence. This gift, he suggested, "places another problem at our door." It was, he said, the most unlikely Christmas present he could have imagined.

Nonetheless, the President took up the challenge, which consisted of giving some tangible educational shape to something described only in the vaguest possible terms by the deed of gift: to wit, an effort intended to "elevate the standards of journalism in the United States." With characteristic intelligence and imagination, President Conant set up a fellowship program not very different in conception from the one we now have.

Not everyone cheered and shouted with unrestrained joy. Walter Lippmann, for example, from his high perch at the *New York Herald Tribune*, said that he felt "[the Nieman] experiment would not be successful if the choice of subjects open to the Fellows" remained so "freely elective."

Lippmann wanted a sort of required core curriculum,

because it seemed to him that the Fellows were wandering into all sorts of subjects and courses for which they had absolutely no preparation. This encouraged them (as Lippmann delicately phrased it) to indulge indiscriminately in the greatest of journalistic vices: the attempt "to deal with very great questions on the assumption that anybody, without previous training, can understand anything."

Fortunately, President Conant stuck to his guns, and that has made all the difference. The obvious strength of the Nieman program is precisely the fact that it has never required that the Fellows should, for whatever obscure reason, be sent back to school.

In fact, if there was ever an era when journalists — to use the term broadly — needed more time, more freedom, and more opportunity to reflect, to read widely, to explore new ideas, and to meet a great diversity of people in an unfettered way, then *this* era of twenty-four-hour-a-day breaking instant news is certainly such a moment.

Nieman Fellows, and others, need that time and freedom because the conditions under which you work have never been more difficult, even ferocious. The rest of us, meanwhile, really do need you to be at your absolute best, because you are — collectively — the crucial filter through which, day in and day out, we try to make sense of contemporary reality as it unfolds. If this is a period when the media have often been subject to criticism from many quarters, I myself want to stress something very different: the depth of your service to society, to free institutions everywhere, and to the indispensable values of open inquiry and free expression.

These happen to be values that are also absolutely critical to the central purposes of universities, and that is clearly one of the reasons why the Nieman program and Harvard have reinforced and energized one another over so many decades. And your role, in guarding the values that we share, is in significant respects the harder one. It involves more uncertainty, more pressure to make instantaneous judgments, more daily public exposure and reaction. Beyond all of that, we have seen, for instance, in the last two or three weeks, what has happened to the "reformist" press in Iran, and each of us could cite any number of similar examples. To create and sustain real freedom of the press remains, in most parts of the world, a job that is filled with hazard and danger. It demands, under even the most favorable circumstances, more than a little courage and deep conviction over long periods of time.

A Sympathetic Imagination

Comments at the Swearing-in of Justice Margaret Marshall
to the Massachusetts Supreme Judicial Court
October 31, 1996

I WANT TO SAY a few things about Margaret Marshall, because I have worked so closely with her these last four years. I
want to single out just three of her qualities — qualities that in
some respects may be obvious, but are worth some reflection.

First, this is a person of remarkable intelligence — an incisive
intelligence — keen, sharpened in relation to the realities of life as
well as the realities of law. So, the very first quality that one needs
in the practice of law and in the art of "judging" (as well as in helping to run a university) is present here in its full power: the capacity to make significant distinctions and to see things clearly, with
a mind that is fully equipped for the task at hand.

The second quality may be somewhat less obvious, but is
essentially nothing more nor less than a sympathetic imagination. We clearly cannot make difficult judgments about situations or people unless we can reach out with our imagination —
with our entire mind, with our full human powers — in order to
understand the people and predicaments that confront us. We

need somehow to enter into them, and to realize how our actions will affect them. This capacity, this activity of the sympathetic imagination, is crucial in the law, and in so many of our endeavors. And Margaret Marshall has it in abundance.

Finally, she has extraordinary judgment. She has not only the insight and ability to imagine situations in human terms; she also is able weigh matters with thoughtfulness, with respect, and with integrity in the light of the law.

Let me mention two additional points. Margaret Marshall is a buoyant person. She approaches the law hopefully, with a sense of its possibilities. There is a Hobbesian point of view which suggests that the law is born of something approximating deep gloom with respect to human nature: people are such that we must find ways to constrain them — must create laws to keep individuals and society under restraint. There is a good deal of truth in this view, but it is far from the whole truth.

Another approach is to view the law as something that cherishes central human values and potentialities: liberty, respect for other individuals, and for the importance of allowing people to find their different pathways in pursuit of happiness. The law — the American constitution and our legal system — enshrines these values and hopes, and is as committed to their realization as it is aware of the need for constraint. Margaret Marshall is sensitive to both perspectives, but she understands wonderfully the importance of the liberating capacities of the law to help and sustain people, to persuade them that freedom is a reality — that individuals will be fairly treated, that societies and their laws can be equitable, that the aspirations and ideals of people are in fact part of our very conception of justice. Justice is not only a constraining but also an enabling power.

Several great justices in our legal tradition have been named Marshall. One of the very first, of course, actually established for all time the idea that the court is the final interpreter of the law in our society. It was once said of Justice Marshall — John Marshall, that is — that he possessed "a mind that created something; a heart that adored something; a faith that believed something; a hope that expected something; a life that was lived for something." These are the qualities, energies, and commitments that Margaret Marshall will bring to this distinguished Court.

Casting and Recasting

Senator Edward M. Kennedy Dinner Speech
17 Quincy Street, October 20, 1992

THIS IS INTENDED as a chance for all of us to express our special appreciation to Senator Kennedy and to Congressman William Ford, as well as to their staffs, for what they have accomplished this year on behalf of higher education — specifically in leading the long effort to design and finally pass the Higher Education Reauthorization Act.

Many of us know that this major piece of legislation was signed in July. But few of us appreciate how much was involved in casting and recasting, debating and re-debating, and finally coaxing Congress into a sufficient state of convergence so that this fiendishly complicated bill could become law. Having watched parts of the drama from a distance and having read the relevant pages in the *Congressional Record*, I can unequivocally say how much higher education (especially students and their families) will benefit from the eighteen months of analysis, negotiation, and persistent hard work that were necessary to bring about this formidable achievement.

I want to take a moment to outline some of the main provisions of the new Act.

First, it authorizes increases in the stipend for Pell Grants, allowing them to rise incrementally every year, from $3,700 in 1993 to $4,500 by 1997. It also increases the authorization for College Work-Study Programs.

Second, the new Act raises the allowable loan limits for college students, simplifies the needs-analysis process, and removes family home-equity as an item that is taken into account in federal needs analysis.

Next, it takes a major step by creating a "direct lending" demonstration project. This will allow many students and families to borrow funds directly from universities under the federal Guaranteed Student Loan Program, rather than requiring them first to seek their loans from banks. The new process will not only be far simpler but also less expensive for everyone.

Finally (and this is important, and it took literally months of discussion), new provisions were passed to allow colleges and universities to enter into purely voluntary agreements to award students financial aid on the basis of need. The institutions are also permitted to discuss broad principles that serve as a means of determining eligibility for student aid. There can be no discussion or comparison of offers to individual students, but the newly passed legislation goes a considerable distance toward correcting some of the potentially damaging effects of the situation created by the recent antitrust rulings of the Justice Department.

These are only a few of the important provisions of the new bill, and none of them, during a recession and during the difficulties of an election year, was even remotely easy to manage. The effort was bipartisan, with strong help from both sides of the aisle. But it would never have happened at all had it not been for several critical people.

In one sense, we know a great deal about how much Senator Kennedy does — and *has* done for so many years. In addition to his work on higher education, he has oversight (as chairman of the Committee on Labor and Human Resources) of all biomedical research and training legislation in the Senate. He has been enormously influential in helping to set directions for the National Institutes of Health and has had a great effect on other health-related legislation, including childhood nutrition and the pursuit of national health insurance programs. Although he is not a member of the Senate Committee on Finance, his stature is such that he has consistently made a difference in setting priorities for tax legislation and funding.

Yet all of this – plus his work in the field of immigration legislation, his steady support for the full participation and advancement of women and minorities in our society, and his more direct work on behalf of the Commonwealth of Massachusetts – all of this gives us only an inkling of the major role he plays in our national public life. That is because a tally of his specific accomplishments and official positions doesn't really convey what seem to me to be his most important contributions.

Senator Kennedy, true to the tradition of his family, has always approached his work as if there were more to do than could be accomplished, and far too little time to do what might be attempted. Managing legislation on the Senate floor or in conference is not an activity that lends itself to portrayal in terms of the bold, broad strokes and utterances associated with heroic political leadership. As we know, it is a process that is saturated with details, that depends on the cooperation and agreement of many people, that requires months and months of patience and perseverance, and that often results in legislation so complex that the public may not recognize its significance.

Under such conditions, many members of Congress – even excellent members – are pleased if they are able to pass any legislation at all. What is rare about Senator Kennedy is his extraordinary intuition, guided by deep conviction: an intuition that enables him to sense where the critical issues and the large opportunities really lie, waiting to be realized and turned into action. He is practical, he gets things done, but he doesn't see politics as merely the art of the possible. Instead, he presses more forcefully to see what might *conceivably* be possible if our angle of vision were shifted, if some of the apparently fixed points were moved. Walter Bagehot once remarked that "the great pleasure in life is doing what people say you cannot do." Approaching life from this vantage point does change our sense of its probabilities, and that is exactly what Senator Kennedy does as a matter of course.

If you had asked me a year ago what the odds were of passing the Higher Education Reauthorization Act with all the major provisions I described earlier — especially those related to need-based aid — I doubt I would have given the idea more than a 25 percent chance. It simply didn't seem to me as if it could be done. But the Senator saw that it just perhaps *might* be done — and it was.

There is one last point that I would like to make. So much of what Ted Kennedy achieves is the result of a commitment not to a set of abstract ideals or goals but to actual people and their welfare, to individuals and their daily lives, to the ways in which things can be made better for everyone. On a purely personal note, I remember that one of the first telephone calls I received after being appointed last year came from Ted. He was calling from his car, having just left a meeting. It was 11:30 at night. He simply wanted to congratulate me, to say hello, and to say how much he looked forward to meeting Angelica and me. We were still feeling slightly like displaced persons, and the call gave us very much the sense that there was someone at the other end of the telephone line who had not only sent a genuinely friendly greeting, but who was ready to help out if needed.

I am certain that Ted has touched countless other people in the same way. In this respect, he shares some of the qualities that were once described by Isaiah Berlin in an essay about an American political leader from an earlier era:

> *[He evoked] an obscure feeling on the part of the majority of the citizens ... that he was on their side, that he wished them well, and that he would do something for them.... He showed that it was possible to be politically effective and yet ... human.*[1]

1 Isaiah Berlin, *Personal Impressions* (New York: Viking, 1981), 28, 31.

Contributing to the Life of
Our Community

Boston Chamber of Commerce Speech
September 29, 1999

I WOULD LIKE, in the time available to me today, to say something about our common purposes: how Harvard (as well as
other universities and colleges) and Boston work together, and
contribute significantly to one another. And I will do this by
focusing on just three questions.

First, what are some of the most important ways in which
Boston makes a major difference to my own university's well-
being, including some of the less obvious ways that we often
overlook?

Second, what can Harvard and other universities contribute
to the city and region, especially economically, but also in other
ways?

And finally, given the fact that all of our different institutional
fates are linked to one another, because many of our institutions
have been here a long time and most of us expect to stay — what
are some of the common problems we now face, and what are

some of the concrete ways that we can continue to work together in the future?

✦ ✦ ✦

Let me begin by saying that, fortunately, a great deal has changed in the relationship between Boston and Harvard over the past decades and even centuries. For instance, when Benjamin Franklin started out as a young Boston reporter in the early 1700s, nothing gave him more pleasure than writing articles excoriating Harvard. Franklin said our eighteenth-century students were rich, vain, lazy, arrogant, and not worth any of the time and money lavished on them. None of our present-day newspapers would ever engage in anything like this kind of behavior.

Life for Harvard presidents was apparently not all that cheerful, either. The University managed to go through quite a large number of them at a few points in its earlier years. I am sure the members of the faculty were as soft-spoken, uncontroversial, and modest then as they are now, so that could not have been the source of difficulty.

If Harvard had its problems, Boston itself, at least in the eighteenth and nineteenth centuries, was not necessarily all that it is now. In 1788, a French visitor to Harvard noted with satisfaction that the University was far enough distanced from the big city to escape what he called "the contagion of licentious manners common in commercial towns." Seventy-five years later, however, modern transportation had dramatically changed the situation. In 1863, President Thomas Hill lamented the fact that "the passage of horse-cars to and from Boston, nearly, if not quite, a hundred times a day, has rendered it practically impossible for the government of the College to prevent our young men from being exposed to the temptations of the city."

✦ ✦ ✦

There will always be people who bewail the present, and prefer the past. But in the case of Boston and Harvard, my own view is that any serious look at the historical record suggests that, for all our current problems and challenges, the health, well-being, and general state of our institutions, and their interrelationships, are in fact far better than ever before.

I want to elaborate a bit more on this point, because it relates directly to the first question I posed earlier: what are some of the chief ways – not always the most obvious ones – in which Boston makes a major difference to the well-being of Harvard?

First, it matters that there is a strong civic society here, a sense of pride about the city, and the urge to be involved in its life. All of you care about and create the economic health of the city and region, and you have created a modern economy that is as enviable as it is impressive. You also care about the vitality of Boston's not-for-profit sector. And you give with amazing generosity your time, effort, advice, and financial help toward keeping all our institutions in an extraordinary state.

It also matters that we have an enlightened, progressive, and strong city government, with a mayor who has clear priorities, and who is willing and able to act effectively. This is vital. We know only too well the plight of many cities around the country where leadership is sorely lacking, and where the results are painfully visible.

Next – and here I want to mention some intangibles – we need to remember that Harvard is by design a residential university, which brings students and faculty and others here from all over the country and the globe. That means we depend critically on an environment which is attractive and welcoming. Our students, faculty, and staff come here to live, and they want to live in a place that is in different ways appealing and stimulating.

From this point of view, Harvard, along with our other local colleges and universities, enjoys advantages that are clearly unsurpassed, and largely unrivaled. We are able to draw, disproportionately, the most talented people to the University for many reasons, but one of them is unquestionably the fact that from Harvard Square to Copley Square we are fortunate to be surrounded by a vital and robust urban environment that is inviting, interesting, humane, and responsive. There is no way to place an exact value on this intangible (but crucial) factor, but, I can assure you, it is a very high value indeed.

It also matters that there is a real mix — a real diversity — of people and neighborhoods in Boston: that there is a North End, a South End, a Chinatown, a Roxbury, and so many other strong, distinctive communities.

This means that people from the University (who are themselves very diverse) can be in touch with people throughout the city from all backgrounds and walks of life. That kind of interaction is one of the most important characteristics of our society — and Boston fosters it and embodies it in action.

Let me mention just one statistical indicator of how the larger Boston environment can help draw people to Harvard. In undergraduate admissions, we have a term called the "yield rate": that is, of all the offers of admission that we make for places in the freshman class, how many accept our offer, and how does that compare with the yield at other major universities?

The answer is just about 80 percent — four out of five — accept our offer, a far higher percentage than our closest rivals, and nearly 10 percentage points higher than Harvard itself had in 1990. Part of this extraordinary yield rate may have something to do with Harvard and its educational programs. But I have no doubt at all that the City of Boston and the whole area in which we are located also play a very significant role in producing our powerful results.

✦ ✦ ✦

I want now to focus on some of the ways that I believe Harvard can and does contribute to Boston and other neighboring communities. I do this not to claim any credit, but to emphasize that we consider ourselves to be active partners in the community, and that we care about its well-being.

This week, we have released the first comprehensive directory of public and community service at Harvard University. Even a glance at the document conveys how strongly our students and faculty feel that a deep commitment to our cities is a major part of their education. I won't take you through the more than 240 public service programs now in operation at Harvard. Just a few highlights:

First, more than two-thirds of all Harvard undergraduates choose to do some significant form of uncompensated, purely voluntary, and often quite demanding public service work each year in Boston, Cambridge, and other local communities. And a very large number of our professional school students — in business, law, divinity, education, public health, medicine, government, and other fields — do at least as much.

These initiatives range from a very serious English language program for recent Southeast Asian immigrant children, to a special public-school enrichment program, to an imaginative and effective project called "Peace Games," started by Harvard students, which has enrolled literally hundreds of elementary school students in a creatively designed program of violence prevention and conflict resolution. In addition, there are the Jimmy Fund, Arts Boston, and several other major efforts.

Meanwhile, the Law School operates significant legal clinics, including the Hale and Dorr Legal Services Center in Jamaica Plain, which provides legal representation to more than 2,500 clients every year.

Our School of Education is part of the Fleet Leadership Development Initiative, working with Boston public schools. And, of course, Phillips Brooks House has a whole array of volunteer programs that have been functioning throughout this past century.

If we were to visit hospitals, elderly care facilities, schools, youth centers, churches, and many other organizations around the metropolitan area, the chances are quite high that we would meet Harvard volunteers – at different times of the day – in a good number of them.

Or, to put it another way, we estimate that about half a million volunteer public-service hours are contributed every year, mostly in Boston and Cambridge, by our undergraduate students alone. If we add graduate students, faculty, and staff hours, it is likely that the figure would be more in the range of a million hours per year.

All of this is important for the spirit of service that it represents. But it also does add up to something very substantial in purely quantitative and practical terms – a concrete contribution on the part of many committed and trained volunteers, from all parts of Harvard.

A second contribution is much more in line with our traditional educational mission, but the level of our investment is now much higher than ever before, and the potential for positive results is also so much higher. Nearly all the fields of the basic sciences, applied sciences, and health sciences are at a point of unprecedented development, and we are already in the early stages of the greatest era of discovery and socially significant applications that the world has ever known.

The potential importance to our society is incalculable – whether measured in terms of further economic development, international competitiveness, or of gains in human health, in education, and in many aspects of the quality of ordinary daily life.

But these gains cannot be realized without very substantial investments – in laboratory space, equipment, research funds, faculty, students, staff, and in the whole process of how we teach and how we learn. For Harvard, such investments will include (in the next four to six years) full operation and staffing of our computer science building; more faculty and growth in other applied areas such as materials science and bioengineering; new major interdisciplinary science centers in genomics, neuroscience, and other important areas; major investments in a new research building at the Medical School; coordinated cancer research at the Medical School in collaboration with the Dana-Farber Cancer Institute and the major teaching hospitals; and major new initiatives in infectious diseases (among other areas) at our School of Public Health. And this is only a partial list.

These are investments that the University needs to make in expanding knowledge, in the cure of disease, and in the discovery of devices and technologies that can lead to the creation of new industries — and finally to the education of exceptional individuals and leaders who can help to forge our future.

We know that a very large portion of the total dollars invested will be spent here, and that will be good for the local economy. We hope, in addition, that the total effort will also add to Boston's already great strength as a leader in research in many fields: in health care, financial services, and technology, among others.

Harvard recently commissioned a study by an outside agency to examine the University's relationship to the Boston-area economy: it is clear that higher education is an economic colossus in Boston — and Harvard plays a large role.

First, we are the area's second largest private employer. We have about 15,000 permanent employees, and just over 80 percent of them live in the Boston metropolitan area. These are talented people; they contribute in many ways to the life of our community; and they tend to spend their earnings, and pay their taxes, right here.

Second, we estimate that the University itself spent about $1.15 billion on payroll, goods, and services in the metropolitan area over the last year — a considerable help to many local businesses, companies, and suppliers of all kinds.

Third, most of the University's annual revenue — about $1 billion of our total operating budget of about $1.8 billion — comes into the state from outside. In other words, we import significant capital in the form of government and other research grants, annual gifts, and student fees, among other things. And that $1 billion is of course spent here, and helps the economy in any number of ways. Harvard is certainly not alone in this respect, but the level of net inflow is simply very high compared to other institutions.

So this is important "business" for Boston. Even more interesting, however, are the dynamic connections between Harvard, higher education, and the rest of the economy — the "knowledge economy" that we are building together.

A recent study by the Progressive Policy Institute finds that among the nation's fifty states, Massachusetts is the "farthest along the path to the new economy": first in percentage of workforce employed in "knowledge jobs," and also first in "capacity for innovation." The dense concentration of colleges and universities we possess is in this sense our premier regional asset. We should be doing all we can to leverage it further. That will require broad conversations across all sectors: education, business, government, and community.

We will also need to work in partnership to meet serious threats as they present themselves, and there are several.

Boston's major teaching hospitals are facing deficits of truly critical proportions, largely because of the steep and progressive federal cuts in Medicare reimbursements. These cuts were mandated by the Balanced Budget Act of 1997, and they are continuing, deeper and deeper every year, in spite of the fact that the federal budget has long since been balanced. Altogether, these cuts are estimated to cost Massachusetts hospitals an estimated $2 billion cumulatively, and they are already producing critical financial situations in several of Boston's major hospitals. We have to turn this situation around. Many are helping. But there is a long way still to go.

Dr. Joseph Martin, Dean of the Harvard Medical School, has been working hard on this issue, and Harvard recently made a special increase in endowment spending to help cover the costs of teaching at the Harvard-affiliated hospitals. This predicament has placed several of our major public institutions — irreplaceable, and unsurpassed in quality — at serious risk. They need all the help that we can collectively give them.

Finally, the affordable housing issue also needs more (and continuing) attention. Just yesterday, at a ceremony Mayor Menino and I attended, Harvard transferred ownership of 775 units of high-quality, affordable housing to the non-profit Roxbury Tenants of Harvard association in Mission Park. And we have recently committed to build an additional large graduate-student housing complex, in order to increase the already large proportion of Harvard students whom we ourselves house. More joint efforts and initiatives can and will be undertaken, here and in other areas.

So let me say that I believe stronger and better partnerships can and must be created among the private sector, government, and our not-for-profits, including Harvard. Each of us may be involved with just one institution, or perhaps a few. But we all know that, fundamentally, communities do not work, cities do not work, and each of our own separate institutions will not work, unless we have a large shared vision and design, and a commitment to doing what each of us can appropriately do, working together. I think there is a genuine opportunity at the moment for us to step back, think more strategically about the future, take a long view, and do even better than we are already doing.

Let me conclude by thanking all of you — and the City of Boston — for the many ways in which you help and support Harvard. I want to say again how much the University is committed to continuing the kinds of contributions it is already making, while also finding ways to do more.

THINKING INTERNATIONALLY

Engaging Global Realities

An Excerpt from the Robert H. Atwell Distinguished Lecture
American Council on Education
Washington, D.C., February 23, 1997

N EARLY A CENTURY AGO, Henry Adams tried to trace what he had learned over the course of a lifetime dedicated to education. And by education, he meant not simply formal study but all his efforts — including involvement in the world of affairs — to understand as much of his universe as possible.

By the end of his odyssey, he felt that he had largely failed. There was simply too much to comprehend. Too many changes were happening too rapidly, and nearly all the forces were centrifugal.

Adams was certainly right in believing that, in his words, the "multiple" would become a dominant part of our twentieth-century reality, and that we would have to take that fact into account in any design for education.

But we are not likely today to think that any single educational design might "fit" all or even most individuals. And we have probably come to accept (more than Adams did) the idea that multiplicity is and will remain a fundamental part of our experience.

I want to discuss several topics that bear on the theme of

multiplicity. Each represents a significant challenge for higher education. None can be definitively "solved." But each can be addressed in ways that can strengthen our institutions — both as centers of teaching and research, and as human communities.

I would like to highlight a few of the major changes that are taking place in national and international affairs. The question in this case is how we should organize (or reorganize) our educational agenda to take these changes into better account.

Recent studies suggest that we are a less trusting people than we used to be. We are more inclined to be suspicious of our government and indeed of many established institutions and professions. We even trust our neighbors less. We also vote less. Fewer of us join community and neighborhood organizations. Volunteerism is still a vital American tradition, but we are now more likely to write checks and donate money than we are to invest blood, sweat, or tears in support of activities and causes that matter to us.

All of this represents a major change from the immediate post-World War II decades, when participation rates in virtually all civic associations were higher. The Cold War may have bifurcated the world then, but within our own sphere we tended to believe that consensus, based on mutual trust, was a desirable and largely achievable goal. In fact, one of our greatest national concerns was the problem of too much conformity and dull conventionality: those were the days of *The Man in the Gray Flannel Suit*, *The Organization Man*, *The Status Seekers*, and *The Lonely Crowd*.

The titles of several recent books dramatize what has happened: *The Clash of Civilizations*, *Democracy and Disagreement*, *Ethnic Groups in Conflict*, *Democracy and Its Discontents*, and Senator Moynihan's pithy little volume, with its understated rubric, *Pandæmonium*.

In short, multiplicity and fragmentation are major themes that are clearly in evidence. Nor is this simply an American phenomenon. The English philosopher Stuart Hampshire concluded his latest book, *Innocence and Experience*, by stating that "life consists in perpetual conflicts between rival impulses and ideals."

Has the shift to a world that sometimes seems full, in the

words of Isaiah Berlin, of "intolerable choices" been monolithic? Certainly not. But have the temper and outlook of the times changed, and have some of our presuppositions altered? On the whole, yes.

Moreover, all of us recognize that we are now actors in a drama that has become global in nature. We must take into account powerful new systems and forces that operate fairly autonomously "above" and "through" and "around" the traditional geographic grid of nation-states and regions. This development has obviously not superseded the previous structure. The two coexist, and together they create a set of dynamics that are far more complex, more difficult to identify, to trace, to describe, and to understand, let alone to control.

Economic capital flows electronically, twenty-four hours a day. Ideas, information, and disinformation move equally quickly to many more places, and from an incalculably greater number of sources, than ever before. Different phenomena — including various forms of religious fundamentalism, the shift to open markets and free trade, or the emergence of international terrorism — suddenly appear and seem to spread, in ways we scarcely begin to understand, from nation to nation or region to region.

All of this is simply another way of saying that reality itself is changing, and at an accelerating rate. There are many reasons for this, but the new technologies we now possess play an important role. These technologies make it possible for an unlimited number of events to reverberate instantaneously around the world in real time. As a result, the pace of life quickens. The number of interactions increases. And our ability to identify coherent patterns behind and beyond individual events is tested more severely.

There is, as I said earlier, no way to "solve" the problems I have been describing. The challenge for our colleges and universities is an educational one: how to deepen our understanding of the transformations now under way in the hope that we can then prepare our students and ourselves to live more effective and satisfying lives in the decades ahead.

I want to stress one particular aspect of this broad educational challenge: the need to reexamine the adequacy of our programs in international studies, as well as the international dimensions of our other programs. To what extent do our research and teaching reflect the fact that many events and systems are now global, not merely national or regional, in their scope? What steps should we be taking to achieve a better alignment?

In fact, there is a great deal already happening. For instance, more than 450,000 students from abroad, representing virtually every country or territory on earth, are now in residence at American colleges and universities. A good number of them are undergraduates, but there is strong and growing demand at the graduate and professional level. The largest "sender" nations are located, increasingly, in East and Southeast Asia.

That is the prevailing pattern at my own university. About 6 percent of our undergraduates come from abroad, but in several of our graduate and professional schools — in arts and sciences, government, business, design, and public health — the figure is well over 20 percent. And of our 3,000 full-time foreign students, nearly 1,000 come from Japan, China, and other parts of Asia. Europe, by comparison, sends us about 750 students a year. Meanwhile, a larger number of our American students now wish to work or study overseas: as summer interns, visiting students, young professionals, or simply as interested travelers.

As these figures only begin to suggest, our institutions have already gone far to engage with and come to terms with global realities. And this, in turn, is forcing significant, sometimes unanticipated changes in how we teach and what research we do.

For example, anyone who has visited a professional school class in constitutional law, or medical ethics, or environmental health knows that the presence and participation of talented students from several different countries can immediately change the whole nature of the discussion. Virtually any issue can provoke debate — whether the question involves limits that might be placed on free speech, or a patient's right to make certain choices in medical treatment, or the extent to which all countries should be bound by a single set of environmental health guidelines.

As a result, course materials begin to change, research projects become more complex, and the number of variables that must be taken into account quickly increases. This process is healthy and actually quite effective. But it is not in itself enough: we need a more coordinated and well-supported approach – an updated version of the initiatives launched so successfully in the 1950s and 1960s.

At that time, we created new departments and centers for regional and area studies. Because of that, we now have a reasonable number of professionals in our society who are knowledgeable about regions and nations such as the Middle East, the Far East, Russia, and India – including a knowledge of their languages. Had we not made that earlier investment, our ability to function with any real effectiveness in world affairs today would be far more limited than it is.

If we now want to consider a revised agenda for the coming decades, what are some of the main possible priorities?

First, in spite of all the criticism surrounding this point, we must sustain our commitment to international student and faculty exchange programs. There is no substitute for direct contact with talented people from other countries and cultures. As I have suggested, we benefit enormously from our overseas students. They add to our base of knowledge. They help to drive teaching and research in new and fruitful directions.

Second, we need to create flexible structures to stimulate the study of important topics that transcend the boundaries of individual nations and regions. I have already mentioned such topics in passing, but any one of us could easily expand the list: for example, the problems and obstacles faced by emerging democracies in different parts of the world; or the causes of, and possible resolution of, ethnic or religious conflict in a wide variety of countries; or the attempt to promote economic development in ways that are sensitive to environmental protection.

Some of these subjects are already being taught because they are of special interest to individual faculty members. But we have to build more effective institutional structures to focus more concentrated and sustained attention on these and similar issues.

Finally, while we ourselves have much to learn about the rest of the world, we are also at this particular moment in history in an unusual position to help others. We have the largest and most effective higher educational system in the world, and we have the capacity — at all levels, but especially in professional and graduate education — to offer advanced and mid-career programs that are invaluable to foreign students and their countries, and that are scarcely available elsewhere.

This kind of education in business, public management, urban design, public health, and law, among other fields, is desperately needed in most parts of the world: more and more, our institutions are being asked if we can provide it. Students from abroad who participate in such programs will come to understand America, its people, and its values better. They will also take back to their homelands new insights and capabilities that can make their own institutions and societies more effective: more productive, more stable, more open, and more ready to reach out to become partners in joint enterprises with others.

In a year when we are recognizing the fiftieth anniversary of the Marshall Plan, it is time to reconsider our own international planning in education. Initiatives that focus explicitly on global affairs are now very much in order. And more intensive efforts to provide education — especially professional education — to students from abroad can make a significant difference to our future.

These efforts represent only a modest part of what might be done. But they are an important part, if we want to make the world more whole — a little more of a unity, however much it will also remain a "multiple."

Indigenously American
but Simultaneously Global

Excerpt from Remarks to Alumni Gatherings
Düsseldorf, Paris, and London, June 27 – July 1, 1997

W E A R E – and will remain – a fundamentally American institution, but we have also rapidly become an international university. Or, to put it another way, we are a place where people of many different nationalities and geographic regions, religious and political convictions, cultural, racial, ethnic, and socioeconomic backgrounds gather, meet, congregate, study, and come to know one another – learning from each other, and teaching each other, year after year.

In fact, beyond our more than 18,000 degree students, Harvard also has approximately 60,000 more students each year, of all ages, who attend short-term mid-career and advanced executive education courses or who enroll in the extension school or summer school. A large proportion of these students come from abroad to attend special programs in business, law, government, public health, and other fields. Most of these programs are heavily oversubscribed, mainly because there are so few universities in the world that offer high-quality advanced education and training of this kind. These initiatives represent a critical part of Harvard's future, and will – I am certain – continue to grow.

Meanwhile, the reverse current – Harvard students and faculty spending time overseas – is also substantial. And these various flows and movements ultimately have, of course, a deep effect on the nature of classroom discussions, on the formulation of new research projects, and on the kind of learning that takes place in hundreds of conversations daily, outside the confines of the classrooms and the formal curriculum.

In short, this enlarged range of different human and intellectual contacts and perspectives increases the richness of interchange at every level and at every turn. The questions that are asked, the problems posed, and the answers volunteered alter, expand, and vary in response to the nature of the enhanced international and diverse educational community that is Harvard.

All of this represents a major stride forward from half a century ago, when the United States was just beginning to realize that it could not withdraw, again, from world affairs; when the Marshall Plan had barely been conceived; and when Harvard – indeed, most universities – had only a very modest investment in international studies. Yet in spite of all that has been achieved since that time, much more remains to be done, because the world is, I believe, at another major turning point: we face an international situation that is dramatically different from, but no less challenging than, that which existed just after World War II (and for decades afterward).

✦   ✦   ✦

We are experiencing one of the most far-reaching transformations in modern history. Today's world is more open to positive developments, more free, more fluid and robust, more interconnected, and more collaborative – at least potentially – across national and regional boundaries.

There is, of course, another side to the ledger. Openness and freedom can lead to fierce ethnic, religious, and nationalist conflict; to highly unstable political regimes and economic conditions; and to the unleashing of powerful centrifugal forces that intensify distrust and divisiveness.

The question, then, is whether we can capitalize on the present moment in order to build stronger international relationships at every level, beginning with individuals and institutions. Can we also create more effective regional and international organizations, to help maintain the positive momentum that has been generated since the end of the Cold War?

I believe that we can, but it will certainly not be easy. It will, in addition to the other things, require a significantly larger supply of educated human talent: people who understand the dynamics and the added complexities of this new world we have entered, with all its fluidity and unpredictability as well as promise.

In 1943, Winston Churchill made a secret visit to Harvard, while World War II was still raging. He received an honorary degree, and in his address he declared that "the empires of the future will be empires of the mind." That future has now arrived. It is clear that finely tuned human intelligence and skill, grounded in humane values, represent the world's most valuable — as well as its most scarce — resource. This resource is vital to every aspect of international affairs today. Fortunately, we have the power to increase its supply, as long as our universities (and our governments) are willing to make a substantial renewed investment in international and regional studies. The goal is to educate leaders, in all walks of life, who are informed about the world at large, responsive to its dilemmas, and imaginative as well as realistic in their search for solutions, and in their capacity to take action.

The need for such an investment cannot be taken for granted. Many nations (including the United States) have been largely self-absorbed for a good number of years. Funds to support research abroad, student exchange programs, technical assistance and aid projects, or advanced mid-career and executive education programs for participants from different countries — such funds, whether from government or other sources, have declined, in real terms, for more than two decades. And this decline is continuing, just when the opportunity for genuine international progress is so clearly open to us.

Reversing so strong a trend will be very difficult. But if we want to make a beginning, we should ask ourselves about some of the concrete steps that universities might consider. Let me give you a brief outline of Harvard's own plans, as just one example.

First, as more countries than ever before play an active role on the international stage, we must at the very least increase our store of fundamental knowledge about them. There may have been a time when it seemed safe to operate with comparatively little understanding of Chechnya, Zaire, Kazakhstan, Colombia, Chiapas, Rwanda, Yemen, Burundi, or even Afghanistan. But the plain fact now is that virtually any region of the world, however distant, can instantaneously become a flash point for serious concern. Or, conversely, it can become a constructive partner in the effort to sustain a durable peace.

Our relative ignorance is not, alas, limited to the most remote or inconspicuous corners of the world. We also know far too little about many major nations and cultures, including parts of the Middle East, China, much of Latin America, Africa, and sizable portions of the former Soviet Union.

Therefore, one challenge for us is to take maximum advantage of the new climate of openness which now exists and which has no real precedent in the modern era. To do so, we need the resources to enable students, scholars, and others to consult the large number of archives, documents, and other research materials that are now accessible in hundreds of cities and regions that have long been effectively closed. Equally important, scholars and students can talk at length with (and interview) ordinary people and officials in these regions, and can travel quite freely to see, at first hand, the texture and crosscurrents of life in these societies.

The objective is a simple and fundamental one: to achieve as deep an understanding as we can of other cultures, for the sake of knowledge itself, but also to make more of the world comprehensible, less impenetrable, and therefore less threatening.

Next, we need to enlarge our student and faculty exchange programs. Little progress has been made in recent years, not for lack of interest, but for lack of funds. In Harvard's current fundraising campaign, we are seeking to increase our endowment to support more students and visiting faculty from abroad. In this connection, our European exchange programs are critical to us, precisely because the nature of the dilemmas we face in common has changed. One of the most effective ways to move forward is by educating more of our young people together. It is one thing to study other countries and cultures; it is quite another thing — and a very powerful one — for people from different nations to study together and to learn reciprocally.

Finally, Harvard has begun to focus even more of its energy on the search for better ways to address some of society's most complex and pressing problems. This can be done only by encouraging people from different specialized fields, professions, and countries to collaborate. We have embarked on a program to increase the endowments of our regional and international research centers, emphasizing their University-wide capacity — that is, their ability to bring together individuals from all our professional schools, and all of Arts and Sciences, to work on projects of unusual importance.

Few if any of the most difficult real-world problems that confront us can be addressed from a single perspective. To understand (and try to solve) a serious environmental health problem in a particular region, for example, we need scientists, political figures, public health officials, and people who understand the economics of the situation and the legal regulations that may apply. If the project is an international one, there must also be individuals who understand the local languages and culture.

Otherwise, factors that are rooted in social behavior, as much as in the external environment, can be easily overlooked, or remedies may be recommended that run counter to important indigenous beliefs and customs.

More and more, Harvard is working to make the most of its total intellectual and other resources, from across the entire University, cooperating with universities and other institutions abroad. We are seeking to learn more about alternative paths to successful economic development, about the roots of ethnic conflict, the serious issues created when immigrant and refugee populations cross national boundaries, the upheaval in many health care systems, and the difficulty of creating democratic institutions in countries where such institutions have never really existed before.

These and any number of other dilemmas require the kind of collaborative (and often international) approaches that I have been describing. Such efforts (indeed our entire international agenda) are among the highest of Harvard's priorities for the future. We will be investing the better part of $200 million in the next few years to create a significant new international studies complex as well as to secure new endowment funds to support increased international research, more student exchanges, and new curricular developments.

If we now step back for a moment, we can see that Harvard is in the midst of evolving toward a new form of university that builds in fundamental ways on its history and heritage, but that will also, over time, incorporate the most significant aspects of the technological and international changes I have been discussing.

The Harvard of a half century from now will represent an intricate web of connections between our permanent, physical, tangible university and the electronic "virtual" university that is now emerging. It will also represent a vastly expanded web of national and international connections. It will be indigenously American and local, but simultaneously global.

The challenge before us, therefore, is very significant and will demand major investments of time, thought, and energy. We must succeed, because I am persuaded that the leading universities of the next century will be those that have carried out this transformation most effectively.

Let me stress the underlying concerns that are the real motive for everything we are trying to achieve. Terms such as "information technology" and "international studies" are at best clumsy and abstract.

In the end, we must focus on the fundamental simplicity of our purposes: to educate our students, and ourselves, to help prepare individuals to live satisfying and generous lives in the complex world they are now inheriting. We want them to be able to address intelligently and decently the difficult, interesting, sometimes hazardous, often rewarding situations that are part of our personal, national, and increasingly international existence.

It would be astonishingly naïve to think that everything can be solved simply by bringing together more of our students and colleagues from different countries in the enterprise of education. It would be equally naïve to think that improved information systems, or a greatly expanded number of international friendships and institutional relationships will carry the day. But conversely it would be folly to believe that strong and lasting relationships, and the values they embody, are negligible or irrelevant. Whatever differences may at times divide us, we know that there are deep and strong foundations of trust and affection, founded upon generations of shared experiences that keep us together in spirit and cannot be shaken.

Exchanging Differences

Address to Commemorate the Centennial of Peking University
March 23, 1998

I COME TO YOU in the spirit of friendship and learning. This is my first visit to China, so I am at the beginning of a voyage of discovery, one I have looked forward to for many years. Our universities, as well as our societies, have different cultures and traditions, and much still to learn about one another. At the same time, we hold many things in common.

One of them, perhaps the most important, is our belief in the power of education: a belief that all of us, through a devotion to learning, can lead lives of value to the societies in which we live. In this sense, I am visiting you not as a representative of another nation or culture, but as a fellow member of the international academic community – concerned, like you, about the advancement of education and knowledge within our own countries, but also across national and cultural borders, in a spirit of true exchange.

I am especially honored to be able to participate in the events marking Peking University's centennial year. Just as your university is the oldest institution of its kind in China, Harvard is the oldest in North America. Harvard was founded in 1636 – just a few years before the end of the Ming Dynasty, late in the long history of China; but very early in our own history: a full 140 years before the United States became a nation. Over the centuries, Harvard has grown from a small rural college with nine students and one faculty member in its first year, to an institution that is now home to more than 30,000 faculty, students, and staff.

Our largest faculty, the Faculty of Arts and Sciences, ranges across more than fifty fields, from biology to economics, from philosophy to physics, from anthropology and music to mathematics, psychology, and literature. We have, in addition, eight other faculties – architecture, business, divinity, education, government, law, medicine, and public health.

This spring marks a special occasion not only for your university, now one hundred years old, but also for my own. Earlier this month, I had the privilege of helping to inaugurate Harvard's Asia Center. The Center represents a major new initiative (building on the strong programs that already exist at Harvard) to think more broadly and deeply about the many interconnections among countries and cultures in Asia. Equally important, we wish to enlarge the avenues for mutual education and scholarly exchange between Asia and the United States.

It was in 1877 that Mr. Francis Knight, an American who had been living for years in China, returned to his home in Boston for an extended visit. He suggested, and Harvard agreed, that our university should hire its first teacher of Mandarin Chinese. Mr. Knight returned to China and engaged the services of Mr. Ko Kun-hua of Ningpo, who came, very bravely, to the wilderness of Harvard in 1879 (with his wife and six small children) to begin instruction in the elegant intricacies of your venerable language. Fortunately, perhaps, we have little record of whether our earliest students made any progress at all in their study of Mandarin. But we do know that Harvard was not easily discouraged.

Quite the opposite: that modest beginning set in motion a major venture which continues powerfully to this day. For example, we now offer intensive instruction in both Mandarin and Cantonese, and approximately five hundred Harvard students elect to study in these courses each year. In addition, more than three hundred different academic courses across Harvard relate to some aspect of Asian studies — including many on Chinese history, literature, archaeology, economics, and many other fields. Harvard is also fortunate to be home to the single largest university library for East Asian research in the Western world: the Harvard-Yenching Library, founded in 1928, which contains approximately 880,000 books, nearly half a million of them in Chinese.

We are also proud of the growing presence of many students and scholars from other nations. Across Harvard, there are now approximately 2,800 students who are citizens of more than 125 different countries and territories outside the United States. Nearly one thousand of these students are from Asia. And of those one thousand students, two hundred are from China: more than any other country except Canada. In addition, nearly one-fifth of our undergraduate students are Americans of Asian descent.

We also have many Harvard faculty and students working on projects to address challenges that are important to both our societies. There is, for instance, a major University-wide research project in which individuals from Harvard and China are working together on the challenge of reconciling environmental protection with economic development. There are also cooperative efforts, involving members of Harvard's Faculty of Public Health, to help improve systems of health care delivery. A number of years ago, Chinese scholars worked with our law faculty to help create, at Harvard, the first U.S. program on Chinese law. More recently, we have collaborated to establish the first modern program on U.S. law here in China. Members of our Faculty of Government have, in the last year alone, worked with Chinese scholars to organize joint conferences on United States-China relations, both here in Beijing and at Harvard, as well as a conference on the Hong Kong transition.

These few examples, and many others that could be mentioned, show how strongly we are committed to a wider understanding of China and to a broader dialogue with colleagues in China on other matters of common interest. I would like to focus on one such matter by discussing some of the major challenges confronting institutions of higher education, particularly those of Harvard and other American universities. These challenges may not be very different from some of those you are facing in China.

✦   ✦   ✦

Let me say something about the importance of what we might refer to as "humane" learning. As we all know, higher education at a high level of quality is a very expensive undertaking – whether it is paid for by the government, or by individuals, or by a mixture of different sources. Partly as a result, there has been growing pressure, in the United States and elsewhere, to demonstrate the value of university education and research in terms of its immediate, tangible, economic benefits.

It is certainly important that university research contribute to economic well-being, as it surely does. And it is certainly important that a university education help students to pursue useful and satisfying work, as it does. At the same time, however, there is much more to excellent education than can be measured in dollars or renminbi. The best education not only helps us to be more productive in our professions; it also makes us more reflective, more inquiring and insightful, more complete and fulfilled human beings. It helps scientists to appreciate the arts, and artists to appreciate the sciences. It helps us to see connections across different fields of learning that we otherwise might not grasp. It helps us to lead more interesting and valuable lives – as individuals, and as members of our communities.

And so, at Harvard and elsewhere in the United States, we are working exceptionally hard, under complicated conditions, to sustain a tradition of what we call a "liberal education" in the arts and sciences. Our undergraduate students, during their four years in residence, do intensively pursue a major field of study, whether in chemistry, economics, political science, art, or some other field of knowledge. But they are also expected to study broadly across several different subjects – from moral philosophy and ethics to mathematical reasoning, from the natural sciences to literature, from history to the study of other cultures. Most of Harvard's undergraduate students also spend a great deal of time on activities outside the classroom: helping to provide social services to members of our neighboring communities, or writing for newspapers and journals, or playing in orchestras or other musical groups. Indeed, relatively few of our students embark on their actual professional training until they have completed four years of undergraduate education in the liberal arts and sciences.

This model is unusual compared to others in the world, and I certainly do not suggest that it is suitable for all systems of higher education – or even for all colleges and universities in the United States. But behind the model lies a powerful philosophy: a strong belief that a university education should stimulate our curiosity and open our minds to new ideas and experiences. It should encourage us to think about our unexamined assumptions, and about our values and beliefs. That is one reason we study the philosophy, customs, and ways of life of other countries and cultures. In doing so, we learn more not only about other peoples but also about ourselves. Such learning presents a difficult educational challenge, but one that represents an ideal to which we can all aspire.

In a similar vein, let me emphasize the importance of what in the United States we refer to as basic or fundamental research. By that I mean research which is not undertaken with a particular practical application in mind, but that is rooted in the passion which we all share to understand nature, and human nature, at the deepest possible level. Universities certainly have a responsibility to produce useful knowledge. But useful knowledge can take a great many different forms.

For example, when scholars at Harvard first began to study China and Asia in a serious way, early in this century, questions were raised about whether the University was using its resources wisely. At the time, China seemed to many Americans to be very remote — large and populous, yet far removed from the day-to-day concerns of people in the United States.

Now, at the end of this century, in our increasingly interconnected world, it is impossible to imagine how China could *not* be a significant focus of study at American universities. It is hard to imagine anyone questioning the importance and even "usefulness" of studying China. Yet Harvard would not have been able to do this effectively if our predecessors, long ago, had taken a narrow view of what constitutes significant knowledge. Excellent academic programs do not spring up overnight. They take decades of careful nurturing — to develop the right faculty, to build great libraries and provide other academic resources, and to attract the most promising students. Without the conviction, and the willingness, to take risks many decades ago, without the broad and even "impractical" intellectual curiosity of our forebears, Harvard would not have the strong foundations now in place for intensified efforts to learn about China and Asia. And this story is one that could be told in any number of other fields.

It is also worth remembering that many of the most practical scientific discoveries of our century have come about because university scholars embarked not in pursuit of useful inventions, but in search of fundamental knowledge about our natural world. The advances now being made in the field of genetics are traceable to the discovery of DNA almost half a century ago, when few people could have imagined what that discovery might generate. Powerful tools such as lasers and silicon chips, superconductors and satellites, optical fibers and magnetic resonance imaging — each can be traced, directly or indirectly, to the search for knowledge at a very basic level, without an immediate practical application in sight.

Without a commitment to intensive research at the most fundamental level, driven by our curiosity and our sheer desire to learn, many inventions of immense social and human value would never have been created. Our universities have played a critical role in this process throughout the course of this century, and I believe we must continue to stress basic research as a high priority in the century ahead — not only in American universities but in an increasingly cooperative way throughout the world.

✦   ✦   ✦

That brings me to another major challenge I want to stress: the need to adapt our universities to a world where so many fields of learning, as well as so many important societal problems, have obvious international dimensions and where the search for new insights can benefit from the collaborative efforts of knowledgeable scholars around the globe.

Let me mention one example to illustrate my point. As I indicated earlier, Harvard has recently launched a major University-wide program to study the environment. The program is concerned with both environmental science and public policy, and with difficult environmental issues in the United States, in Europe, and in Asia. One of its first significant research projects is a collaborative effort on "Energy and Environment in China." The project involves more than one hundred scholars from both China and the United States. They span a wide range of academic disciplines and professional fields, and they are working on the complicated interplay among economic development, energy use, and environmental protection.

The purpose is not to take a model or an approach that may already exist in one part of the world and simply transplant it to another. Instead, the idea is to try to understand issues and problems in the context of the actual place where they arise, and to seek solutions that are appropriate to these specific conditions and circumstances. The hope is to draw on the special insights of individuals who can bring different perspectives and expertise to the discussion: people, for example, who may be specialists in economic development together with people who understand environmental science; people who are deeply rooted in Chinese culture and values together with people who understand the nature of commerce, politics, and law in an increasingly international world.

The same cooperative, multidisciplinary spirit underlies many of the initiatives of our new Asia Center. One of them, for instance, the Asia Pacific Forum, will gather together high-level officials from China, Japan, Korea, and the United States each year, in order to discuss challenges that will confront Pacific Rim countries in the first decade of the twenty-first century. The intention is to convene people from our different societies, in the hope of taking account of our various perspectives while examining together important long-term issues of mutual concern.

How can we manage rapid changes in the global economy, so that we can minimize the dangers and difficulties that have the potential to affect all of us? How do we prevent the spread of terrible infectious diseases? Given the major changes in the international landscape in recent years, how can we build a framework for a durable peace in the future? These and many other questions can be intelligently addressed only if we strengthen our capacity to work together across traditional academic borders and across traditional national and regional boundaries. We are fortunate that advances in information technology make it easier now than ever before to communicate with colleagues who live and work in distant places. At the same time, there is often no real substitute for the power of direct, sustained, face-to-face exchange among knowledgeable people of good will.

Such exchanges can and must be carried out in many forums — government, business, and others. Our universities, however, have a special role that is increasingly significant: we can work to create "neutral spaces" for serious discussion, based on a shared commitment to open inquiry, and to rigorous research, analysis, and continuing dialogue.

✦   ✦   ✦

During the past few decades in particular, Harvard and many other American universities have taken significant steps to open their doors more widely to people from many different walks of life: talented students across the entire economic spectrum; men and women from a broad mix of racial, ethnic, and religious groups, as well as from nations around the world. We have made progress. But we still face many problems in our own country, and we will have to work increasingly hard to sustain and extend what has been achieved.

While this challenge has been addressed with considerable force in America, it is one that I believe is becoming far more pervasive, touching a great many nations. As the world continues to "shrink" — as so many aspects of life become more international — our universities, and those of us within them, will be drawn into closer contact. All of us will need to consider how to incorporate and accommodate a greater diversity of people and a greater variety of attitudes, customs, and ideas. We will all have to learn how to sustain our own deepest cultural and human values, while also living more closely with others who have different values — and attempting to learn from them.

This kind of experiment in diversity is complicated and often very difficult. At least at first, it can lead to greater social fragmentation. It can involve all the pain and struggle that comes from misunderstanding. But the longer-term rewards of extending ourselves in this way can be very great indeed, particularly when the stakes are so high, and when the alternative may be greater and greater conflict, on a planet that is already very crowded and has witnessed more than its share of conflict over the centuries.

Let those of us in our universities join together, with others around the world, in an open and vigorous exchange of opinions. Let us do our best to reconcile differences whenever we can and to understand better the reasons for the differences that remain. Let us encourage collaborative contacts between our students as well as the members of our faculties. Let us work to make our libraries, museums, and other academic resources widely accessible. Perhaps most important, let us welcome one another in a spirit of mutual respect, energetically pursuing the ideals of openness, free inquiry, and the free exchange of ideas that lie at the heart of the search for new knowledge and deeper understanding. In this important effort, we must succeed — because we cannot afford to fail.

A Democrat Who Has Learned
from a King

Introduction of His Excellency Nelson Mandela,
President of the Republic of South Africa,
Before Conferring on Him an Honorary Doctor of Laws Degree
Tercentenary Theatre, September 18, 1998

NELSON MANDELA'S remarkable life has shaped, in absolutely decisive ways, the course of his country's history since the early decades of our century.

Born eighty years ago into a royal lineage in South Africa's Eastern Cape, he went as a boy to live in the household of the regent of his own Thembu people. He has often said how much he learned about leadership from those early years. He learned, he has said, that "a leader ... is like a shepherd. He stays behind the flock, letting the most nimble go on ahead, whereupon the others follow, not realizing that all along they are being directed from behind." President Mandela is a democrat who has learned from a king.

He also took from his background a deep sense of his own dignity and the dignity of all men and women: a conviction that led him to suspend his university studies because of a dispute about the rights of students, that drew him to his work as a lawyer, that guided him to his eventual decision to join the African National Congress.

As a founder of the ANC's Youth League, Mr. Mandela was in the forefront of the struggle against the system that came to be known as apartheid: what he called, simply, "a struggle for the right to live." He was often banned from public appearances, and after his acquittal of treason charges in 1961, he went underground.

Captured and then imprisoned in 1962, he was in 1964 sentenced to life imprisonment without possibility of parole. At trial, he did not deny his actions against the government. Instead, he argued that apartheid had "imposed a state of outlawry" on him. "All lawful modes of expressing opposition," he said, "had been closed by legislation, and we were placed in a position in which we had either to accept a permanent state of inferiority or defy the government.... We believed that South Africa belonged to all the people who lived in it," he told the court, "and not to one group, be it black or white."

Despite the extraordinary suffering to which he and his fellow prisoners were subjected, Nelson Mandela never turned away from the vision of a nonracial South Africa.

And so it was that, as his country's most famous political prisoner, he was willing to engage in dialogue with the National Party government that still held him in bondage. A decade of dialogue began in prison, continued after his release, and ended with the historic agreement with President de Klerk that led, of course, to South Africa's first democratic constitution and his own inauguration as the first president of a democratic South Africa.

For many people around the world, one of the most enduring memories of our time is the image of Nelson Mandela emerging from prison, with a vigor in his step that belied his years of suffering, "free at last." We knew that we were watching not simply one man walking out of bondage, but the emancipation of a whole nation.

As his country's president, he has never sought to harm those who had previously injured him. He was imprisoned and abused, but he has not sought to punish his abusers. He has always looked forward toward justice, never backward for vengeance. He has taught us all that there is "no easy walk to freedom"; but he has also shown us that, however hard, it is one of the only walks worth taking. In doing so he has reinvigorated the democratic ideal for all of us.

Pitching into Commitments

Remarks in Honor of David Rockefeller, Marshall Award Dinner
New York Public Library, May 17, 1999

IT MAY SURPRISE US to think that David Rockefeller and Charles Darwin grew up with a good deal in common. But they were both in fact bewitched by beetles, which they collected extravagantly.

One of David's teachers in secondary school, in a letter of recommendation to Harvard College, mentioned that although David's "spelling tends to be somewhat Chaucerian," he "has a unique collection of *coleoptera*," and his knowledge of this entomological group is "surprising in so young" a person.

Later, of course, Darwin and David came to a slight parting of the ways. Darwin concluded that mankind was descended from countless generations of evolving anthropoids. David, by contrast, decided that he derived from a line of devoted philanthropists. And while philanthropy has been only one of his many callings, it has characterized a life in which a natural spirit of generosity has been strengthened and deepened by an equally strong sense of responsibility for the common good — and for the health of institutions and societies around the world.

How to build and rebuild; how to initiate, motivate, and rejuvenate; how to create and sustain relationships even when conditions are adverse; how to encourage others to develop their own distinctive capacities for growth, for fruitful collaboration, and for the wise exercise of freedom: these have been the chief principles guiding David for many decades.

It is this unusual vision — whether in philanthropy, business, education, or international affairs — that links David most clearly and directly with General George C. Marshall, and with the General's own values.

You may remember that in his brief Commencement address at Harvard in June of 1947, General Marshall offered a startling plan, completely at odds with the way that victorious nations had behaved in the wake of virtually every previous major war in history. There was no hint of imposing punitive reparations or using territorial gains to extend one's own power. In other words, there was to be no repeat of the disastrous policies followed by the Allies in the wake of World War I.

Instead, the General stated that the most important problem facing the world was the fact that the long war had led to the complete "dislocation of the entire fabric of [the] European economy." It was imperative, therefore, that the United States

> *assist in the return of normal economic health in the world, without which there can be no political stability and no assured peace. Our policy is directed not against any country or doctrine but against hunger, poverty, desperation, and chaos.*[1]

"The initiative," he added, "must come from Europe"; "the role of this country should be one of friendly aid."

So it was that the nations that were so recently our enemies, Germany and Italy, were rehabilitated rather than degraded. Economic health was identified as crucial to the survival and the creation of free institutions and international peace. And American aid was transformed — by an army general — from military to humanitarian assistance.

These principles defined a new conception of enlightened international investment and philanthropy similar in its fundamentals to David Rockefeller's own.

David's instincts are ecumenical. He travels inexhaustibly, and (as has been said more than once) he has come to know more heads of state than any of our actual presidents have managed to do. But then, David has been "in office" for nearly as long as our last ten presidents combined. Which office? His own, of course: an office and a role created purely by his integrity, intelligence, tireless work, naturalness of manner, and breadth of vision.

There are many, many wealthy people in the world, and many with well-known names. But neither riches nor lineage guarantees anything in our society. Too often, indeed, they lead to forms of self-indulgence and self-promotion that are mainly a prelude to public notoriety.

If David is received everywhere around the globe as Ambassador Plenipotentiary without Explicit Portfolio, or as unofficial Head of State, it is because he is an informed, observant, experienced, modest, and generous citizen of the world, interested in the welfare of all.

In this role, he has taken more than his share of risks. In 1973, he flew to Beijing to meet with Premier Chou En-lai, to open channels that could be broader and deeper than those of our government. Much earlier, in 1964, he traveled to see Premier Nikita Khrushchev for a set of far-ranging discussions. He concluded that the "Soviets would rather deal with [someone] they consider to be a real capitalist...." Furthermore, said David, they seem to "believe their own propaganda": they apparently assume that "I really [do] run the United States."

Moving from abroad, closer to home, I want to say a few words about David's long-standing loyalty to Harvard University — deriving not simply from his status as an alumnus but from his belief in the radiating power of excellent institutions.

When he was first nominated for Harvard's Board of Overseers in 1954, he garnered the largest number of votes ever recorded in an Overseer election during the entire history of the University. Soon thereafter, he was elected President of the Board, and he later held important positions on more committees across all of Harvard than one could possibly list here.

Then, after more than half a century of dedicated participation, David made his most dramatic contribution to the future of the University just five years ago, when he took the lead in establishing a major new interdisciplinary Center for Latin American Studies.

This initiative, in itself, gives powerful expression to all of David's extraordinary qualities. He had, of course, been personally involved with the countries of Latin America for decades and had created and sustained friendships, in good times and in bad, throughout the entire region.

Earlier than most people, he sensed the movement in many of these countries toward more open and democratic regimes, toward greater economic productivity and free trade. He also knew that the people of the United States had far too little knowledge about the cultures, the capacities, and the rapidly growing significance of Latin America. It seemed clear to him that Harvard could and should play a much more visible and focused role in research and teaching about the region, as well as in helping to address some of its complex problems. He envisaged opportunities for mid-career education programs at Harvard for Latin American practitioners in many professional fields, and he hoped for the creation of closer partnerships between the North and the South of our shared Americas.

We can think of this new initiative — the David Rockefeller Center for Latin American Studies — as an act of philanthropy, or of enlightened international relations, or of educational and cultural development, or of durable institution building. It has represented not only an investment of significant financial resources on David's part, but (equally important) a continuing investment of his own time, energy, and advice in order to help ensure the success of this new enterprise.

When making such investments, one always gives something away: one spends part of what one has and what one is. But if we invest wisely, we also find ourselves gaining satisfaction from what we create, and even identifying with the venture and all that it stands for. In this sense, we actually retain what we have given, because through our own efforts we become part of the new creation.

In a wonderful essay about the writing of poetry, Robert Frost once talked about this particular paradox in terms of his own calling. "Every single poem," he said,

> *is a symbol small or great of the way the will has to pitch into commitments deeper and deeper to a rounded conclusion and then be judged for whether any original intention it had has been strongly spent or weakly lost; be it in art, politics, school, church, business, love, or marriage — in a piece of work or in a career. Strongly spent is synonymous with kept.*[2]

David Rockefeller, very much like General Marshall, has demonstrated through a lifetime of practice what it means to give "strongly," openly, wisely, fruitfully. He has long known that if one spends or gives in the right spirit — involving oneself in the entire activity and its purposes — one also gains, and in effect retains what one has given. "Strongly spent," as Frost said, "is synonymous with kept."

1 George C. Marshall, *Commencement Day Address*, Harvard University, June 5, 1947.

2 Robert Frost, "The Constant Symbol," in *Selected Prose of Robert Frost* (New York: Holt, Rinehart & Winston, 1966), 24. Orig. pub. *Atlantic Monthly*, October 1946.

Transforming Situations

Yitzhak Rabin Memorial Service
John F. Kennedy School of Government,
November 15, 1995

THIS MEETING – now a commemoration and memorial tribute – was originally to have been a welcome. We had hoped and expected to greet and warmly receive one of the world's significant leaders, as well as one of the most important figures in the history of the State of Israel.

Now, all of our early and eager preparations have been changed, changed by a terrible event that will leave its deep mark on the memory and spirit of us all. Tasks that were already difficult and dangerous are now likely to be even more so.

As we look across nations and peoples, there are never enough individuals and leaders who are courageous and yet also human in their sensitivities, strong and even unyielding when necessary, but also willing to grasp essential opportunities, and to transform situations in response to changing circumstances and to a new vision of what may be possible. Yitzhak Rabin was such a person. The loss of any such person, at any time, is a grave blow for everyone, everywhere. The loss of *this* extraordinary person, at this hazardous and uncertain time, has struck suddenly, with a gravity that all of us will feel for a very long time to come.

Although we are familiar with Prime Minister Rabin's remarkable achievements, it is nonetheless important to recall some of his accomplishments. When he was very young, he risked his life to help establish the State of Israel. Later, as a general, he was one of the architects of the Six-Day War. As an ambassador, he sustained and deepened the commitment of the United States to Israel. As a defense minister, he helped to forge the agreement with Egypt that paved the way for the Camp David accord. Then, most recently as Prime Minister, he found, slowly and painfully, his own pathway, and that of his nation, toward a difficult and demanding peace, and he found himself often alone in the midst of honest doubt and defiant opposition.

He was a soldier dedicated to victory but ambivalent about war, a statesman devoted to peace but anxious about its fragility, as well as about his nation's security. We admire him the more, precisely because he was not always absolutely single-minded, or utterly self-confident, or fully persuaded that he knew firmly what was right, or what was the true will of his people, or of God.

Now he has been swept away by those who have, unfortunately, no such hesitations. The contrast is blinding in its clarity and power to all except those, now so numerous, and in many lands, who have far less difficulty than did Yitzhak Rabin in distinguishing at all between their own vision of truth and God's vision.

There are also no simple, clear lessons that we can learn from this terrible event. But I do strongly believe that this is a time for everyone to reassert – with renewed force – a commitment to democratic forms of government, which require not only freedom of expression and the vigorous exchange of different views in order to prosper, but also a significant level of tolerance and mutual understanding and an uncompromising commitment to the rule of law: not one's own view of the law but the established law of any civil and legitimate democratic state. Those individuals who wish to bear witness to what they believe to be a higher law, or a more sacred truth, should choose paths that very great religious and moral leaders have long since taught us to choose: nonviolence and forbearance, let us say, require more courage, more patience and steadfastness, more religious spirit, and certainly more humility in relation to God, than acts such as those we see now carried out almost daily in the names of the different gods of different peoples. Surely it is time to remind ourselves that we are citizens who live among other citizens; that our civic duties involve civility; that we belong to democracies which deserve to be cherished, not desecrated.

Next, and here I speak for myself since there may be others in our university who have a different view, I believe that we must now pursue the process of peace in the Middle East (and elsewhere) with even greater intensity. It may be more difficult to do so. But we cannot let those who are committed to disruption and violence prevail. Of course the peace process must take every responsible caution, on every side, to insure the security of Israel and of all people. But moments and leaps of faith will at points be required. Moments of faith on behalf of peace, properly prepared, simply must be preferred to actions in the service of wars that have no end and that now offer only the mere illusion of victory.

As we go forward, let us remember the deeds and life of Yitzhak Rabin. Let us celebrate the very conflicts of his sometimes divided mind and heart, as well as his decisiveness and strength. And even when events may be discouraging, when the odds in favor of peace may be at their very lowest point, let us have hope and the will to realize our hopes. "Either we have hope within us," wrote Václav Havel not long ago, "or we do not." Hope, he said:

> is a dimension of the soul, and it's not essentially dependent on some particular… estimate of the situation…. It is an orientation of the spirit, an orientation of the heart…. It is not the conviction that something will turn out well, but the certainty that something makes sense, regardless of how it turns out.[1]

Yitzhak Rabin concluded that peace makes sense. That conclusion had become the orientation of his spirit and heart. We are grateful to him for that, and we must now dedicate ourselves to ensuring that his hope does indeed become reality.

---

1 Václav Havel, *Disturbing the Peace: A Conversation with Karel Hvíždala*, trans. Paul Wilson (New York: Alfred A. Knopf, 1990), 181.

A Major Turning Point
in International Studies

Speech to the Committee on University Resources
March 22, 1997

VIRTUALLY EVERYONE in any field of "regional studies" or "area studies" is a virtuoso more or less by definition: there are so few of them to cover so much of what is "out there," and each faculty member may have to cope with an entire string of dynasties, or a large bundle of rebellions and revolutions. I myself once specialized in English lyric poetry from the 1530s to about the 1630s, and even that seemed quite a stretch at times. But we ask our East Asian scholars (as well as those in Middle Eastern studies, Latin American studies, and other analogous fields) to bestride whole centuries and even continents. And they carry it off in a remarkable way.

Therefore, the first point worth remembering when we discuss regional and international studies is that they present unusually difficult challenges. They require versatility and elasticity. They also typically involve the ability to manage, deftly and fluently, two, three, or more languages (often complicated languages). And the people, cultures, and documents to be studied are not nearby. It is difficult enough for the rest of us to understand the pattern and meaning of events close to home, where we speak the language and know the customs. To try to do the same in China, or Korea, or Japan, or Vietnam demands formidable scholarship, a special kind of imagination and human perceptiveness, decades of experience, and great perseverance against what are sometimes heavy odds.

It is not surprising, therefore, that these fields of study are far from easy to launch, and are usually very slow to develop. Harvard had been in existence approximately 250 years before the first course in Mandarin Chinese was taught, and it was not at all clear whether anyone was actually interested in taking it. Finding students, developing faculty, acquiring books and scholarly journals and other research materials, raising funds to endow professorships, or to support travel and research, or to create fellowships for graduate students — all of these matters take literally decades.

Harvard's first real library and research center on China (and I will focus to some extent on China, mainly because it was the first Asian country to receive serious academic attention here and in several other American universities) was the Harvard-Yenching Institute, founded in 1928. That was rather early for higher education in the United States, but perhaps rather late from the point of view of China. By the mid-1930s, we had laid modest foundations for work in the earlier periods of Chinese history, literature, art, and related subjects. But it was still a slender enterprise, and might well have continued so indefinitely, if the external world had not erupted in ways that changed the course of history dramatically.

Let me focus for a moment on a single day in 1935. A Harvard freshman studying European history found himself cramming for examinations in a Boylston Hall room that he described as "crowded, sweaty, and steamy." He noticed, on the other side of the corridor, a large chamber that looked empty and tranquil, so he quietly slipped across the way, where the air seemed more fragrant. The room turned out to be the library of the Harvard-Yenching Institute. The shelves were lined with handsome blue-bound volumes, printed on fine rice paper and studded with unfamiliar characters. Years later, the one-time freshman recalled his experience:

> *As I became more and more and more accustomed to the ... atmosphere, and my eyes rested on the scrolls of calligraphy on the walls, I began to feel at home. The Boston Latin School had given me reading knowledge of Latin, German, and French.... Hebrew was the language ... I spoke best after my native English. Why not, then, take a giant step, and add Chinese to my languages — and find out what the blue-bound volumes said.*[1]

So began the journey of one young student (ultimately a distinguished writer and a member of our Board of Overseers) to learn about China and Asia. At the time, undergraduates had just been granted (against the will of many faculty) the right to study the Chinese language. Only graduate students had been eligible before then. A grand total of five students (three at the doctoral level, and just two undergraduates) were enrolled in the introductory course. One of the two undergraduates failed, more or less immediately. Our hero survived and received an A. He then went on to be the only person in his Harvard class concentrating in Chinese studies. His tutor was a recently minted Ph.D. — the only person on the Harvard faculty teaching any topics in Chinese history beyond the eighteenth century. The tutor was convinced that the recent "Long March" of Mao Tse-tung was an epoch-making event.

The young undergraduate and the youthful instructor became an adventurous pair of exploratory modernists. They worked intensively together, even as wars in the Pacific and in Europe were beginning. In his senior year, the student won a Sheldon Traveling Fellowship. He left New York in September 1938, on a bunk bed deep in the hold of the SS *President Roosevelt*. He wrote:

My sense of history was drawing me outward [toward Asia].... I hoped eventually to come back to Harvard. But first I must satisfy curiosity, my absolute lust to see what was happening in the China I had studied. How did *history actually happen?*[2]

The student was Theodore White, who gradually shifted his focus from China to the United States, and later wrote *The Making of the President, 1960*, among other volumes. And the young tutor was John King Fairbank, magister of modern Chinese studies for decades afterward.

That was how the second half century of Harvard Chinese studies, from the late 1930s to the 1980s, began: one undergraduate who was interested in languages and history, a peaceful room with intriguing books in the Yenching library, a committed young teacher and scholar, earth-shattering events in the world outside, and a fellowship grant that allowed the student, after his tutelage, to set off on his own to see for himself what was actually happening on the other side of the globe.

Here, in this one vignette, we can see how a number of different factors can sometimes converge and catalyze entire fields of learning. Fortunately, Chinese studies at Harvard had progressed just enough to provide the basis for that next major leap, to a new phase of rapid and intensive development. But that leap would never have happened if far-reaching transformations had not already been under way in China, and in Asia more generally.

As we know, within the space of a single short decade (between the late 1930s and the late 1940s), Japan had begun and lost the war in the Pacific; that earlier and relatively tranquil China, which included merchant traders and Christian missionaries, had been replaced by the new revolutionary China of Mao Tse-tung; and a previously isolationist America had become an engaged international power. In addition, by the late 1940s, a small but growing number of people in the United States had begun to believe that the study of China, Japan, and other Asian countries was important, not only for itself; it now seemed increasingly essential in terms of national security and world politics.

For the next three decades, international studies enjoyed a boom, made possible by the strong support of the federal government, several foundations, and many individual donors. Departments, research centers, and institutes were established. The governing purpose was to focus not only on individual countries, but also on specific regions of the world: East or Southeast Asia, the Middle East or the Near East, the Soviet Union and Eastern Europe, Africa, Latin America, and other areas. The growth was spectacular compared to anything and everything that had ever happened before in such studies. But it still fell short when compared to the real needs or to the substantial resources available in much more established fields of knowledge. And that is why we must still rely so much on professorial virtuosity.

In fact, the needs and the demands are now so great that the gap between our present number of faculty and the mission to be accomplished has widened since even a decade ago. Why is this the case? The reason is quite clear: the world has changed dramatically (and the pace of technological innovation has accelerated) in ways that have created far more pressure for more information and knowledge, with less response time and more demand for precision. We are at another major turning point in international studies, and we need to think clearly about our educational goals for the period ahead.

Think for a moment about the real-world changes that have taken place since the late 1980s. The combination of them is more deeply transformative than at first we might suspect. The breakup of the Soviet Union, ending forty years of superpower Cold War, was certainly the single most significant event. In addition, there have been the different but steady effort to create peace in the Middle East, the sudden sea change in South Africa, the continued opening up of China, the shift throughout much of Latin America toward more democratic governments. The list goes on:

powerful changes, sometimes happening simultaneously, that even in 1980 would have seemed unimaginable.

We have also witnessed the widespread shift in the direction of free-market economies, the privatization of many state monopolies and services, the increasing belief that economic entrepreneurship and controlled growth are crucial to political and other forms of stability.

Then, there is the revolution in modern information technologies, including telecommunications. Suddenly, it is essentially impossible to insulate any nation or people from ideas, news, video, and the free flow of e-mail or satellite broadcasts to (and from) the most remote corners of the world. There can still be, and there is, much oppression in the world. But there can no longer be impenetrable iron curtains that isolate entire areas or regions from world opinion. That single fact marks an enormous shift in human history.

Finally, in spite of the strife and even war that we continue to witness in so many places (the Middle East, the former Yugoslavia, Chechnya, Afghanistan, Zaire, Albania, Nigeria, Rwanda, Bulgaria, Peru, Ireland, and elsewhere), it is nonetheless clear that most of the world community has developed a strong consensus in favor of limiting such conflicts and attempting somehow to resolve them, rather than exploit them in order to provoke larger-scale war.

For at least the past two centuries, and in fact much longer, many nations have operated on the assumption that war was an effective instrument of state power, so long as there seemed a reasonable chance of coming out ahead. But for several years now, most major powers appear to have concluded that aggressive full-scale war in the nuclear age makes it difficult to imagine how anyone can conceivably come out ahead. The stakes are simply too high.

Most, if not all, of the developments I have just described have been positive. And yet, it is also obvious that they have not resulted in a New World Order. They have unleashed a multitude of old rivalries — political, religious, ethnic, racial, tribal, economic, and territorial. They have also demonstrated again how exceptionally difficult it is to create and sustain successful institutions of government — or effective legal systems, or a private economic sector that operates with a high degree of stability and integrity. The alternative to totalitarian or authoritarian regimes may possibly be some form of democracy. But it may also be the equivalent of a social and political vacuum, leading to a process of civic chaos and collapse, followed by a return to authoritarianism. How to create a strong infrastructure, how to build effective and participatory structures for governing, how to reduce the ferocity of age-old hostilities among different groups, and how to do this across the entire globe: these are some of the most formidable challenges of the present moment.

Fifty years ago, it took great vision and determination to recognize that it would be far better to help reconstruct Germany, and all of Europe, far better to help Japan regain its strength as a society, than to seek the kind of immense vindictive reparations that followed in the wake of World War I. In the 1920s and 1930s, we discovered what can happen to nations that are crippled economically and embittered politically. As an antidote to that earlier experience, the Marshall Plan and similar efforts were born.

Today's situation is more complex — less clearly focused and more diffuse — but it is no less difficult. The number of countries and peoples at risk has multiplied substantially. The number of nations where provocative or violent events can create a crisis of international proportions has also grown. The challenge of constructing and maintaining an intricately balanced and cooperative international system, or a constantly negotiated process that might result in a reasonable degree of world order, is huge in its dimensions and unpredictable in its likely outcomes. What policies do we follow in order to realize such a vision? We are beginning to learn some of the essential tasks, but we still know far too little about other nations, regions, and peoples of the world.

Without such knowledge and experience, we cannot possibly act in an informed and effective way in order to achieve the broad goals that I have been discussing.

Meanwhile, the amount of information available to everyone is greater by far than ever before. Many more archives, libraries, and other institutional sources of information are now open. Many societies are more accessible: people in dozens and dozens of countries can now be interviewed easily, and they discuss matters more freely than a brief decade ago. For universities, therefore, the job of seeking to understand and reinterpret the history and culture of many "known" nations and peoples is itself a massive undertaking, even as we also try to understand enough about the many less familiar societies with which we now interact.

In other words, we must now expect to survey a scene that is essentially worldwide or global in nature. And we ourselves are an inescapable part of that scene yet we understand far too little about it. Given the fact that the world has changed significantly in the last decade, it is clear that the university's international agenda must also change.

What, then, are some of the implications for Harvard? Education in itself can do only so much. But education has come to be seen, correctly, as indispensable if we are to have any chance at all of analyzing and addressing exceptionally difficult problems and situations that confront the world today. Allow me to sketch the barest outlines of a provisional agenda for the future.

First, we must continue to deepen our knowledge of individual cultures, nations, and regions. Otherwise, we will have no real basis for understanding the fundamental attitudes, beliefs, viewpoints, and expectations of people in other countries. A "global" perspective is not a substitute for "local" or regional perspectives.

Second, we must make it easier for faculty in the various regional centers based in the arts and sciences to collaborate with faculty in our professional schools — business, divinity, design, education, government, law, medicine, and public health. We must develop a more comprehensive and complex view of particular societies and regions. That can be achieved only by drawing together individuals from a wide number of disciplines and fields across the entire University.

Fortunately, our regional centers and departments in Arts and Sciences are already doing precisely that: creating stronger relationships with colleagues throughout Harvard, in order to share knowledge; seeking a deeper understanding of issues and problems that require an interdisciplinary and interfaculty approach.

Third, we need to make it easier for faculty and students who are studying one particular region, such as Asia, to work more closely with those involved in other regions, such as Latin America or Eastern Europe. Not all such connections make sense. But as regional economies develop (and become more intertwined), or as religious or political ideas and movements migrate across boundaries, there is obviously a greater need to study such developments at a transregional or worldwide level. It is an oversimplification to say that this is the moment in modern history when we are expanding our vision from a predominantly regional approach, which has been the governing model in international studies since World War II, to one that is essentially global. But there is more than a single grain of truth in the idea.

Fourth, we must continue to identify those important topics that are in fact transregional, so that we can give them the sustained attention they deserve. Environmental issues are obviously one such subject. Pollution and ozone loss affect everyone, everywhere, not simply the people in a particular country or area. The emergence of powerful, widespread religious movements is another significant topic. The complex problems faced by emerging and fragile democracies or developing economies constitute additional topics. The multiple causes of ethnic, religious, or racial strife in different societies are yet another subject. The analysis of conflict resolution and of the essential factors in creating a successful peace process is another fertile field for greater exploration. All these subjects (and others) can benefit greatly from research and discussion by individuals who approach them from different points of view, with different skills and methodologies, and who can therefore pool their insights and ways of thinking in order to extend their scope and reach.

Fifth, we should encourage more of our own students to study, work, and travel abroad during some part of their education. Similarly, we have to continue to bring students from foreign countries to Harvard, both to widen our own perspectives and to enable students from abroad to have contact with American students and the United States, including its institutions and values. Nothing, absolutely nothing, can replace the sustained, direct contact that takes place within a diverse community of students and faculty if we want to increase mutual understanding and the chances for cooperation in the world at large.

Finally, I believe we must think more carefully about the contribution that Harvard can make at advanced levels of education — at mid-career or executive levels in the professional schools, as well as in Arts and Sciences. If we consider our own comparative advantage and examine what we are best able to offer other countries in the form of assistance in higher education, then it seems clear that we are in a position to help educate and train individuals from abroad who are already in positions of some responsibility and leadership but who need to strengthen their skills and deepen their insights in order to be even more effective.

There is now a vast need in dozens and dozens of countries for well-trained government officials, institutional managers and leaders, business entrepreneurs, public health officials and doctors, urban planners, international lawyers, and economists, as well as academics and educators. Without such people, there is very little hope that many of the world's societies can become, or remain, stable. There is little prospect that they will be able to achieve levels of basic political and economic well-being. Relatively few nations have higher education systems that are sufficiently developed. Even fewer offer graduate and professional education opportunities of the highest quality. And fewer still can create exceptional programs for individuals in mid-career or in positions of significant responsibility. The investment in such individuals can have a powerful "multiplier effect" in societies that desperately need people capable of managing complex institutions – including entire nations or economies or health care systems.

The agenda I have just outlined is very substantial. It will not be easy to achieve, and it will take time. But our new Asia Center is taking shape. In addition, Harvard has (in the past five years) established the David Rockefeller Center for Latin American Studies; it has strengthened the Korea Institute and been helped by a substantial endowment for the Kathryn W. and Shelby Cullom Davis Center for Russian Studies; it has created the Reginald F. Lewis Center for International Law and is beginning to establish an Islamic Law Center. In addition, a new international studies complex will help to bring many individual units into closer working relationship with one another.

We are well on the way. But we lag in relation to our own goals – and to what our times will require. We will need (and demand) a great deal more knowledge about the world which we now inhabit in order to help ensure that the world itself remains habitable and hospitable in the century ahead. The challenge is a formidable one, particularly at a time when the nation's attention is focused inward, and when the federal government's investment in international affairs has declined drastically in the last decade and a half.

As we explore ways of developing our international responsibilities, it is important to bear in mind that, in an era of instantaneous communication, current events and the historical past can act upon one another in new and unpredictable ways. On January 6, Angelica and I received a personal e-mail from a friend in Serbia, titled "Declaration of Professional Walkers in Belgrade." These were the days of massive protest against the government because of its manipulation of recent election results. The letter read, in part:

We have been stirring the conscience of Belgrade, tirelessly march-
ing and persistently walking, whistling and ringing, lighting can-
dles and lamps to illuminate streets and squares of Serbian towns
for more than a month. This act of civil resistance is our choice.
Why?

Because we want to live in peace and freedom, in a parlia-
mentary and democratic state, governed by the rule of law, and not
in chaos and lawlessness, in a primitive, totalitarian, dictatorial
regime. Because we refuse to allow our lives, or our votes and the
laws and all our requests to be ignored; because our children are
arrested and battered.... We want to live in a [place] where all
human rights and all achievements of the civil society shall be
respected, and every [person has] a chance to make a creative con-
tribution. We want to join the world community.

The protest in Belgrade (instantly broadcast throughout the world)
was immediate, current, political; but the ideas were as ancient as
they are contemporary: ideas that come from the past, and that
have now traveled across all boundaries of time and place, stirring
the spirit of people everywhere. And the experience of receiving
such messages is radically different from reading about a distant
political protest in the morning papers.

Yes, the larger world has undergone another significant shrinkage. It can enter our consciousness directly, one way or another,
at any hour. We need, more than ever, to help ourselves, our students, and society to be prepared for this new form of drama,
with all its unpredictability and fluidity. And that is a central part
of our emerging agenda in international studies.

---

1 Theodore H. White, *In Search of History: A Personal Memoir* (New York: Harper
& Row, 1978), 46.

2 Ibid., 55.

THE WORLDS OF HARVARD

Pointing Our Thoughts

Harvard University Campaign Kickoff Speech
Sanders Theatre, May 14, 1994

T HE FIRST TIME I really saw Harvard was in September, 1960. I arrived as a graduate student, on a brilliant autumn day, ready to study Renaissance literature.

Just a few weeks earlier, I had been a first lieutenant, commanding a tattered field artillery battalion at Fort Sill, Oklahoma. Day after day, we had fired 105 millimeter howitzer shells into vacant stretches of desert sand, littered with the extinct Buicks, Chevrolets, and abandoned oil drums that were our targets.

After Fort Sill's acres of silicon, the modest grass and shrubs of Harvard Yard seemed like an unimaginable green oasis.

I sat more or less motionless for two or three hours, perched on the edge of one of those high parapets that flank the front steps of Widener, looking out over Sever Hall, Memorial Church, University Hall, and the buildings beyond.

Those hours on Widener's parapet began my own romance with Harvard. Like many romances, it started as a form of intoxication. But it also contained the sense of something inevitable. It was an encounter that I knew would sooner or later take place,

239

and that I could no longer postpone. The reason, in the end, was very simple.

To my mind, Harvard not only *set* the standard, it *was* the standard. I realized that if I failed to keep a rendezvous with this university, I would always feel as if I had been unwilling to test myself against the very best. Like the uncertain hero in Cole Porter's ballad, I would have constantly wondered, as I wandered through life, looking at things:

> *Is it the good turtle soup, or merely the mock?* …
> *Is it Granada I see, or only Asbury Park?*

I had reached the point when I knew that I wanted the very best turtle soup. And so I found myself perched on Widener's parapet, ready to begin.

Why is it that I (and so many others, before and since) have felt so certain that this journey to Harvard was eventually bound to happen? How did the University move, from its fragile beginnings in the 1630s, to the magnetic institution that it had become three and a half centuries later?

The transformation did not happen by accident. The story is both surprising and absorbing. It also has a great deal to do with the reasons that we find ourselves together in this historic room.

Harvard College started with only one acre of land and just one house. And that single acre was part of a larger cow yard, where all the local bovines were herded every night, to graze or laze or simply slumber.

Harvard Yard was originally Harvard's cow yard: a place where our earliest students and the neighboring beasts of the field co-existed in odoriferous proximity, until the College finally got enough money to buy the cattle out.

Very little went smoothly in those days. After an unsteady beginning in 1636, Harvard literally had to close its doors and remained entirely empty for the academic year 1638–39. In fact, even after the College reopened, the size of the graduating classes varied from somewhere between seven and eleven students per year, and never reached a steady state of more than twenty graduates until nearly a full century later.

With very few exceptions, Harvard's early presidents came and went with all the regularity of a distinct migrating species: seventeenth-century frequent fliers. Dr. Leonard Hoar, for instance, was a learned and pious man. He was also so overbearing that the students (never at a loss for words) parodied and satirized him quite mercilessly. Mr. Hoar became increasingly despondent. Then suddenly, in the winter of 1674–75, literally all the undergraduates packed their bags and left the College *en masse.* Harvard was totally deserted once again. "After Hoar's experience," wrote Samuel Eliot Morison in his wonderful history of Harvard, "the College found great difficulty for the *next thirty-four years* in procuring a President."

Those early days were more than a little precarious. And we must remember, too, that the drama of the College was being played out against the backdrop of an unsettled New World society. There were virulent epidemics; destructive fires; skirmishes, wars, and threats of war; economic recession and depression; harsh winters and severe privations of every kind.

From day to day, one did not know what act of devastation might simply eradicate so tiny and vulnerable an institution of learning — an institution subject to the constant mutations and permutations of every chance and circumstance.

✦   ✦   ✦

Given this situation, we may well wonder how Harvard survived at all, let alone flourished. Three important factors (including some strong prevailing attitudes) made all the difference.

The first had to do with our original chartered purposes.

We decided from the very beginning that we wanted to educate youth to become learned, pious, and useful members of society. We cared, in other words, about service and the public good. We also decided not to become a denominational college or theological seminary. We would be open to a variety of creeds and faiths, committed to a broad liberal education, including "the *advancement* of all good literature, Arts and sciences."

In short, no sphere of knowledge or field of inquiry would be ruled out of bounds. And that single phrase concerning the "advancement" of learning ensured that we would concentrate, not only on the preservation and transmission of knowledge, but also on its extension and creative growth. The process of research and discovery – that determination to press beyond the limits of what we already know – was part of our mission from the very start, and guided all our aspirations.

The second important factor was that Harvard had a clear vision of what a great college (and later, a great university) ought to be. Our founders, many of them graduates of Oxford and Cambridge, brought with them a vivid image of residential college life, and they insisted on nothing less than the best in their new homeland.

Their successors, especially in the nineteenth century, had an equally strong vision of what a major *university* should be: they wanted doctoral studies, professional education, great libraries and museums, and extensive research programs. Gradually, element by element, century by century, Harvard began to give shape to an ideal which drew on the experience of other nations but was also distinctly American.

That brings us to the third main factor: Harvard's boldness in the midst of all of its prudence and sobriety. There was the driving ambition and sense of confidence, the stamina and persistence, to create something unique and unsurpassed. All of this was accompanied by a New England-style directness in asking for help from alumni and friends, as we set out to build our own Georgian, Victorian, and modern temples of learning.

The ambition and drive, however, were anything but indiscriminate. Those original chartered purposes and goals served as constant guiding stars. In addition, the University chose its most important moments carefully, reserving its greatest efforts for just those times of maximum challenge and opportunity.

In fact, the capacity to rise to significant occasions, the ability to sense when major decision points were at hand, has been more critical to Harvard's development than any other single factor in the University's long history. Time and again, when it would have been understandable and even natural to move more slowly, or to avoid a particularly difficult path, Harvard deliberately chose to press further and to reach higher. It refused to be satisfied, or to settle for anything except the most that could be achieved.

✦   ✦   ✦

To watch some of that ambition in action, to see something of the living institution as it struggled and grew, is worth a few minutes of our time.

For instance, the College decided very early that it wanted a printing press, to turn out religious tracts, as well as the first translation of the Bible into a Native American language. Harvard had virtually no buildings at the time, so the press was conveniently located inside the President's house until about 1655. Soon it was turning out "almanacs, law books, broadsides, catechisms, psalm books, sermons, . . . and [even] a few books of poetry by New Englanders such as Anne Bradstreet. . . ."[1]

In fact, this whirling dervish, tucked away in a tiny college, was literally the only printing press in all the colonies for about twenty years. Harvard was not content, in other words, simply to collect books for the use of its faculty and students. True to its purpose of advancing and expanding knowledge, the College began to create new books, and then to distribute them widely.

At that time, we possessed few if any detectable scientific instruments. But in 1672, Governor John Winthrop presented us with a telescope. (We were not able to afford scientific equipment then, any more easily than now.) In 1680, young Thomas Brattle, a recent alumnus, had made and recorded observations of a new comet, observations that were significant enough to be cited later by Newton in his *Principia*. By the 1680s, the Copernican system was freely taught at Harvard: one of those resounding judgments that turned out to be scientifically accurate as well as theoretically correct. Meanwhile, the College's one and only tutor in science compiled all the latest astronomical data, and with the help of our printing press, he began to circulate new almanacs to the farmers of Massachusetts, keeping them fully abreast of the recent discoveries by Galileo, Kepler, and Gassendi.

Of course, the telescope of 1672 was soon hopelessly out of date. We went through a number of "upgrades," thanks to the generosity of a sequence of donors. By the middle of the nineteenth century, we acquired a stunning new instrument, exactly the same size as the one at Pulkova, in Russia. These two instruments were "the largest refracting" telescopes in the entire world. Within months, observers at Harvard had discovered an eighth satellite spinning through space around the planet Saturn, as well as three new stars in the neighborhood of the trapezium in the nebula of Orion.

Even more remarkable, the new telescope enabled us to measure time much more exactly, because we could now record very precise observations of the transit of stars over the meridian. Railroads soon relied on the information from our accurate Harvard Observatory clocks to set their train schedules up and down their lines. In his 1849–50 Report to the Overseers, President Everett reported this fact, and announced astonishingly that "the motion of every railroad car in the Commonwealth [of Massachusetts] is now being regulated by the time at the [Harvard] Observatory."

In other words, the results of what we would today call "basic research" — research propelled by the sheer human desire to discover more and more about the nature of our universe — these results were turned into practical applications. Moving from Copernican theory, to the Harvard telescope, to the regulation of the Commonwealth's clocks and railroad cars, proved to be one of our earliest triumphs in technology transfer.

This was cause for real celebration, but it also brought its share of fiscal woe. The largest of our telescopes turned out to be more expensive than anticipated. Then (inevitably) we needed a building in which to house it; plus a full-time observer; then an assistant to help the observer; then money to publish the data, and so on. Student tuition could obviously not be used to pay for such costs. President Everett acknowledged (in his annual report of 1847) the immense value of the Observatory and the teaching of astronomy. But he also noted that the temporary funds to support most of these new activities would expire by the end of that very year, and there were no obvious alternative funds in sight.

Nonetheless, the president showed no evident sign of panic. "The Corporation," he wrote, "look with a grateful confidence, founded on experience, to the continued existence and operation of that noble public spirit, and enlightened munificence, that have thus far been the greatest resource of the university." Which is to say: he hoped that new gifts would soon be forthcoming. And in due course, with a bit of effort and much generosity, they did indeed come forth.

This tale of the printing press, the sequence of glittering telescopes, the synchronization of an entire railroad system to Harvard time, and the constant push-pull of searching for more resources to pay for the extra reach and drive of the University: this tale epitomizes a great deal of our entire history. Countless additional stories might well be told. Let me mention just one more.

In 1877, Mr. Francis P. Knight, a local merchant, returned from the Far East to Boston for an extended visit. He had decided, essentially on his own, that it would redound to the glory of Harvard, and presumably to all humankind, if he could raise (and I quote now from President Eliot's annual report) "a subscription of $8,750 (mostly payable by installments)" — President Eliot rarely omitted any significant financial detail — "for the purpose of maintaining at Cambridge for a term of five years, a native teacher of Mandarin Chinese."

This proposal was accepted by our intrepid Corporation. Mr. Knight returned to China to find a likely candidate. He finally engaged the services of Mr. Ko Kun-hua of Ningpo, for three years, beginning September 1, 1879.

Upon their arrival, neither Mr. Ko nor his wife nor their six small children spoke a word of English. They came bravely, and with great good grace, into utterly unknown terrain. They moved (with an interpreter) into a house at 10 Mason Street. A Harvard faculty member, observing all this, wrote to a friend: "I never heard of [Mr. Ko] until two days ago, but it seems he is to be our instructor in Chinese for the next three years. Who is going to learn Chinese, and how it is to be got into our College [curriculum] are questions that have not [yet] even been considered."

Here, in action, we see the convergence of mercantile entrepreneurship; institutional aspiration; an imaginative faculty appointment process (surely the most *ad hoc* of all our famous *ad hocs*); an interesting Sears-Roebuck method of funding professorships on an installment plan; and the introduction of a complex non-Western language and culture into the curriculum and the College.

All completely irregular, but also ingenious, risky, spirited, successful, and, in the end, extremely expensive. In time, the University would need additional professors: in Chinese literature, history, art, and other fields. We would also have to purchase the necessary library books, offer fellowships to graduate students, acquire museum collections, and then turn our attention to the study of Japan, Korea, and other neighboring Asian societies.

In the light of all this, we might well ask whether the University should have turned down that original unorthodox proposition back in 1877. Surely not. Might there have been a more prudent way to begin the study of Chinese? Very probably. But the circumstances were opportune. The historical moment was right. Mr. Knight and Mr. Ko proved to be willing instruments of Fate. And so Harvard made another move that was prescient and even profound in terms of its educational consequences, as well as significant in its usefulness to society.

✦　　✦　　✦

That decision may seem similar to those earlier decisions concerning the printing press and the Observatory. But it was actually very different. The religious pamphlets, Bible translations, and sermons — as well as the study of the stars — were very much part of a long-established tradition of learning and inquiry in Europe and later in America.

The study of Chinese language and civilization, however, concerned a different agenda. It was directly related to Harvard's nineteenth-century ambition to be not only a leading undergraduate college, but also a distinguished *university*. The goal was to include every new discipline and field of knowledge that was beginning to demand serious attention. As President Eliot would boldly put it in his 1869 inaugural address: "We would have them all, and at their best."

Harvard quickly expanded to embrace a wider and wider range of subjects. The first clear signs of this larger vision were visible as early as 1860, when the annual report stated (somewhat prematurely) that Harvard College had already grown "from a provincial school to a national university."

Two years later, President Thomas Hill corrected the record, pointing out the gap between our rhetoric and our reality. "No department," he wrote, "either in the College or among the Professional Schools, can be said to stand above the need of improvement, and few, if any, can court comparison with the most thoroughly furnished schools of Europe. No lower ambition is worthy of our age and our people than that which would... at length make Harvard College a University in reality as well as in name."

In his final report, in 1868, Hill again insisted that it was crucial to build a great national university:

> *Such a university does not exist in this country.... The easiest place to found a university of a high order is [here in] Cambridge. The addition of two hundred and fifty thousand dollars a year to our income, or the direct gift of four millions to our capital, would do more toward making Harvard College able to supply the national need than the gift of eight or ten millions to any other college....* [2]

Here, we can see the outline of an emerging plan, including its projected cost, terrifyingly underestimated. There was nothing casual about the objective: to create a university that could take its place among the very greatest in the world. Harvard's educational ambition and confidence, as well as its financial directness, were as plain as daylight. We were challenging ourselves to become something far more than we had ever been. In this way, we began the most decisive transformation in our entire history.

That change in the University's level of aspiration was, by any standard, enormous. We should remember that in 1866, we had only 419 undergraduates in the College, and 542 students in all the graduate and professional schools combined. There was a grand total of approximately fifty faculty members. We were (about a century ago) barely as large as a medium-sized contemporary suburban high school.

In addition, the years of the 1860s were of course years of great national crisis and devastation. They were mainly the years of the Civil War and its immediate aftermath: not a time when many institutions would have seriously considered a bold, expansive, and expensive development. Under these circumstances, Harvard's vision of what it hoped to accomplish does seem, in retrospect, quixotic. It flew in the face of all the reasonable facts. It had the spirit of Marshal Foch's message to headquarters during the Second Battle of the Marne: "My center is giving way, my right is in retreat. Situation excellent, I am attacking."

✦   ✦   ✦

Harvard continued to "attack," taking on successive challenges (some momentous, some less visible) during the past century and a quarter. And the story would be far from complete without some description of the crucial role played by the University's graduates and friends. If the University continued to rise to important occasions, it was the generosity of Harvard's many supporters that made this steady rise possible.

Every donation, large or small, advanced the cause. And this was true well before the mid-nineteenth century, even when some of the gifts were slightly obscure in nature, or highly indeterminate in value. In 1719, for instance, a certain Mr. T. Hollis sent the College twelve casks of iron nails from England, without specifying the precise purpose they should serve. This was one of our earliest and most original unrestricted gifts.

Around 1650, John Newgate of Boston gave five pounds sterling "forever," toward "the maintenance of lawfull, usefull, and good literature" at the College. Later, a certain Mr. Penn wished to make a bequest, but he was extremely suspicious of the religious views of Harvard's governing boards. In his will, he stipulated that "£10 pr. An. are to be given to poor Scholars, out of the Rents of [my] farm at Pulling Point, but this money is to be disposed & [distributed] by the Elders & Deacons of the old church in Boston, so that neither [the] Corporation nor overseers of the College have anything to do" with it.

Every cask of nails, every five or ten pounds sterling, made a difference: just as every five or ten dollars now, every single new library book, and every act of service add to Harvard's strength today.

As for the very large gifts in Harvard's history, they too have mattered, and have often been breathtaking in their transformative power.

There was J. P. Morgan's famous staccato telegram which arrived from London on June 21, 1901: "Referring our conversation and plan submitted I am prepared erect Centre Pavilion and two buildings new Medical School, Harvard University. Said buildings to be ... in memoriam James Spencer Morgan, native of Massachusetts...." And then the important final line of the telegram, upon which everything rested, and which the astute Mr. Morgan knew was essential: "You can," he said, "announce this."

Soon afterward, Mr. John D. Rockefeller gave a sum that equaled Mr. Morgan's, and the two together made it possible for the brightening white Medical School quadrangle to rise from the ground almost overnight.

A few years later, Mrs. Eleanor Elkins Widener decided to construct a memorial to her son. She was modest but also firm in her determination: so modest and firm that she changed irrevocably the idea and image of what a university library might be, creating the centerpiece of an institution that has since become the largest university library in the world.

Finally, there was Mr. Harkness' vision and perseverance. He was determined to introduce, on this side of the Atlantic, an undergraduate House or College system modeled after the Oxbridge residential colleges. He first presented the idea to his alma mater, Yale, but Yale hesitated. Despite his lack of any prior association with Harvard, Mr. Harkness turned to President Lowell. Would Harvard conceivably accept the funds necessary to build all those stately Georgian structures which now grace our salubrious River Charles? Yes, indeed we would. And thus the entire experience of undergraduate life and education was dramatically transformed with one magisterial stroke.

In other words, Harvard not only challenged itself (and its graduates and friends) to reach higher. It soon found that those very graduates and friends were in turn challenging the University to become even better than it was, to scale heights that went beyond its own ambition, and at a pace that was often faster than seemed possible to absorb.

This dynamic between the University and its many supporters

has been critical to all Harvard's achievements. Without the constant interaction of mutual challenge and response — of shared investment, shared risk, and shared achievement — the University's most important goals could never have been realized. Harvard could never have become even a faint shadow of what it is today. Nor could we hope to become, in the years ahead, all that we know we must become in order to remain true to our fundamental purposes, and to ourselves.

+   +   +

Our own future will be very different and obviously far less expansionist than that of our nineteenth-century predecessors. And it will not be at all the same as the second period of major growth in higher education, which began at the end of World War II.

We cannot predict the precise shape of that future. But we know we are at another significant turning point. We are facing major educational and economic challenges, at a time when the need for education and leadership has never been greater, and when the opportunity to make dramatic new discoveries, in many fields, is full of promise. We must not fail to meet those challenges, or to realize that promise.

I want to conclude by saying something more personal about why I believe this venture — this campaign — is so important. It is important because it concerns the essence of what we do, and what we are. It concerns the motives and reasons that led so many of us to Harvard in the first place.

We came because we wanted to test ourselves against the best, and to learn all that we could possibly learn: not simply about particular subjects or disciplines, but also about other people and their points of view. We wanted to learn not only what individuals (often the world's greatest authorities) actually knew, but also what they did *not* know; and where their knowledge began to dissolve into uncertainty, and then slip suddenly into ignorance.

We wanted, in addition, to discover how individuals and great institutions coped with uncertainty and ignorance, because that too was a central part of human experience and reality.

We understood, in other words, that our ability to live lives of value, and to act effectively in the world, would finally depend on much more than the limited stock of actual knowledge we could possibly master. We would also have to rely on what we could only infer, or estimate, or speculate about, or learn later: peering through a glass darkly, and drawing on our all too modest share of human experience, our intuition, and our own personal convictions.

Education in this larger sense is what we sought. It would consist of far more than what we definitively knew. It would represent, as well, the sum total of our capacity to continue to learn, year after year.

This passionate pursuit — this desire to find out what lies just beyond the ideas we have barely understood, beyond the discovery we have just made; this desire to marshal the evidence, tighten the argument, polish the stanza, design exactly the right experiment, and convert ideas into effective actions — this is the primordial energy and motive force of the university, in all its many forms and purposes.

There is a poem by Robert Frost that captures some of the passion that I have been describing. The poem is about a slightly eccentric villager who was determined to buy a telescope in order to probe the universe, and come closer to understanding its mysteries.

As we have already seen, there is almost no way to keep a star-gazer from the instruments he covets, whatever the cost. One evening, the poet joins his friend in order to see, finally, what the new telescope can reveal:

Often he bid me come and have a look
Up the brass barrel, velvet black inside,
At a star quaking in the other end.

I recollect a night of broken clouds
And underfoot snow melted down to ice,
And melting further in the wind to mud.
Bradford and I had out the telescope.
We spread our two legs as we spread its three,
Pointed our thoughts the way we pointed it,
And standing at our leisure till the day broke,
Said some of the best things we ever said.
That telescope was christened the Star-Splitter
Because it didn't do a thing but split
A star in two or three, the way you split
A globule of quicksilver in your hand
With one stroke of your finger in the middle.
It's a star-splitter if there ever was one,
And ought to do some good if splitting stars
'Sa thing to be compared with splitting wood.

We've looked and looked, but after all where are we?
Do we know any better where we are,
And how it stands between the night tonight
And a man with a smoky lantern chimney?
How different from the way it ever stood?[3]

These lines have always seemed to me to be a metaphor for the university. There is the driving curiosity – to split the star, as we might split an atom.

There is the actual revelation: that image of the quaking star at the other end of the telescope, seen more vividly than ever before, as if it were alive and almost within reach.

There is the aspiration – pointing one's thoughts upward. There is also the fact that, because the experience was shared, much more was learned than what the telescope alone could have revealed. Looking through the brass barrel creates a moment when suddenly both seekers after truth spontaneously say "some of the best things [they] ever said."

Finally, there are the difficult, unanswerable questions at the end. How useful is the knowledge we have gained? Do we know any better where we are, or how things stand between ourselves and the surrounding outer darkness?

The questions are real, but they do not erase what has been learned and experienced: the sense of having pressed further, and having seen infinitely more than what we had ever seen before.

That is what universities are created to do.

That is why we come to universities, and why we so often return to them.

That is what prompted generations before us to create this extraordinary institution and to stand watch over it — through the course of centuries — in all its secular sanctity.

That is why Harvard has become what it is today, and why we must make certain it is never diminished: that it prospers, that it flourishes, and that it gives back to the world all that it receives, all, and still more, far into the future.

1 Samuel Eliot Morison, *Three Centuries of Harvard, 1636–1936* (Cambridge: Belknap Press, 1965), 39.

2 Thomas Hill, *Report of the President to the Board of Overseers, 1867–68*, 18.

3 Robert Frost, "The Star-Splitter," in *The Poetry of Robert Frost* (New York: Henry Holt and Company, 1979), 178–179. Orig. pub. *The Century Magazine*, September 1923.

Integrating Knowledge

An Excerpt from the Commencement Day Address
June 10, 1993

HARVARD'S DIFFERENT SCHOOLS share the belief that this is a time when many, though certainly not all, of the most important advances in research and teaching will depend on our success in integrating different fields of knowledge. We live in an age when people who specialize in a single field (or even two) can scarcely hope to come fully to grips with some of the large-scale systems and immensely complex situations that face us, and to understand them in all their dimensions. Thus there's a strong tendency to try to bring different fields closer together.

This point may seem obvious, but it really is not. For most of the past century, our dominant approach has been to divide and subdivide broad fields of knowledge: to pursue teaching and research in an increasingly concentrated and specialized way. As a result, we have multiplied the number of freestanding departments, programs, institutes, and schools. That pattern made good sense for a very long time. It produced excellent results, and we will always need specialized research and special units in order to make progress in particular fields.

At this moment in our history, however, we have much to gain by drawing individuals, groups, and programs closer together, rather than by creating more and more separate entities. Many of our specific proposals for Harvard's next decade are intended to achieve just that goal: to consolidate and coordinate, to integrate, and to lower barriers between units wherever it is productive and feasible to do so. This is true not just in how we conceive our academic programs, but also in how we think about our physical-space needs, and our organizational structures.

The renovation of Morgan Hall at the Business School, for instance, has brought together most of the School's faculty in a single building designed to make the boundaries between different research and teaching groups far more fluid, and to let those boundaries shift as needs and priorities shift in the years ahead.

Similar developments are taking place across the University. At the Kennedy School of Government, separate research centers are now working more closely together, and their research is being linked more effectively to teaching programs. At the Graduate School of Design, the basic curriculum is being reviewed; the focus is on creating some "core courses" that would give students from all of the School's different departments a common, interdisciplinary base of knowledge.

In Arts and Sciences, meanwhile, the Freshman Union building will become the centerpiece of a new center for the humanities, once our Memorial Hall renovations are complete. As things stand, faculty from our humanities departments are scattered among many different buildings. In some departments, the dispersion is so great that faculty hardly have a chance to see one another except at formal meetings. By bringing nearly everyone together, in a single complex or center, we can obviously create a much more collegial environment, and encourage more joint work among teachers and scholars in neighboring disciplines. We can also make sure that currently underutilized buildings will be utilized all day long.

Similar plans are under way in other fields. For example, some new space and facilities will be needed in the basic and applied sciences, and in the School of Public Health. But in nearly every case, the new facilities will be designed to create, quite literally, physical as well as programmatic "bridges" between separate units. We will link together freestanding buildings and departments to encourage greater faculty collaboration in research and more cooperation in teaching, in graduate student supervision, and in curriculum planning.

We also plan to strengthen the links among our many different libraries, and within our increasingly sophisticated information technology network. We have already made great progress with a single on-line electronic catalogue that will eventually include reference data on all the volumes in our vast collections. And we are hard at work on modernizing our other electronic information networks, so that people can have easy access to all sorts of data (on course offerings, current events, and other subjects) from dorm rooms, offices, and other locations all around the University.

+   +   +

Another major theme that has emerged from our planning process is the strong conviction (on everyone's part) that this is a time when the University must work especially hard to help solve some of the most difficult problems facing the larger society. We will do this, in part, by continuing and extending the research and teaching already under way at Harvard. At the same time, we plan to create a stronger organizational framework, and more concentrated focal points of talents and energy, to address carefully chosen topics. Faculty and students from all over the University will be participating in a set of programs to tackle issues of real urgency.

One of these programs will concentrate on public-school education. It will be anchored at the Graduate School of Education but will also bring together people from the Kennedy School, the Business School, Public Health, Arts and Sciences, Law, and elsewhere. It will deal with important public-policy questions, such as school choice and the concept of national testing. It will strengthen advanced training programs for school principals and superintendents. It will examine issues such as the relationship between schools and their neighborhoods, the role of parents in education, and the role of school boards. It will address questions concerning child development (including nutrition and health) and the kinds of teaching that can be most effective in different classroom settings. Our public schools face problems of enormous importance and complexity, and Harvard is determined to be more directly involved in providing real help.

Another program, involving faculty from literally every School at Harvard, will focus on the environment. This program was created only in the past year, and it is already well on its way, with a new undergraduate concentration and a major research agenda. A third program, one of obvious immediacy and importance, is focused on health care and the health care system.

Another, also well under way, concentrates on the difficult ethical and moral questions now faced by individuals and institutions in different professions. For example, advances in technology are continually presenting us with new and difficult choices and dilemmas. What use should be made of sophisticated and expensive life-support systems, in circumstances where there is little or no chance that the patient will be able to resume any semblance of a normal, satisfying life? What can we do to define and protect personal privacy in a world where computer databases contain more and more information about all of us, and where more and more people have ready access to that information? How can we think more clearly about problems like these? And what kinds of courses and teaching materials will help our students to think about them in a more informed and fully responsible way?

The last of the currently planned set of inter-School programs will focus on the mind, the brain, and behavior — how the brain functions, and how it affects the way we think and act. We are rapidly discovering more about how the brain and mind develop: how human beings grasp new ideas, how we learn, how we become "educated." We are also on the threshold of beginning to understand the relationship between brain functions and many behavioral disorders, including addiction and different kinds of substance abuse. These are all rich fields of inquiry, full of important insights as well as potential practical applications. And they are fields where scientists, social scientists, and humanists have much to learn from one another.

The particular inter-School programs I have just described have several things in common. They are part of our general effort to bring together scholars from different disciplines and different parts of the University, to work on multidimensional problems that cannot be solved by people in any one or even two fields. They are not new, freestanding entities but programs that essentially draw on and knit together faculty who are already here. It is critical that we make the most of the human and other resources that we already have in place. Finally, these programs represent a strong commitment on the University's part to be more directly useful to society at a time of real need. Harvard has always taken its public responsibilities with great seriousness; we now plan to give an even more concrete definition to that role in the years ahead.

A Spirit Not to Be Quenched

Thomas Dudley Cabot Memorial Service
June 14, 1995

WE ARE HERE to remember and celebrate a remarkable person, and a remarkable life. Whether one knew Tom Cabot for only four years (as in my own case) or forty, or twice forty, the strength and vividness of the impression, and the depth of the effect, were similar: in half an hour, or half a century, one caught the spirit of all that persuasive energy, driving to explore and inquire, to advance the cause, to find out more — and then to act, and to make things better.

It takes a special genius to understand a university, and especially to know how to work with a university, and through it, and on behalf of it. When the institution happens to be Harvard, even more than genius is required. Tom had all the requisite capacities: he created an inimitable role, and an irreplaceable place, among us.

He was our local neighbor, and Harvard became, so to speak, his other address. In the best possible way, he was ubiquitous. Once last year, he turned up in New York, during the worst moment of the worst of winters, for a meeting whose only purpose was to offer advice about the design of the University's campaign brochure. And at the end of the meeting, having made the journey, he turned to me and said: "Well, you have to have one of those things, but nobody will read it, and it won't raise a dime for you."

Not long afterward, he showed up at our Museum of Comparative Zoology for the celebration of the birthday of a much younger man, the great evolutionary theorist Ernst Mayr, who was just turning ninety.

Wherever something interesting was happening at Harvard, whenever something could be learned, or wherever something useful could be done – in the sciences, or university finance and operations, or undergraduate education, or public health, or the affiliated hospitals – Tom would be there, our Ambassador for Scientific and Medical Affairs, and our unofficial Vice President for Detectable Results.

I have never known an alumnus who was more deeply identified with the daily life and welfare of a university than Tom was with Harvard. That is the record. It will not be easily matched, and certainly never surpassed.

He relished his time with us, and we in turn have relished his presence.

He would not have wanted us to sentimentalize him at this moment.

He would have wanted us to recall that he was not always the soul of reticence – and he had little patience with the conventions of any society that practiced politeness while actually neglecting courtesy. True courtesy of the heart, a sense of unadorned but fitting ceremony, of appropriate deeds and demanding duties – these were his habits, his forms, his own social conventions; so much his own, that he was everywhere himself, everywhere the same, whether at home, or in town, or in the Yard just outside.

Add to these qualities his pleasure in the smallest trace of active intelligence, and his willingness to engage with anyone, on any plausible terms, so long as there was something potentially interesting or useful in the encounter: add all these, and we capture at least part of this vital, open, voyaging, and pioneering person — a person of strong devoted feelings, and deep loyalties. That was Tom: a spirit not to be quenched, either in fact or in our memory.

"If the salt [of the earth] has lost its savour, wherewith shall it be salted?"

We have now lost a portion of that precious salt. And as we look to the years ahead, we must somehow find (for Tom's sake as well as our own) the savour that he has always been at hand to provide.

Deeds, Not Creeds

John Loeb Memorial Service
January 16, 1997

I MET JOHN LOEB, for the first time, barely six years ago. I knew only the smallest fraction of all that he was, and all that he had achieved, in the course of so long a lifetime.

Nonetheless, because of John's receptivity, because he was so attuned to listening and inquiring, he made it easy to establish an immediate rapport.

I remember our first conversation, and it seems hardly weeks, or perhaps at most months, ago. What was striking about it was not anything that either of us said; it was, rather, the tone that John himself set from the very beginning. He somehow made it clear that no agenda was necessary. He was not waiting to hear profound views about the future of higher education. The only order of the day was to meet, to talk, and to begin to know one another.

It was remarked, long ago, about a particularly celebrated personage, that he lacked the power of conversation, but not, alas, the power of speech. With John, of course, it was the reverse. Mere speech, and certainly speeches, were easily dispensed with, but not conversability, not the words and the views and the play of the mildest wit that help to draw and keep people together, rather than set them apart.

As I think back over conversations with John, I do recall some of his views and opinions on various subjects, because he expressed them easily and naturally, and they certainly mattered to him. But I am aware, even more, of his way of *not* pressing his own ideas, not marshaling arguments, not driving toward hard and fast conclusions — at least not over lunch, or even over tea.

He knew, of course, that conclusions and actions were necessary and important. But he had no interest in fostering habits of the mind or heart that might lead to an even more querulous and quarrelsome world than the one we already inhabit. He wanted to play no part in creating even greater antagonisms than already exist among people, or any greater separation of human beings into winners and losers, either in conversation or in life.

When I think about him, I remember, yes, his remarkable strength and that wonderfully natural dignity which never deserted him during these last two or three years. But I remember, and am moved most of all, by the profound modesty and instinctive courtesy which simply emanated from him. It was as if he had come to feel that, although considerateness and common kindness would never cure all of the ills of our planet, they were very likely to help, and at the very least they were not very likely to do harm.

One day, about a year ago, John and I were seated at his customary luncheon table at the Four Seasons, where he was having his customary made-to-order special "Spaghetti Loeb" (which, as far as I could see, bore very little resemblance either to any existing form of spaghetti, or to any existing Loeb). At one point, John said matter-of-factly that he had decided to endow the Humanist Chaplain's position at Harvard. "The ... *what*, John?" I asked, not wanting to quite confess the full extent of my ignorance about Harvard's many ministerial parts and functions. "Yes," John said, "the Humanist Chaplain. He's dedicated to being humane. He makes himself available to students, he gives advice and help, and he has no official doctrine." "Deeds, not creeds," John said, a phrase that he repeated to me several times over the years.

Deeds were indeed what John did. And all the qualities I have mentioned — the receptivity, the interest in the views of others, the mutuality in conversation and in human relations, the avoidance of ideology and dogma, the modesty and considerateness, and finally the emphasis on humane actions: all of these qualities led John intuitively to make philanthropy an inevitable and central part of his life.

His philanthropic concerns, which he shared with Peter [Frances Lehman Loeb], included, as we know, a great many institutions and activities. Much as he cared for all of them, however, I think it is fair to say that his deepest and most abiding commitment — or really, his affection — concerned education, and especially Harvard.

He became a member of his first Harvard advisory committee (to our School of Public Health) nearly fifty years ago. After that, there was scarcely a year when he was not actively involved in one part of the University or another — usually several simultaneously. He was on the Visiting Committee to Harvard College, the Committee on Corporate Relations, the Committees on Fine Arts and the Fogg Museum, Anthropology and the Peabody Museum, Visual and Performing Arts, Visual and Environmental Studies, the Graduate School of Design, the Business School, the Program in Health Sciences, and the Committee on Foundations.

He was vice chair of the fund-raising drive for Harvard College in the late 1950s. He chaired the fund-raising campaign for the School of Design in the mid-1960s. During the tumultuous period of the late 1960s, when alumni support seemed to falter, he stepped in with a challenge grant of his own, urging others to give generously and promptly in order to complete the Harvard campaign which was scheduled to end in 1971. He served with great distinction as one of Harvard's outstanding Overseers, from 1962 to 1968. He was awarded an honorary doctorate of laws by

Harvard in 1971. And, in 1985, he received the "Harvard Medal" for his unparalleled service to the University.

John has been an honorary chair of Harvard's current University-wide fund-raising drive, and until recently, he never missed a meeting. The number and magnitude of his gifts to the University are princely in nature. There is no other word. But it was the quality and character of his giving, which a friend once described as "reverential" in spirit: it was that quality, as well as his care and thoughtfulness, which made John's bounty so deeply impressive.

He created, for example, a fund to improve undergraduate teaching. He provided critical support for associate professors in Arts and Sciences: faculty members who are just at the most difficult point in their academic careers, trying to press forward simultaneously with major research as well as with major teaching responsibilities. In addition, there were the gifts to create the Loeb Drama Center; a major professorship and research fund at the Medical School; basic "core" support at the School of Public Health; an innovative Fellows Program at the Graduate School of Design; the Frances Loeb Library, also at the School of Design; help for the American Repertory Theatre, for Harvard's Villa I Tatti program, and, of course, for the Humanist Chaplain.

A full accounting of John's gifts — made together with Peter, and with generous support from the entire family — would far surpass $100 million. And all of these gifts have come with essentially no concern for public recognition: no monuments, and no monologues, however eloquent, from the donor, only more and more modesty throughout. And so it is that John has emerged, quietly and almost imperceptibly over the decades, as the greatest single benefactor in the history of Harvard University. That is the record, pure and simple.

He is missed, and he will be remembered, in more ways than we can imagine. For myself, the loss can be partly captured in the form of a mental image that continues to recur, and will undoubtedly recur long into the future. I am settled in my seat on the plane, traveling from Boston to New York, preparing for meetings and events that will take place over the next two or three days. Invariably, at some moment, I think of the lunch that is scheduled with John: the customary table; the plate of Spaghetti Loeb; John's eyes, with their reservoirs of kindness; the conversation without an agenda; the hour or two, suspended out of time, like an oasis; and finally, the sense of reassurance that one had a standing invitation, so to speak, to come and share the rarest of all forms of friendship.

A Lifetime of Service and Care

Remarks in Memory of Joseph Pulitzer, Jr.
October 30, 1993

IT IS MY PRIVILEGE to talk about the long association between Joseph Pulitzer, Jr., and Harvard University. You will immediately realize my limited qualifications for this assignment, if I mention that when Joe entered Harvard as a freshman in the fall of 1932, I was a minus 3 years old; and when, in 1949, Joe joined what was then called the Visiting Committee to Fine Arts and the Fogg Art Museum, I was an impressive fourteen years old.

In fact, Angelica and I knew Emmy long before we knew Joe. But fortunately, the compact richness of our decade of friendship with Joe made up for the many lost years that slipped away before we met him. Happily, I suspect that to have known Joe even for an abbreviated time was to know the essence of him, his fundamental human qualities and commitments, because these seem to have remained remarkably constant throughout his remarkable lifetime.

I will not try to describe in detail all of the many ways in which Joe served Harvard and contributed to the University's well-being, decade after decade. Some day, a complete *catalogue raisonné* might be in order. Very few of you may know, however, that Joe was a member of Harvard's Board of Overseers from 1976 to 1982, and served on four major committees, including not only Humanities and Arts, but the Institutional Policy Committee, the Honorary Degrees Committee, and even the Committee on Student Life.

Those years when Joe was on the Board were not easy years for universities. They were the years of what was inelegantly called "stagflation," a cheerless combination of general economic paralysis and double-digit inflation: the worst possible mixture, short of total economic depression and collapse, for universities. It was characteristic of Joe, I think, that he should have chosen to serve on the Overseers at just such a moment, rather than during a more heady "boom" period or an era of tranquility, when there was no heavy weather, no major challenge in sight.

His briefest association with the University was exactly one year of service, in 1951, on the Visiting Committee to the Harvard University Press. History does not record what unspeakable or unpardonable revelations at the Press were sufficient to shatter Joe's ordinary aplomb, and drive him from the field so swiftly. But I feel certain that it was not because the books being published at the time were too provocative or controversial, but rather because they proved to be either impenetrably academic, or simply dull, or both.

Overshadowing all of Joe's many services to Harvard, of course, was his unswerving commitment to our museums and art department. He became a member of the joint Visiting Committee in 1949, and even though the names and the configuration of the committees related to our art department and museums changed periodically, Joe survived all the vicissitudes of Harvard's nomenclature with equanimity, and remained at his post until 1993: a total of forty-five years' service interrupted only by occasional mandatory "rotations off" for a year at a time. I cannot swear to the fact that forty-five years constitutes a Harvard record, but it is hard for me to imagine that any other individual ever *has* done so much, or ever will do more.

Even President Eliot's tenure of forty years as president of Harvard begins to pale before Joe's long-distance sprint. And if we go back to 1932–33, when Joe's connection with art at Harvard really began, we have what is literally a sixty-year span of achievement and sustained relationship to contemplate.

Quite apart from his length of service, it is obviously the *quality* of Joe's total contribution that was so extraordinary, and that made such a very great difference.

The quality showed itself, first of all, in the range and scope of his interests, and in the actual gifts he made, year after year. He cared about the teaching of art history and the capacity of teachers to inspire students, as he himself had been inspired by Paul Sachs, Benjamin Rowland, Frederick Deknatel, and others. He supported exhibitions at the Fogg, and catalogues, as well as the conservation of the museum's collections. And he did not overlook the apparently incidental items that can make such a difference.

In 1987, for instance, he made a contribution to help fund the Fogg Museum's sixtieth anniversary ball; much earlier, he contributed generously to the costs of insurance which the museum could not then afford. And then there was simply a steady stream of generosity: gifts to the Director's Discretionary Fund, the Museum Stabilization Fund, the Agnes Mongan Center, the Building Fund of the early 1980s, and, of course, as a crowning symbolic act, the establishment of the Pulitzer Chair in Modern Art.

If this had been all, it would in itself have been munificent. But there was of course much more. Beginning in 1953 (forty years ago) Joe began making gifts of art to the Fogg: paintings, but also drawings, prints, and sculpture. In that first year, 1953, he gave a beautiful Feininger drawing, a Pissarro oil, and a Henry Moore watercolor.

Thereafter, into the 1980s, scarcely a year went by without some important object arriving, and usually more than one. In

1954 and 1955 alone, there were paintings by Miró, Tamayo, Beckmann, Dufy, Vuillard, and Kokoschka. By the early 1960s, an important Monet; Picasso's *Woman in Blue*; Braque's *Mandolin*; and Cézanne's *Portrait of Jules Peyron* were all added. Later, when Emmy and Joe were giving together, we find, in addition to a Pissarro, a Rouault, and a major Cézanne, *Mont Sainte-Victoire*, drawings or paintings by Richard Serra, Sol Lewitt, Brice Marden, Frank Stella, Cy Twombly, and others.

All in all, by my count, twenty-six paintings (quite apart from the works on paper and the sculpture) entered our collections over the years. It is no exaggeration to say that it was Joe's vision and patronage, steady and clear, that enabled the Fogg's late nineteenth- and twentieth-century collections to take their rightful place among the museum's other great holdings.

That is at least a sketch of the record: a lifetime of service, of care, of faithful attendance, of gifts, of building collections. And everything was done almost imperceptibly, without visible public notice, and with scarcely any awareness except on the part of those closest to the scene. In this sense, Joe's immense contribution to Harvard was utterly consistent with so many other aspects of his life, because the person and the life had at their center a set of undeviating attachments, motivated by interest and affection, but also by strong conviction and an unselfconscious feeling of obligation.

His total commitment to his profession of journalism and to the *St. Louis Post-Dispatch*; to the civic and cultural life of St. Louis itself; to the art of his time; to Harvard; and of course to his radiant partnership with Emmy — all these were expressions of the single person who seemed to know, even as an undergraduate, that his life would be a life of constancies, of values that, once discovered, would only be deepened and strengthened as the years and decades unfolded.

Some time ago, John Coolidge said of Joe: "No other patron in the Fogg's history has contributed to the institution so faith-

fully and in such a variety of ways, each of them unique, imaginative, and helpful." Let me only add, in concluding, a few of Joe's
own words — words that he used to describe two works of art
which he owned, but words that might well serve as miniature
partial portraits of Joe himself. In the first passage, Joe characterized a particular painting for its

> *assurance; craftsmanship . . . finesse rather than bravura in brush-
> work; exclusion of intrusive detail; restraint, contemplation, com-
> posure, rather than romantic or expressionist fervor.*

Elsewhere, in discussing a piece of sculpture, he said:

> *As I live with this presence, I become more impressed daily with its
> . . . authority.*

It might disconcert some people, he added,

> *but in time they will appreciate its displacement of space, its scale, . . .
> and its definition of the land it occupies.*[1]

Joe possessed a sense of assurance that was somehow as modest
as it was assured, his brushwork was admirable for its finesse rather
than any bravura, there was that welcome air of restraint, the quiet
authority, an appreciation of scale; and most of all, his always
engaging presence with its combination of poise and passion,
which gave such unmistakable definition to whatever space he
inhabited, or landscape he occupied.

---

1 *Modern Painting, Drawing, & Sculpture, Collected by Louise and Joseph Pulitzer, Jr.*
(Cambridge: Fogg Art Museum, 1971), III: 349, 442.

Her Own Poetics

Judith Nisse Shklar Memorial Service
November 6, 1992

IT WAS NOT my good fortune to know Judith Shklar well. Our few encounters were brief, but the darting, rapid exchanges, with all the intellectual and human intensity that Dita brought to them, always made up in height for whatever they may have lacked in length. A totally forgettable French eighteenth-century poet once sent what he believed to be his most brilliant epigrammatic couplet (two short lines) to the Comte de Rivarol. "Very nice," came the immediate reply from the Count, "but there are some dull stretches." Anyone who ever encountered Dita, for even the most fleeting of moments, knew that there were no dull stretches in any of her couplets. She was the inventor of her own poetics: powerful, vivacious, pointed, and inimitable.

I have been asked to say a few words about Dita's contribution to the University as a whole, as well as to her profession. She came to Harvard as a graduate student in 1950, and remained here throughout her entire career. This was not at all her original intention. As she said (in a wonderful talk given in 1989), she had expected to work in what she called "high-class literary journalism"; "I would have liked," she said, "to be a literary editor of the *Atlantic* or some such publication." Instead, she was taken by surprise by the offer of an instructorship in the Government Department, and she then surprised herself by accepting the offer.

The road, as she readily acknowledged, was far from easy. Women academics were not at all part of the Harvard scene at that time, and Dita was teaching, writing books, and raising a family simultaneously. "The crunch came," as she put it, "when the matter of tenure finally came up. My department could not bring itself to say either yes or no.... [So] I went to the dean and asked him if I could have a half-time appointment with effective tenure and lecturer's title. It was not exactly what I wanted, but it was what I decided to arrange for myself, rather than wait for others to tell me what I was worth."

Without undue self-consciousness, but with that spontaneous habit of choosing freely and decisively to determine her own fate, Dita pioneered, making her own way, but also making the way smoother for women and many others who came later.

In 1971, President Derek Bok (only recently inaugurated) worked with the Government Department to see that Dita was soon awarded the tenured full professorship that she had long since earned.

Over the course of her decades at Harvard, she wrote eight books that were invariably singled out for honors and acclaim. In 1984, she won a MacArthur Fellowship, which enabled her to do the scholarship and writing that she relished so much, traveling, as she did, from Harvard to Oxford and Cambridge Universities. In 1989, she became president of the American Political Science Association, the first woman to serve in that capacity.

She was not, I think, what we would normally call a "committee person." She was always ready to do her fair share and more, but if we were to sum up her contribution to the larger University community, it would surely be in terms of the way that she embodied the values — in all their distilled purity — of a great university: the example of independence matched with integrity, passion with analytic power, engagement balanced by a wise skepticism and detachment, a commitment to teaching but a primary driving desire to discover new ways and new ideas to help us understand reality.

Let me conclude with a passage in which Dita characterized herself and her role: "The reason why I teach political theory," she said, "is not that I just like the company of young people, but that I love the subject unconditionally.... As I look at myself, I see that I have often been moved to oppose theories that did not only seem wrong to me, but also excessively fashionable. I do not simply reject, out of hand, the prevailing notions and doctrines, but complacency, metaphysical comforts, and the protection of either sheltered despair or cozy optimism drive me into intellectual action. I do not want to settle down with one of the available conventions." It is hard to think of any better way to describe Dita Shklar's contribution to Harvard than as a continuous example of "intellectual action" in the vibrant form of someone who refused to settle down in complacency or conformity.

Our Lean Galbraithian Hero

Remarks on the Occasion of John Kenneth Galbraith's 90th Birthday
October 15, 1998

KEN GALBRAITH and I, and Angelica and Kitty, met for the first time, and dined together as a quartet, in the autumn of 1991, soon after Angelica and I had returned to Harvard after a lapse of more than twenty years.

I cannot, therefore, speak with firsthand knowledge about anything that happened during the first eighty-three years of Ken's several lives and careers. I know, for instance, only from secondary-source materials, that Ken managed his shift from youth to official manhood brilliantly: it coincided perfectly with the most spectacular of the many seismic, tectonic events of 1929.

On October 15, 1929, Ken's twenty-first birthday, there was a spontaneous celebratory chorus of public good cheer from major figures in the financial world, despite several previous months of acute distress signals. Charles E. Mitchell and Professor Irving Fisher declared that the United States economy was more or less indestructible, and that the stock market was poised once again to rise euphorically.

Within one hundred hours of Ken's twenty-first, when the

last traces of icing on his birthday cake had scarcely had time to deliquesce, the United States Secretary of Commerce said that he was having difficulty "finding the $100,000 in public funds that would be required to pay for the upkeep of the yacht *Corsair*, which J. P. Morgan had just given" to the nation. Within another couple of hundred hours, the New York Stock Exchange had essentially disappeared into a black hole, plummeting through its worst day in recorded history.

Ken's market timing has, of course, always been faultless. And so it was that our lean Galbraithian hero, barely moments after attaining his majority, toppled the House and capsized the Yacht of Morgan; blasted the money changers from the temple; and cleansed what little remained in the Augean stables at the heart of lower Manhattan's stock and bond yards.

This long-ago battle with the madness of the markets has been on my mind, not only because I recently reread Ken's marvelous book, *The Great Crash* — in fact, the specific references and quotations I just borrowed are all from his volume — but also because two of Ken's most recent works, both written *this* October, on the brink of *this* birthday, happen to be on the very same great-crashing subject.

The first of these pieces was his elegant *New York Times* op-ed essay, just a few days ago. The second is an unpublished letter to me. It arrived about two hundred hours ago, and it had to do with our modest university endowment, as viewed in the light of recent market disturbances. Our institutional net worth, Ken seemed to be suggesting, might just possibly be mutable, and it was not necessarily predestined to be always upwardly mobile.

But what struck me most about the letter was the fact that, while the theme was certainly a familiar one, the style was anything but Ken's public Enlightenment voice, a voice in the approximate range of a twentieth-century Voltaire. Instead, there was something more comradely, and almost solicitous, about the tone: a sort of "Watch out! Don't let yourself be hedged!" This companionable message, this uncondescending solicitousness, this real concern for the institution and the people who comprise it — all of these nuances and inflections, as well as others, seemed suddenly to epitomize what Angelica and I have been fortunate enough to experience in our friendship with Ken and Kitty these past few years. And we have felt immeasurably enriched, as well as buoyed, by what they have given us.

When I see Ken striding toward Widener Library or the Faculty Club, his head above the treetops, I feel reassured that the spirit of the University is happily abroad in the Yard: the sanity and the great good sense; the irony and wit; the edge, the clarity, the skepticism and the conviction, as well as the sense of affectionate identity with Harvard. I feel reassured that all these qualities and relationships are still vital and present, embodied, kinetically, in this remarkable person who is celebrating not only his birthday, but also his fiftieth anniversary as a tenured member of the Harvard faculty, our Paul M. Warburg Professor of Economics, Emeritus.

To Ken, a toast:

To your constancy — whether to friends, to Harvard, or to Houghton Mifflin;

To your persistent vision, and your unwillingness to forget those in our society who are, for whatever reason, disenfranchised and dis-inherited;

To this evening, which finds you surrounded by so many who care so much about you and about Kitty;

On the eve of your 90th, let me simply say this:

> *The shrewdest eye discerns no sign*
> *You are no longer eighty-nine.*

Thou Art a Wonder Gome

Celebration of the Reverend Peter Gomes'
Twenty-five Years in the Ministry of Memorial Church
Adolphus Busch Hall, October 14, 1995

SOME TIME AGO, in 1982, Peter Gomes was delivering one of his Commencement-morning utterances to the graduating senior class. He said that he realized the seniors were probably quite surprised to find themselves in Memorial Church at such a time.

Indeed, they might well feel they were well past the point where prayer could be of any assistance to them. Nonetheless, said Peter, they should try to do their best. Besides, chapel (like the glass flowers) should be visited at least once.

People generally do visit Memorial Church, not only once but rather more. And often, they do so because of Peter. He is our own perpetual multiplier effect: our pastoral exponent, as well as our elegantly worldly host, our Crimson cicerone, our Master of Loaves, Fishes, and Chandon Brut champagne.

I know that Peter's surname Gomes probably relates to Gomez, via his Portuguese ancestry. But I prefer to think of it as the plural of "gome," because I assume that (in his ubiquity) there must certainly be more than one Peter. Everywhere I stray, in different parts of the campus, I see gomes galore in different roles fulfilling different functions.

It occurred to me that I ought to know more precisely what a gome actually is. As I'm sure you know, the *Oxford English Dictionary* (there is, alas, no *Emmanuel College Cambridge Dictionary*) tells us that "gome" derives from the Anglo-Saxon *guma*, found as early as *Beowulf*. *Guma* meant literally *man*, and is connected to our own *human*. In *Beowulf*, of course, a gome tended to be a warrior type, a heroic battler: the sort of person who went galloping after Grendels.

Later, in the medieval period, a gome became rather more refined, Arthurian, and chivalric. There's a charming fourteenth-century poem, in which, at one point, the narrator salutes a stranger riding toward him in shining armor. The image seems to me the very picture of our young Peter:

> *"Christian knight," quoth Ferumbras,*
> *"thou art a wonder gome."*[1]

Finally, from ancient to recent times, in different languages, "gome" has referred to several important qualities associated with people who carry responsibilities and who are likely to be spiritual as well as secular leaders. It means heed, or attention, or care; and it also has meant good sense, wit, tact. Whether we think of Peter as a singular gome, or as many plural gomes, he is our *guma*, our man; our heedful hero; our Christian knight whose real armor is in fact his care for others, his good sense, his wit, and his tact.

✦   ✦   ✦

The special capacity for human and spiritual interlocution is what I most associate with Peter: his ability to transform the modest everyday experiences and events of life into so much more than they might otherwise become.

In the 1982 Commencement sermon that I mentioned earlier, Peter told the seniors that they should expect virtue and other important moral or spiritual qualities to be

> *demonstrated in the ... unexciting ... side of life. Tempting as it may be to perform virtue at a cosmic moment in world affairs, ... more often than not the test of your character will come ... in the ordinary circumstances of living, being, and doing.*

So, he said, try to make as much as possible of your daily, mundane existence, by turning it into something "civil, gracious, and humane."

There are many occasions, of course, when Peter lifts us, with the gift of his eloquence, far above the mundane. But I like to think that his other gift is equally great: the gift of somehow blessing and giving significance to all the incidentals of our experience. He reminds us that in the many mansions of our Father's house, there are rooms where Gilbert and Sullivan as well as Mozart, Josquin des Prés – and even Elgar – are played; rooms where butternut squash, baby carrots, and even cranberries, as well as *crème anglaise* and Chardonnay, are served; where Emmanuel College, Tuskegee Institute, Bates College, and Harvard University all convivially coexist; and where all of these are as holy as they are worldly.

Peter has been Minister of the Memorial Church a full twenty-five years; and he has not long ago passed his fiftieth birthday. I would like to conclude these remarks with a brief lyric by William Butler Yeats. It is a poem that is set in England – a place Peter loves. The poet is about fifty, and that seems appropriate. The subject has to do with moments of grace and how they can come unexpectedly, illuminating and transfiguring the most ordinary particulars of our life. This is not so much a poem about a person, as it is about the ways in which mundane life can, at moments, be experienced intensely, when we have a gome to remind us of what is possible:

My fiftieth year had come and gone,
I sat, a solitary man,
In a crowded London shop,
An open book and empty cup
On the marble table-top.

While on the shop and street I gazed
My body of a sudden blazed;
And twenty minutes more or less
It seemed, so great my happiness,
That I was blessèd and could bless.[2]

Thank you, Peter, for what you have done at Harvard, these twenty-five years, to bless the life that surrounds us.

---

1 "Sir Ferumbras," in *Ashmole MS.* 33 circa 1380, ed. Sidney J. Herrtage (London: Early English Text Society, 1879), 14. (Modernized spelling added.)

2 W. B. Yeats, "Vacillation" IV, in *The Collected Poems of W. B. Yeats*, rev. 2nd ed., ed. Richard J. Finneran (New York: Scribner, 1996), 255.

This Singular Place

Mid-Campaign Speech
October 25, 1997

WELCOME BACK to Sanders Theatre, now restored and burnished, but no less familiar than when many of us met here more than three years ago, to begin the first University-wide campaign in Harvard's history.

The campaign has gone remarkably well by any conceivable standard. And our endowment has been bounding through a period of uninhibited robustness, especially since 1994. As a result, we might well be tempted to relax our campaign efforts, on the theory that we can comfortably coast the rest of the way home. Or we might well ask whether Harvard actually has a compelling need for any more resources at this point.

I take these considerations very seriously, but I admit that I have no real doubt about my own conclusions. I would like to start with a backward glance, if only to recall where we began, and how quickly, as well as unpredictably, so many things have changed in the brief time since we set out together.

In 1992, I had read far less of the history of Harvard than I would have wished. But even from my modest store of knowl-

283

edge, I remembered one (among many) of President Conant's most authoritative utterances: uncompromising words, portentous and ominous, that haunted me with all the wit and charm of a Greek tragic chorus: "Decentralization in fund-raising," said President Conant nearly fifty years ago, "is essential here at Harvard. Tentative proposals . . . to emphasize this point are now under consideration." And, President Conant stressed, it will be "extremely difficult to present an adequate picture of what we plan and hope to the alumni as a body, or even to the Board of Overseers."

For weeks on end, Mr. Conant's declamation echoed in the chambers of my mind. Could we possibly succeed with a full-fledged, collaborative, University-wide campaign? Could we conceivably create a plan that would be even faintly intelligible to alumni and friends, or to the Overseers and Corporation, or even to ourselves — those of us inside Harvard? Moreover, President Conant's words seemed all the more sobering because of the difficult economic conditions that prevailed in the late 1980s and early 1990s.

We may have forgotten that the entire nation was then in a state of considerable recession: severe downsizing; massive job losses; a burgeoning federal deficit; pervasive uncertainty about the future: about Social Security, social services, and health care; and, perhaps most of all, there were serious worries about America's ability to compete effectively in the new global economy.

Let us also remember not just the national scene, but Harvard's own predicament. It was far from encouraging. In 1991, several of our schools, institutes, and other units were showing negative financial results. The Faculty of Arts and Sciences had an annual operating deficit of about $12 million. The total University-wide deficit was about $42 million. We began our own regime of downsizing and economies, which has finally, during the last two years, produced a balanced budget.

Then too, the financial markets were inscrutable at best — not at all obviously bullish – back in 1991. Harvard wrote off $200 million in endowment losses that year, and we had a total return of exactly 1.1 percent. Nor was that single year a fluke: the University's average total return for the four years from 1988 through 1991 was 6.6 percent per year, a level which, if it had continued, would have quickly led to a steady erosion of our endowment's actual purchasing power. It was not so very long afterward that I (speaking to many of you) paraphrased Marshal Foch's spirited staccato telegraphic communiqué, which he dispatched during the most somber hours of the Second Battle of the Marne in 1918: Our center is giving way, our right is in retreat; situation excellent; we are attacking.

What can we learn from the tale of these past several years? At least one or two useful home truths.

First, we should never expect any existing situation, whether gloomy or glittery, to last indefinitely, or even for very long. This seems self-evident. But our collective memory is often short-lived, and we have to keep reminding ourselves that today's economic euphoria tends to anaesthetize any trace of yesterday's lugubriousness. Also, vice versa. Certain kinds of institutions (and especially universities) cannot exist or thrive if they allow themselves to ride too closely the ups and downs of every minor or major boom and bust. They simply have to plan and operate in terms of the long run, and they have to take the long view. They need to be sensibly prudent in heady times, just as they must be seaworthy and steady when the going gets rough. That means setting a course that can be maintained with real consistency through any number of vicissitudes: "Calm rising," as our hymn has it, "through change and through storm."

From this perspective, it makes no more sense to allow our expectations (or plans) concerning Harvard's extended future to be based on the surreal, favorable financial circumstances of the last three to four years, than it would have been sensible to base them on the totally different (and far more discouraging) conditions of 1991 or 1992. *Harv-ars longa, fortuna breva, pecunia fugienta*, which, roughly translated (inside out), means "Fortune is fickle, the markets will falter, but Harvard must be here forever."

So if we are asked whether we can coast through the rest of the campaign, with $500 million still to raise, or whether we can rest, soporifically tranquilized, on our endowment laurels, then our reply, I feel certain, must be that we dare not.

Not only should we expect our share of down times ahead, but we also need to keep in mind that several major campaign priorities are still lagging. These include resources for Widener Library and other parts of our extraordinary library system; endowments for important new professorships in several fields, especially to strengthen the College and undergraduate teaching; support for our most hard-pressed professional schools, such as Education and Divinity; funds to maintain our momentum in information technology and international studies; plus financial aid — at the graduate and professional school level, as well as for undergraduates.

In other words, we will not really have succeeded if we achieve our overall "dollar goal," formidable as that is, but fail to complete some of the most significant projects that we identified, at the very beginning of this campaign, as essential to Harvard's future.

This is not the moment to talk about the case for each of those specific projects. But I do want to suggest that these (and other) priorities clearly relate, in their scale and variety and reach, to the purposes of a national and international university, as well as those of a great undergraduate college. They also signal to me (and this is something that I want to stress today) that higher education has now entered what is really a new era, with new and difficult conditions as well as stimulating but imposing challenges.

Navigating the new global, intergalactic spaces, and interpreting our unfolding genomic future (so that we make the right judgments, and take the right actions), is the most important task we face as we enter the final phases of the campaign and begin to think about the landscape that lies beyond.

Let me elaborate a little about what I mean when I say we are now in a new era. If we scan the history of American higher education, it is clear that there have been two major periods of great transformation and expansion.

The first began in the latter part of the nineteenth century, and continued into the early part of the twentieth. This was our heroic, Homeric, epic age. At the heart of this ancient saga was the struggle (led by Harvard) to turn miniature colleges into emergent universities. Graduate studies were created on the Germanic model, and advanced students, in growing numbers, soon began to undertake their winding and often dolorous, Dantesque sojourn in pursuit of the Ph.D.

Professional school education, meanwhile, was reinvented. Serious research began to be respected, although it was in many quarters still highly suspect. Undergraduates were suddenly placed in direct contact with major scholars. Teaching began to be more a matter of asking questions than transmitting prefabricated answers. Dozens of new fields of knowledge were opened up.

In short, another age of discovery — a sort of academic Magellan-like efflorescence — had begun.

There was a more or less unstoppable urge on the part of compulsive tycoons, middle-class classicists, pecunious as well as impecunious botanists, insatiable bibliophiles, and indomitable entomologists and archaeologists to travel, search, unearth, possess, organize, display, study, and, in effect, conquer everything in sight, by amassing collections of every conceivable kind of artifact, manuscript, glacial pebble, rare or well-done book, organic specimen, art object, anatomical revelation, astronomical observation, and countless other phenomena. At Harvard, the Peabody Museum, the art museum, the Warren Museum at the Medical School, the new observatory, and the Museum of Comparative Zoology were only a few of the tangible structures created by this powerful surge of sustained inquiry and acquisition.

If we wanted to generalize, succinctly, about this entire era, when so many Giants walked our Earth, we might well say that aspirations grew, knowledge grew, the curriculum grew, buildings grew, and the budget grew. In addition, at least one penetrating fundamental financial insight remained as a significant legacy, well into the future.

That insight appears simple in retrospect but was less obvious at the time and has turned out to be crucial. It was the recognition that the only way to create a major university (with major museums, libraries, research institutes, and fields of learning that were important but not necessarily populous) was to endow, as far as possible, every new activity. In that way, the total educational program – and total intellectual capacity – of the University could be vastly enriched and intensified without requiring student tuition and fees to bear more than a fraction of the cost.

As we ponder why fund-raising campaigns are important, and why large endowments are essential, it is helpful to remember that it is precisely these endowments, together with unrestricted gifts, that undergird (just as one example) the resources of the entire Harvard library system: ninety-two libraries of thirteen million volumes, with on-line access to the total catalogue as well as to a great deal of text, constituting the greatest university library in the world. All of this is available to our students, with only a small fraction of the cost being charged to tuition.

I want to shift now to that second major transformation (and expansion) of American higher education, which I mentioned earlier. This came right after World War II. At the risk of great oversimplification, I believe we can say that the war demonstrated, as never before, that brains – motivated, marshaled, and focused – matter infinitely more than brawn. Human commitment and great courage were certainly indispensable. But the war showed us that a very great concentration of intelligence – in advanced cryptography, in the invention and refinement of radar, in the skill that can manage complex organizations (including the difficult process of collaborative strategic decision making), or in the discovery of nuclear fission and fusion – concentrated intelligence at work in all these and other areas mattered decisively, and made it possible for our own nation and others to move forward from a state of almost complete unpreparedness to the point where talent and determination, with enough raw materials and production capacity, could finally prevail.

By 1945, many people realized that what worked in war could also work in peace. So it was not surprising that education and research were at the top of our national agenda by the late 1940s. Probably the most crucial turning point here, reached by 1950, was the decision to rely primarily on our already existing major universities for America's basic research effort, rather than to build a separate government system of research institutes (on the model of some European and other countries). Since the universities represented high-quality assets-in-being, the United States had, almost immediately, a powerful, competitive, and immensely successful research enterprise under way, operating at full tilt. The program included many disciplines and fields of knowledge. It soon began to produce an unprecedented number of discoveries and new insights. In fact, by far the largest number of significant breakthroughs since World War II — from the elucidation of DNA, in all its intricacy and brilliant simplicity, to the creation of high-speed computer networks, to the dramatic unmasking (not so long ago) of the Top Quark, in the deep obscurity of its remote hideaway — all of these had their origin in university-based research projects, supported mainly by our federal government.

But research alone was not, of course, enough. However much we needed ideas, we certainly did not need them disembodied. As a result, the government (together with the major private foundations and individual universities) began a program during the 1950s to expand graduate and professional education so that there would be a steady flow of well-educated and trained people who were prepared to take up, throughout our society, the increasing number of positions that required new kinds of talent and leadership ability.

Therefore, when we utter the word "research," we ought to

link it immediately to the word "education," at least when we are talking about a major university. The two activities, at their best, have always been linked together. The fact that they reinforce one another, at all levels, from the undergraduate college through to our executive education programs, is exactly what has made the American model of a university — and certainly Harvard — so distinctive, and so effective.

All of this may sound as if the postwar system were somehow invincible. But we know of course that it was not. To understand why, we simply have to remember the long rainy monsoon season (or was it a drought?) from about 1969 to 1982. Either way, there were far too many economic phenomena of one kind, and far too few of another, producing more than a decade of what we poetically dubbed "stagflation."

Those were the years when many colleges and universities posted almost daily deficits. Physical plant maintenance was often deferred. Institutions watched endowments erode and saw faculty and staff salaries shrink steadily in the face of a double-digitizing CPI. That was also the era when need-blind admissions and need-based student financial aid first began to falter, and when major foundation support for graduate student fellowships literally plummeted from one year to the next (and it has never really rebounded). State universities and colleges had some of their first seismic shocks; over the years since then, circumstances have become worse for them, rather than better.

These changes (and others) were really structural, not transient, in nature: that is, we were not just watching blips on a screen, but were experiencing much deeper tectonic shifts in the economics of higher education, compared with the period between 1950 and 1970. Of course, there have been fluctuations since then, some ups and some downs. But the basic underlying situation has not changed. For some time now there have been fewer flexible federal and state revenues available, and there are many more claimants (some of them with very urgent needs) for government as well as foundation dollars. All of this represents an absolutely major change. In the new era that we have entered, there will continue to be less external financial support, in "real" terms, from several key sources, just at a moment when the need and the demand for education (as well as for new ideas and discoveries in research) are at their maximum. That is the essence of our current situation.

So the question for all of us, and certainly for Harvard, is how we move ahead, keeping our impetus and our edge, to meet the challenges that are surely there, and do so under conditions that will probably be more difficult, not less.

We certainly can not allow ourselves to suffer the fate of Lord Rosebery, whom Bernard Shaw characterized as "someone who never missed an occasion to let slip an opportunity."

Our challenges, and opportunities, are real, and they have to be seen in relation to long-term changes already taking place in society. In this way, the larger pattern of events may become more clear to us and may help us to chart our own directions with more certainty.

For instance, the strong forces that have recently made our world so thoroughly interconnected are unlikely to be reversed. The Internet, instantaneous worldwide satellite connections, and rapid transportation systems are here to stay. Similar developments have produced fluid global financial markets, and have led to many more open, penetrable societies that can no longer be shielded behind iron curtains. Porous boundaries permit the quick movement of people, ideas, goods, economic capital, particles of culture (or particles of sulfur dioxide) from country to country. More societies are less authoritarian and more democratic than even half a decade ago. One possible result of all these changes is greater cooperation among peoples and nations. But another might be a growing number of close encounters that are as likely to end in collision and conflict as in collaboration.

We also know that over the next quarter century to half century, there will be major demographic changes in our own country, and throughout the world. There will almost certainly be, over time, more major centers of power, certainly in Asia, and perhaps elsewhere. Some "minority" groups will become majorities. Women will play a greater and greater role in public life, even, I believe, in those societies that now seem to be moving in quite the opposite direction. All in all, it will be essential for people to be able to work effectively, on an almost daily basis, with a widening range of fellow human beings from different national and other backgrounds.

This will not be easy. The history of our species does not suggest that we have often managed to get on so very swimmingly together, in the same little pond, over the centuries. When he was President of France, Charles de Gaulle (not always impeccably patient in the face of contrary views) once asked in exasperation: "How can you [possibly] govern a country which has 246 varieties of cheese?" Well, our little planet is now much farther along the path toward an infinite number of anthropoid specimens, and we need to learn how to cope with that.

If the future turns out to be anything like this rough sketch, what are the implications concerning an educational agenda for Harvard – not only through the end of this campaign, but also well beyond? What steps should we be taking to make certain that the University stays abreast: to ensure that those who follow us will feel that we have done as much for them as our predecessors did for us?

First, it means that we have no choice but to keep up our momentum in the field of international studies. If the world will be a more crowded and interdependent place, then our students and our faculty must have better opportunities to travel, explore, and learn about what is "out there." And we also need to keep up the flow of students, scholars, and professionals who come to Cambridge from abroad to study at Harvard and learn about the United States.

Let's not forget that since the end of the Cold War, vast

archives that had been closed for generations have now become accessible, and hundreds of thousands of people, in countries around the globe, are for the first time able and willing to speak freely about their own histories, their societies, and their experiences. This situation represents a prodigious opportunity, and an immense challenge, for our scholars and students. The historical record (and the living presence) of dozens of nations and cultures can now be examined, and is already in the process of being reassessed, reinterpreted, and rewritten.

Therefore, we need research, travel, and fellowship funds, as well as endowed faculty positions, to carry this major project forward. We also need to complete the funding for, and then create, our projected new Center for International Studies. Sidney Knafel has given us an exceptional lead gift, but there is a substantial distance still to go. This complex of buildings will bring together, in improved and expanded space, most of our regional and international institutes. It will take us far toward achieving a greater level of integration in all our international programs. It will, in fact, represent the first significant visible presence in Harvard's history of our commitment to international studies, conceived on a worldwide scale.

I believe this is also the moment for Harvard to consider locating a limited number of outposts overseas, the main purpose of which would be to facilitate research and study by the many Harvard faculty and students who now undertake fieldwork in countries around the world. We need to be able to sustain their projects over time, to build longer-term relationships with people and nations abroad, and to place ourselves more directly in touch with the societies that we study. In other words, we need to extend our wings — tentatively, carefully, but with some sense of real excitement.

A second major priority is the further development of our modern information systems. It is hard to make this enterprise sound poetic. Even so, the new networks make a difference to every part of education, because they open up limitless sources of information and knowledge, and unlike other media, such as television or radio or film, these technologies could scarcely be more versatile or interactive.

They are already creating the equivalent of an enormous electronic research library whose volumes are on line rather than on shelves. They virtually force users to take a position of command, the driver's seat, compelling them to search, to seek, to find, and not to yield. In this way, they not only provide us with data, images, and information, but they also help to transform our pedagogy, placing the emphasis on the process of framing questions and looking for relevant evidence in order to test ideas: a form of what President Lowell called "self-education under guidance," and what President Conant referred to as "education by self-directed study."

If we are interested in advancing the cause of excellent teaching and learning in Harvard College and throughout the University, then the new technologies, properly used, are very much on our side. They also remind us of the ideal I mentioned earlier: the goal of integrating research, exploration, teaching, discovering, and learning in a way that dissolves the lines between them, bringing faculty and students together in what is really a common pursuit.

As these technologies develop, faculty and students will participate more frequently in discussion groups and joint classes on-line with students and faculty at other institutions — even in other countries. Harvard will be invisibly but significantly connected to all parts of the world through this filament-like network, where time and space are immediately collapsed. Here and elsewhere we can sense the obvious parallels with the revolution in international studies that I discussed a minute ago.

The next agenda topic concerns the question of diversity in its largest terms: how we manage to live our lives in some reasonable state of national and international harmony, given all the factors that I have already described — including the coming demographic changes — as well as the possibilities for conflict as the world shrinks and the pace of life continues to quicken.

Here I want only to say again, as I have before, that unless we are willing to continue our commitment to diversity in our colleges and universities, bringing together students from different backgrounds — from many geographic regions, from a variety of religious, ethnic, and racial groups representing a wide span of interests and talents — unless we can create the conditions in college that will allow our students to learn directly from one another, to discuss and test their different beliefs and points of view, outside the classroom as well as inside, then we will not have educated them fully, or prepared them to take on the role of leaders, either in our own diverse democratic society or in the larger, complicated, international arena.

From a financial point of view, the key to ensuring diversity in all its dimensions is the very same one that allows us to enroll, year after year, the best entering classes in the nation: need-blind admissions and need-based financial aid. This offers the most direct way to bring down the actual cost of college to students and parents alike. Nearly half of our undergraduates are awarded scholarships which average (on a sliding scale) about $13,500 per student this year, for a total of almost $40 million in undergraduate student aid alone. The system is equitable. It means that we have enough tuition income to help protect the quality of our programs, but it is also cost-effective institutionally. Most of all, it keeps Harvard well in the lead in the drive to attract the very best talent.

Let me also add at this moment a word about Harvard's commitment to the education and advancement of women. Recently, the Kennedy School inaugurated a new initiative in the field of "Women and Public Policy." The Women's Studies program in Arts and Sciences continues to grow, increasing its range of subjects and disciplines. Last spring, Professor Shirley Williams organized a major international conference on "Women and Leadership," including an ambitious research agenda which has already begun to develop. Meanwhile, during the past six years, the rate at which women are being appointed to tenure positions in the Faculty of Arts and Sciences has increased by more than 50 percent.

Collaborative work with Radcliffe has helped Harvard to make progress in several of these areas. There is still much to be done, but the signals are pointing in the right direction. I am also happy to report that we have, during the past year and a half, received a number of campaign commitments, amounting to more than $5 million, that are specifically intended to support some of the Harvard initiatives I have just described, as well as others that may evolve. This is a real boost, and points the way forward.

So our unfolding University agenda is ambitious, the needs are real, and we must keep pressing.

In closing, let me mention a few of the things that lie at the very heart of what we are and what we do. It matters that we are a residential college and university. The energy we feel in the air; the excitement and intensity that are the essence of our life here; the visible history present in our buildings, and our walkways; the friendships that have grown from the days and years spent together in this singular place: these depend deeply on the fact that we are rooted here, that we are a residential community whose values still echo the independent and questing spirit of our founders — their determination to build an institution that would last, that would have a far-reaching effect on learning, on education, and on the life of its society.

Consequently, as we think about a future in which Harvard will be more extended in time and space (electronically as well as tangibly), in which there will be more complexity, more networks and worldwide webs (some of our own making), it is important to remember that we are strongly grounded, right here, as well as being far-flung and international. And the challenges, great as they are, are not new for this institution. In fact, every major stride forward in our history has left us with a surprised sense of how much had been accomplished, and how much more still remained to be done.

As he contemplated the occasion of Harvard's three hundredth anniversary, in 1936, President Conant wondered about the fate of Harvard – and other private universities – during the coming century:

> *As compared with even one hundred years ago, our universities are [now] startlingly large and complex; their buildings and equipment are great beyond the imagination of our ancestors; their faculties and students alike have facilities never before at the disposal of any body of scholars. What will be the fate of these institutions thus suddenly developed to such dimensions? Can they escape the curse which has so often plagued large human enterprises well established by a significant history, – the curse of complacent mediocrity? What will be written and said about the role of the university ... [particularly Harvard], when the four hundredth celebration draws near?*[1]

Well, the four hundredth anniversary has drawn a good deal closer since 1936, and, so far at least, I do not see signs of "complacent mediocrity." For that, we owe thanks to many who have preceded us. But today I want most of all to express my debt – Harvard's debt – to all of you.

These last years have achieved much of what we hoped. They have drawn us together, have created fast friendships among us, and have already set standards beyond what we imagined when we first began. The time has not been always easy. We have lost – sadly, sometimes tragically – wonderful partners along the way: Tom and Virginia Cabot, John and Peter Loeb, and others who have made such a great difference in spirit to us. "Complacent mediocrity" was certainly not their style, and it cannot be ours. So as we conclude, and look to tomorrow, let us remember that we are, for this generation, the trustees of this very great university, and we need to reach as far and as high as we can – through calm, through change, and even through storm.

---

1   James B. Conant, *Report of the President to the Board of Overseers 1934–35*, 6.

A Class By Itself

Remarks to the Harvard College Class of 1949 50th Reunion
June 7, 1999

ALL HARVARD REUNIONS are, of course, equal. But some are more equal than others, and the fiftieth is a class that is in a class by itself.

The tenth reunion is always astonished to find that it has just passed the age of thirty, and can no longer be trusted. The twenty-fifth seems solemnly preoccupied with start-ups and productivity gains – their motto this year is "Sleep faster, we need the pillows." The thirty-fifth is neither fish nor fowl. But you, the fiftieth, are splendidly philosophical. You care deeply about Harvard, but you were not necessarily sure – before opening your programs – whether you would be addressed by President Pusey or Lowell, or Dean Rosovsky or Bundy.

No matter, it is refreshing to arrive under an assumed name, more or less incognito, footloose and even garrulously free – happy to talk about the University as if it were a sort of remote, shimmering Platonic Idea, rather than that perpetual seething cauldron of daily campus life – whose stew is constantly stirred, whose fire never goes out, and whose lid must always be on.

I would like to say a few words about Radcliffe. I am enthusiastic about – and deeply committed to – our merger and our joint creation of the new Radcliffe Institute for Advanced Study. But as you must know, there have been any number of storms along the way since Radcliffe was created a century ago – and many slings and arrows that Radcliffe has had to bear.

When the idea of educating women undergraduates first came up in the late 1860s, you may remember that President Eliot said:

> *The Corporation will not receive women as students into the College proper, nor into [any of Harvard's schools] . . . that requires residence near the school. The difficulties involved in a common residence of hundreds of young men and women of immature character and marriageable age are very grave. The necessary police regulations [would be] exceedingly burdensome.*[1]

Thus it was that Radcliffe College came to be established as a chartered, coordinate, residential institution on its own – linked closely to Harvard, but definitely possessing its own distinct, distant dormitories and its own eloquent police regulations.

During your years at Harvard, because of overcrowding and other unnamed contingencies, some Radcliffe and some Harvard students were actually allowed to take a few courses together. In addition, in the fall of 1945, two women teaching fellows were reported (by the *Harvard Alumni Bulletin*) to have "invaded" the History Department. There was such a large enrollment in History 1 that more instructors had to be dragooned, or perhaps merely conscripted, to lead small-group discussion classes. The coming of these women, said the *Bulletin*, "was accepted philosophically by a freshman class heavily weighted by returned veterans."

In addition, during your senior year, the first women ever (twelve of them) graduated from Harvard Medical School – whether as a result of overcrowding or not, the *Alumni Bulletin* fails to record.

All of you should take pride in the fact that, because of the sheer power of your flood-tide numbers, Harvard had its first serious beginnings of coeducation – if only in miniature – vigorously thrust upon it.

The creation of the new Radcliffe Institute carries to fulfillment the long, hundred-year process of bringing Radcliffe and Harvard to the point where they are to be formally and legally merged. The Institute will be an integral part of the University, attracting the very best visiting fellows and scholars from this country and abroad, and advancing research across all fields of learning, in the arts and sciences as well as in the professions.

In addition, an important part of the Institute's work will focus on the study of women, gender, and society – from an international, as well as a national, perspective.

The Radcliffe Institute will provide a flow of superb annual visitors, bringing fresh impetus to subjects that are already on the University's broad agenda. Meanwhile, Harvard's various Schools and Faculties will in turn contribute substantially to the intellectual vitality of the Institute and to its important work.

+ + +

The very large size of your class, together with your inventiveness and restless energy, had in addition to mini-coeducation, several other presumably unintended consequences.

You begat, for example, a housing crisis of unprecedented proportions, as well as a traffic crisis, and an academic degree crisis. In the fall of 1945, when you arrived, the city manager of Cambridge concluded wearily that "no permanent solution [to Harvard Square congestion] is possible" – at least not without drastic measures that seemed to lie well beyond the scope of everyone's collective ken.

As for housing, essentially everything imaginable was tried. Some ideas were rather conventional: Harvard took a three-year lease on the Hotel Brunswick, located in Boston on Boylston Street. "Among [other] possible dwellings," reported the *Alumni Bulletin*, "are counted two country clubs and one sanatorium."

Then, as a special concession, the Federal Public Housing Authority assigned four hundred family units – to create what was called
a "Harvard colony" – at the U.S. Army base, Fort Devens, conveniently located just thirty-two miles from Cambridge. Finally, "at
the height of the tumult," the *Crimson* reported, one freshman
"sailed his twenty-three-foot sloop from Nahant to the Charles
River, and then proceeded to make his home" right there on
board.

Academically, you also flooded the market. In your senior
year, 3,064 degrees – a record-breaking number beyond anyone's
nightmares – were awarded at Commencement. Your class walked
away with 1,054 of them, and it is not at all clear who got the
remaining 2,010 – or even in what subjects this riotous horde of
extra degrees were awarded.

Moreover, 35 percent of your class graduated with honors – a
percentage considerably higher than any previous known figure
in Harvard's history. Therefore, we are now finally in a position to
state precisely when grade inflation started – and by whom.

On the other hand, it may well have been the case – and I suspect it was – that you were in fact brighter, more talented, and
more honorific than all the classes that had ever preceded you.
And you were obviously more brilliant than our slower-witted,
lackluster, but wonderfully good-natured undergraduates of
today who, like Ferdinand, browse gently among the flowers in
the Yard, undisturbed and imperturbable.

✦   ✦   ✦

You came to Harvard at a moment of great historical significance:
higher education in this country was about to expand exponen-
tially – and many of you were in the GI vanguard. Federally funded
research was really just beginning – in fact, the National Science
Foundation was in the midst of being created when you were
enrolled. Standardized tests were beginning to be used on a much
larger scale. The library contained about 5 million books, but was

about to grow in the next few decades to the 13 million volumes we now possess.

And despite all the hurly-burly, yours were great vintage years for teaching, learning, and research at Harvard. The new General Education curriculum was in its beginnings, and among the extraordinary Harvard faculty members who were given tenure in your last two years were: Walter Jackson Bate, Sam Beer, Jerry Bruner, Helen Maud Cam, John Fairbank, Sidney Farber, Ken Galbraith, Oscar Handlin, Harry Levin, Archibald MacLeish, Agnes Mongan, Frederick Mosteller, and Willard Quine.

✦   ✦   ✦

I have told you very little about the Harvard of today. But I can say with real conviction that your University remains invigorating, stimulating, robust, and as committed as ever to the view that we should settle for nothing less than the best in choosing our faculty and students and in making certain that they have the academic and other resources that they need — whether scientific labs and equipment, archives and libraries, computers and networks, museums and creative arts facilities — whatever is necessary for them to do their work at the highest possible level of quality.

Because *that* is our only mission and justification: to educate broadly, deeply, and well; to be as certain as possible that the leaders who graduate from these courtyards will be resilient, inquiring, skillful, articulate individuals and citizens who — in the words of President Conant — have been "inoculated" with "the virus of a self-perpetuating liberal education." "It seems to me," he wrote,

> *a hopeless task to provide a complete and finished liberal education suitable to this century [with just] four years of college work. The only worth-while liberal education today is one which is a continuing process going on throughout life.... Has the smattering acquired in college worn thinner and thinner with each succeeding year?...*

Or has it provided a basis for continued intellectual and spiritual growth?[2]

My own sense is that Harvard then and Harvard now is in fact offering its students the kind of education that has its eye, so to speak, on the long run, enabling its graduates to grow intellectually and spiritually, throughout their lives.

1   *Inaugural Address of Charles William Eliot as President of Harvard College,* October 19, 1869, 17.
2.   James B. Conant, *Report of the President to the Board of Overseers, 1935–36,* 10.

AN EDUCATION

Reaching Out

Letter to the Incoming Harvard College Class of 2004
July 2000

B Y NOW, you will have received more information and advice than any innocent mortal should be asked to absorb. All of this information is useful. And the last thing you need, at this point, is anything more. Allow me to write to you some words that are more personal and that grow out of my own educational experience.

The most important part of your years at Harvard will be those moments and activities that help you understand what your real interests and abilities are and how you want to live your life.

Such moments can happen in academic courses that you take, or in conversations with friends, on solitary walks, in extracurricular pursuits, or in the ways that you begin to discover new patterns of meaning in the variety of your experiences. Harvard can provide you with a very great deal — teachers, advisers, laboratories, libraries, programs, computers, museums, residential Houses, and wonderfully stimulating fellow students. In the end, however, you yourself will inevitably be the person who evaluates and integrates everything. You will perceive your own meanings, develop your own values, and make your own choices.

The education that you are now beginning will certainly not be complete after four brief years as an undergraduate. It is bound, in fact, to continue to unfold throughout your entire life. Nonetheless, your Harvard years will, I hope, be an exceptionally creative, concentrated, and often intense period — at least that is what many, many, students have discovered in the generations before you, throughout Harvard's history. In addition to the intensity, I hope your time here will also be enjoyable, reflective, expansive, and even occasionally relaxing.

I have little advice to offer. But let me suggest a few ideas that may be as helpful to you as they have been to me.

First, you may well want to try your hand at many different things during your Harvard years and may not have time to be able to do all of them as well as you would like. Try to be sure, therefore, to pursue at least two or three things energetically and persistently. Try to get as close as possible to the bottom of even a few significant intellectual and human dilemmas or challenges. Only by probing deeply and by following one or two pathways or lines of exploration, for a very long distance, will you ever begin to discover the extent — as well as the limits — of what you can really create, or master, or understand.

Next, try to read some number of significant books that can help you to learn as much as possible about American culture as well as other cultures — and, perhaps, even about New England and Harvard. There is, for instance, a wonderful book by Isaiah Berlin called *The Crooked Timber of Humanity: Chapters in the History of Ideas*. Berlin was an intellectual historian with deep philosophic interests. He lived through many of the most tumultuous as well as devastating events of the last century. He was brilliant, omnivorous, and wise, and he writes with a fine unforced eloquence.

One of the greatest of all American intellectual autobiographies — which is also a tale about Boston, Quincy, Harvard, Washington, and London — is Henry Adams' *The Education of Henry Adams*. It is a book about education, in the largest meaning of the word, and tells us a great deal about the major political, scientific, and more general intellectual currents of the nineteenth and early twentieth centuries. It is not an easy book, but it is one that can be read, with immense value, at different times in one's life.

Two interesting books about science — and especially science at Harvard — are James Watson's *The Double Helix* and E. O. Wilson's *Naturalist*. Both have to do with significant discoveries and theories in the biological sciences. Both are wonderfully readable. And both are by present or former Harvard faculty members.

Another book — brief and very moving — is W. E. B. Du Bois' *The Souls of Black Folk*. This is a personal odyssey but also a book about politics, education, and the experience of many African Americans through the Reconstruction period into the early years of the twentieth century. Du Bois graduated from Harvard, was one of the founders of the NAACP, and is as fine a prose stylist as he is an observer of American life.

Finally, the diary of Alice James (in addition to Jean Strouse's biography of Alice James) is a truly extraordinary book about a remarkable person and also a remarkable family. Both volumes chart the experience of an astonishingly observant person who lived an intensely private life in a highly public milieu. Alice James' portrait of herself, as well as Jean Strouse's evocation of the Jamesian world, are arresting, absorbing, and deeply affecting.

I am not sure that any of these books qualify as "light summer reading." But all of them are formidable human documents that can expand the imagination, and they have helped me at least to enlarge my own understanding of life and its possibilities as well as its exigencies.

I am not a scientist, and I continue to regret that I did not press myself harder to study more science in secondary school and college. Most of what I have learned in science and mathematics has unfortunately been gained amateurishly. Yet even that little makes a very substantial difference to my intellectual and everyday practical life.

It is nowadays impossible — as I am sure you know — to think very intelligently about many questions in the humanities or the social sciences without knowing about mathematics and the sciences. Complex theories of justice, for instance, are virtually impossible to understand without some sophisticated knowledge of economics as well as statistics. Concepts of the mind – and descriptions of what we call "mental acts" – must take into account our increasingly detailed knowledge of the physiology of the brain and how we believe the brain is organized. In other words, mathematics and the sciences are not only deeply absorbing and compelling in themselves; they are linked in fundamental ways to the structure of knowledge and understanding in many fields of learning. Those of you who are scientists already know this. Those of you who are not scientists have the happy possibility of exploring new connections and ideas that are waiting to be discovered.

Are there any parting shots in such a letter? Not many. Try to write a very great deal while you are at Harvard and experiment with different kinds of writing – because experimentation forces one to develop new forms of perception and thought, a new and more complex sensibility. And try to rewrite your essays more than once or even twice: it is in the rewriting that coherence usually comes, if at all. Whatever your chosen field of study, you will not be able to proceed very far unless you constantly master new vocabularies, experiment with new forms of syntax, and try to see how precisely and sensitively your use of words can begin to reflect the very best movements of your own mind and imagination as well as your most penetrating observations of the world around you. It goes without saying that the more widely you can read – and the more intricate the materials that you read – the more you are likely to comprehend the breadth of human experience and creativity in its immense variety.

Finally, you are entering a community of peers that is likely to be more talented and more diverse – at least in its highly concentrated form – than any similar community you may ever again have the chance to be associated with. It would be a pity not to reach out in order to meet, understand, and simply enjoy the company of individuals who are very different from yourself (as well as those who are rather like yourself) and who will be your class-mates and associates for the next few years.

This form of "reaching out" is easier said than done. When you are tired of writing essays, or rowing on the river, or playing the cello, or doing a difficult laboratory experiment, you may quite naturally want to relax and spend time with just those few friends whom you know best and feel most instinctively at ease with. In fact, it would often be foolish not to do so. But it would also be a great loss if you could not find many occasions to make that extra extension outward in order to create new friendships with people from different backgrounds who may have very different views from your own. This usually requires real effort. It can sometimes lead to misunderstandings — and even to painful experiences. But it is one of the most important and profound opportunities that Harvard can offer you.

The Act of Reading

Dedication, John D. Verdery Library
Wooster School, October 6, 1990

WHEN I ARRIVED at Wooster as a freshman in the fall of 1948, the School's only buildings were the Chapel, the two cottages used as dormitories, and one "wing" – called the New Building – on the far side of the Chapel. We used the old farm-house at the bottom of the hill as another dormitory, and the red barn as our basketball court. Coburn Hall did not exist. There was no science building, no music building, no art center, and no gymnasium. There were about ninety students, and my own Class of 1952 jumped from about fourteen strong to nineteen when a nearby school went out of business and sent us reinforcements.

What this meant, of course, was that it was very easy to bring the entire Wooster school together frequently. In fact, it was almost impossible to do anything without bringing the entire school together: three times a day for communal meals with everyone present; daily chapel, every evening just before dinner, with everyone there; evening study hall after dinner, with virtually everyone there. Even athletics, which were compulsory, were essentially the same: since there were so few of us, almost everyone had to play on every team. In football, there were hardly enough members from the junior and senior classes combined to field a varsity squad that had both an offense and a defense. No one was allowed to be ill. A few wayward bacteria or stray streptococci could cost us a whole season.

So we were all together almost all of the time. Not only that, we were cast in a fairly similar mold. With rare exceptions, we were all boarding students; we were all males, all white Caucasians of one sort or another; we were not always charming, and it often must have been exasperating for the faculty to try to teach us anything, or even to be around us so continually, day after day after day. Somehow they stuck it out, and so did we: an untidy band of adolescents watched over by some very extraordinary teachers, inhabiting a group of distinctly unimposing buildings on a steep hillside in the midst of still unsettled woodlands in western Connecticut. How did we land here? Why on earth did everyone stay? What did we learn? And how does any of this relate to the new library we are dedicating?

These are not easy questions. But it seems clear that one reason so many exceptional people chose to associate themselves with Wooster, and then held fast to that association — as teachers and staff, as trustees, as parents and students and alumni — was the elementary fact that John Verdery was the headmaster, and that he and Suzanne Verdery drew such people to them. To those who were secure in themselves and who had, so to speak, a room or a spiritual home of their own, John and Sue somehow enhanced what was already there, enlarging the sense of what was possible in life, what values and what energies might lie beyond self-certainty or self-sufficiency. For those who were adrift or at sea — wanderers without a clear destination — John and Sue were a place of haven, an anchorage, a restorative and revivifying center to which one could always return, where one might hope to find one's bearings yet again.

Of course, all this was grounded on the fact that Wooster was a school, that its ostensible business was academic education, and that John Verdery was its headmaster. But the process of formal learning, of reading books and writing essays, or working in the library, seemed to be mainly the vehicle — the necessary engine and the occasion — that simply made it possible for everyone to get the real work of the School somehow accomplished.

To try to understand that real work better, I recently reread John's last book, which he entitled *Partial Recall*, published in the early 1980s. It is an informal memoir of his first forty years at Wooster, and it covers virtually every conceivable problem or issue relevant to private schools. Yet I could not find in the whole book a single reference to either Wooster's library or anybody else's. In fact, only a small handful of books or writers were mentioned at all: E. B. White, Robert Benchley, Theodore Dreiser's *Sister Carrie*, and of course the Bible. Whatever else might be said about them, these were distinctly not the kind of volumes for which one would need a well-stocked academic library and a brand new building.

I began to ask myself why it was that the new library was John's most important project during his last years: the project he cared most passionately about and the one he pursued so persistently. And why is it so appropriate, as it surely is, that we should choose the new library — rather than some other significant part of Wooster — to name in John's memory and honor?

Again, there are no clear answers, but let me suggest two possible ones. First, as I mentioned at the beginning of this talk, one of Wooster's most powerful and inescapable characteristics, during its early years, was the tangible compact unity and wholeness of the School. It was possible to bring everyone together in a single room, several times a day; one could literally see the entire school made visible in an endless series of formal and informal rituals of confirmation and reunion.

But of course that characteristic became increasingly difficult to sustain, and for very good reasons. Beginning in the late 1950s, there were a few more day students, and there was a strong program to attract minority students to Wooster. Within another decade and a half, the size of the School had more than doubled, coeducation had arrived, the day students began to outnumber the boarders, daily chapel was no longer compulsory, and there were formal academic departments and several more buildings. The one-room schoolhouse had given way to something more interesting and rich in its human and educational possibilities, much more responsive to the real needs of life as we now live it, but also much larger, more complicated, and more subject to the discontinuities that punctuate the rhythm of our current daily existence.

John Verdery recognized this clearly, accepting it and indeed embracing it. But he obviously did not want to give up the effort to create new ways of sustaining the fundamental unity of Wooster, even if that unity could no longer be captured in quite the same fashion as before. The new library, I think, was the unifying space — not merely physical but human, intellectual, and spiritual — that John began to focus upon. When he spoke about the library, he naturally mentioned the importance of books and proper study facilities. But he returned most often to his hope that there would be a large, inviting lounge where faculty and others could meet informally and frequently, outside their departments and classrooms. And he wanted, if it could be afforded, a large auditorium in the library: a place that could accommodate the whole school, whether for lectures or films or meetings and discussions. The location of the building and its shape also became critical: it was to be near the very center of everything, facing outward in several directions; it would be a crossroad, a place where anyone could easily stop by for a few moments, or study, or meet friends. In contrast to the Chapel of three or four decades ago, where literally everyone gathered in just one room for religious services every day, the library would be a mansion of *many* rooms, where attendance would be voluntary. It would obviously be less communal in many ways; but perhaps it would be ultimately no less binding in its cumulative subliminal effect on the lives and minds of students and faculty alike.

The second reason that the library meant so much to John, I believe, is the very unusual value he placed on individual books, as opposed to great shelf-loads of volumes. He told me more than once that he was a slow reader, and this was a great comfort to me when I was young, because I was and still am the slowest reader I know. For John, this fact meant that he approached every book, whatever its subject matter, as if it were a kind of sacred text: to read it meant investing a good deal of time, and time was always in short supply. He would choose his books very carefully. Once under way, nothing would escape him: the meaning of every anecdote, every turn of plot, every human vicissitude — all would be absorbed. Where some people might skim, John would virtually memorize what was on the page, just as he memorized, after writing out by hand, every one of the sermons he preached week after week. In this special way, John restored to books and to the act of reading some sense of the preciousness that they held in much earlier times, when books were scarcer and harder to obtain, and when they were valued as exceptional sources of knowledge and wisdom, not only to be carefully treasured, but to be incorporated and integrated into one's own life as one tried to live it and give meaning to it.

I like to think of the new library as a form of secular chapel which John can preside over, with bright spaces that can bring together the different parts of Wooster, and with books that can — if approached in the right spirit — take on the character of sacred texts. This is the kind of testament which I believe John wanted to leave Wooster: the last building from a man who never believed that a school should have very many buildings.

In closing, I want only to add a brief coda. For all the changes that have taken place since Aaron Coburn first set up his school in the farmhouse at the bottom of the hill, and since John Verdery came as Aaron Coburn's successor in 1942, Wooster is of course still a small place as the world goes, and it still maintains its appointed but unobtrusive vigil on a steep hill in the countryside of western Connecticut. It still has virtually no endowment. It lives, as it has always lived, close to the edge of financial peril. Yet it has always resisted the temptation to try to build very fancy facilities in order to attract a wealthier clientele in order to be able to build even fancier facilities to attract an even wealthier clientele. It has gone its own way, sticking to its essential human values. The same holds true, of course, if we think of John and Suzanne Verdery, of Donald Schwartz, Joe Grover, Hobart Warner, Korb Eynon, and so many other people who came and stayed — and stayed, and stayed. When John turned down the headmastership of Groton twenty-five years ago in order to remain at Wooster, I understood; but it was certainly not an easy decision for him, and he gave up a great deal when he decided to remain just where he was.

And of course Joe Grover, like John Verdery, was also offered any number of headmasterships, and virtually every member of the Wooster faculty let more glittering opportunities slide by. There must have been, with all the satisfactions, some occasional second thoughts, some regrets about what else one might have done. Underlying everything, however, there was also a deep sense of the inevitability of these decisions: after all, could one really imagine John anywhere else? Or Donald or Hobart or Joe? They knew what was important, and they had the self-confidence, clarity of vision, and redeeming simplicity to recognize that they were involved in creating a very extraordinary school on a small patch of land where they could be free to pursue their own special errand in the wilderness.

All of them as individuals, and the School as an institution, chose a path that was anything but the usual one. I want to finish by reading a short poem that sums up for me a great deal about Wooster and John Verdery: about the difficult choices which, because they were made, have kept so many of us together for so many years and have brought us here. As we listen to the poem, we should imagine that the speaker is a kind of collective Wooster voice, a voice of the whole School reaching back to include Aaron Coburn and John Verdery, as well as John and Michael Coburn, Peter O'Neill, and all the faculty and students who continue to carry the School forward:

> *Two roads diverged in a yellow wood,*
> *And sorry I could not travel both*
> *And be one traveler, long I stood*
> *And looked down one as far as I could*
> *To where it bent in the undergrowth;*
>
> *Then took the other, as just as fair,*
> *And having perhaps the better claim,*
> *Because it was grassy and wanted wear;*
> *Though as for that, the passing there*
> *Had worn them really about the same,*
>
> *And both that morning equally lay*
> *In leaves no step had trodden black.*
> *Oh, I kept the first for another day!*
> *Yet knowing how way leads on to way,*
> *I doubted if I should ever come back.*
>
> *I shall be telling this with a sigh*
> *Somewhere ages and ages hence:*
> *Two roads diverged in a wood, and I —*
> *I took the one less traveled by,*
> *And that has made all the difference.*[1]

Wooster and those who have given themselves to it have always chosen to take the road less traveled by. And that has made all the difference, not only to them, but to the rest of us who have benefited so incalculably from everything they have done.

---

1 Robert Frost, "The Road Not Taken," in *The Poetry of Robert Frost* (New York: Henry Holt and Company, 1979), 105. Orig. pub. in the *Atlantic Monthly*, August, 1915.

Designed to Be a Genuine Community

Belmont Hill School Speech
October 9, 1998

W HEN I WAS thirteen years old, about to finish eighth grade in the public school of my hometown, my school principal — a tall, stern man, with a quick temper that was itself tempered by kindness and intelligence — summoned me to his office one day.

In 1948, there were a very limited number of reasons one might be summoned to the principal's office, and none of them, I assure you, was considered by students to be even remotely benign.

I showed up at the designated hour, and Mr. Maginley (for that was his name) asked me if I would like to go to boarding school, instead of high school, on a scholarship. Conversations with Mr. Maginley were usually not long, exploratory, informal, probing dialogues. In fact, the question just put to me had nearly exceeded all by itself the outer limits of the expected length of time for an interview between pupil and principal. I replied, "Yes, sir, I think I would." "Fine," he said.

Such was our faith in figures of authority, in institutions (even if completely unknown), and in the general power of education, that I went off to the Wooster School as a "first former" (or ninth grader) in the autumn of 1948, exactly half a century ago. And the experience, without a doubt, completely changed my life: it changed my sense of life's possibilities, my sense of what it means to learn something, and — most of all — my ideas about what a valuable life might be, and how one might try to lead such a life.

I mention all of this because, despite their differences, there are important parallels between Belmont Hill and the school that I attended. For one thing, they were both part of the New England private school movement that began in earnest during the late nineteenth century and continued for at least another four decades. Both schools were also relatively late entries: Belmont Hill started in 1923, and Wooster in 1927. Both were small, unendowed, pioneering schools, whose founders were driven by a sense of mission — inspired by the Grotons, Kents, and Deerfields that were already well established by then.

The approach to learning was basically simple and sound: find teachers who love their subjects and who also care about individual students, helping them to grow as people, not only as minds; keep the regimen of daily school life fairly spartan; think of education as a process in which the school is seen as a true community, and where many activities — in the arts, or athletics, or public service — are all viewed as genuinely educational.

The original goal, unchanged since the 1920s, was to teach young people how to participate and to lead, as well as to learn: or rather, to show how teaching, participating, leading, and learning could actually all be part of a single dynamic and humane experience.

While I cannot speak with anything approaching authority, I suspect that my years at Wooster had at least some of the features that are clearly in evidence at Belmont Hill. It is obvious from my friends among your alumni (as well as among the parents of your students and alumni) that this institution has been extraordinarily important in shaping the lives of its graduates: during their actual years on campus, and long afterward.

In fact, it is just this "shaping" role that is so distinctive and crucial: a role that represents the special and increasingly important contribution that a Belmont Hill can — and does — make during a time when so many schools, and school systems, are in such deep trouble, with so little ability to achieve coherence or a strong sense of direction, or to gain the active involvement of communities that care for them and expect the best from them. A school like Belmont Hill really does "work," and it is worth taking a few minutes this evening to ask why, trying to identify some of the less visible reasons as well as the more visible ones.

Those less visible factors — often by-products and even accidents of a school's formal educational activities — can make an enormous difference to individual students. And despite the accidental, unpredictable nature of such factors, they actually turn out to be part of the entire system, so to speak, because the school has been created and structured in such a way as to make such experiences more likely, rather than less likely, to happen. Let me mention just one or two such experiences from my own past, starting as a "first former" back in 1948.

One of the most startling events of my first autumn term was something that I'm certain did not seem to be an "event" at all to anyone else, least of all to my academic advisor, who was responsible for it. I simply showed up at his office, as scheduled, and was stunned to see that the entire side wall of his study consisted of ceiling-to-floor shelves that were absolutely crammed with books.

Yes, I had seen shelves of books before — in the slightly gloomy, Victorian brownstone public library in Danbury, Connecticut, where I had grown up. But it had never occurred to me that any individual human being might buy, read, and actually possess large numbers of books as a part of normal, everyday existence. Even more striking, it was clear that these were, so to speak, "real" books, not textbooks or ordinary school books. And they seemed, collectively, to touch upon every conceivable subject: at least, every subject that I could conceive of.

I still remember names and titles, even though most of them

were names and titles that I had not heard of before, or had barely heard of. There was Darwin's *Descent of Man*, which puzzled me. Descent from where, and when? There was a book by Groucho Marx, not very far from something by Karl Marx. There was a large volume of Eugene O'Neill's plays, Plato's *Dialogues*, and Evelyn Waugh's *Decline and Fall*, which was just two shelves down from Gibbon's *Decline and Fall of the Roman Empire* — to which was added, later, Will Cuppy's *Decline and Fall of Practically Everybody*.

This seismic, tectonic event happened totally silently, inside me, and I know that my advisor did not have even the remotest idea that he was at that time (or on my later office-hour visits) actively engaged in teaching me anything in particular, or anything at all. On my side of the desk, however, I was experiencing a kind of revelation. Here were all these writers, ideas, poems, novels, histories, works of science, and heaven knows what: and I suddenly realized that anyone, even I, could own them and begin to explore them.

It was also soon obvious to me that my advisor knew exactly where every individual book was placed, and that he could find more or less whatever he wanted to look up, simply by flipping the pages quickly. In other words, there was an invisible order, not at all decipherable, to the arrangement on the shelves, and it must have been important because it never really changed (except for the addition of more books) during my four years at school.

I don't remember trying to articulate for myself, at the time, what this entire experience actually meant to me. But I'm certain that it is not at all an accident that I have been buying books ever since; that I have spent untold hours shelving the books in ways that make complete sense to me, but probably to no one else; and that, whenever our family has moved house, I have not really been able to begin work (or do anything else) until the cartons of books have been emptied and the library has been put back in order: because until *that* happens, it is hard for me to feel that my mind is back in order.

Therefore, if I'm asked what I learned at my school, one of the most powerful things was having a teacher who simply assumed that reading, and asking questions, and creating interesting conversations; that being curious about the world, looking at how the world and societies seem to function, or didn't function; that reaching for the relevant book (often a dictionary), as well as reading books, and owning books, because you somehow needed them near at hand: that all these and many related things could be, legitimately, just a natural part of life — not just a part of school, or of being a teacher, but a part of one's total existence.

It took a special teacher at a particular kind of school for all that to happen. It took a school where there was enough time, and the right kind of atmosphere, so that students and teachers could carry on real conversations, outside the classroom as well as inside: a school where teachers considered students to be people, as well as pupils.

Those are simply some of the ways in which teaching — in many shapes and forms, in the most unexpected ways — takes place in a school that is robust. Thousands of Belmont Hill students (and parents) could recount similar, as well as different, tales because these are the kinds of incidents and events — often not fully appreciated, or even understood until years later — that create the texture of life in a place that is genuinely dedicated to learning in all its dimensions.

I have just slipped from teachers and teaching to the subject of learning, and I want to say something about this other side of the equation for a minute or two. Teachers can, as we know, teach from dawn to dusk; but, ultimately, it is only the student who can learn. And learning is, of course, the heart of the whole matter. Learning is also astonishingly difficult: nearly the hardest, most difficult activity that we ever try to do, at least at the deepest levels, where the really important work needs to take place.

The process of learning is complicated and subtle, and while it clearly has something to do with teaching, it also has its own dynamics and obscurities. Our very best efforts at formal instruction can fail dramatically, or at least they may not quite succeed. We still know all too little about how people learn, or why, or under what conditions.

If it is often a little discouraging to see how much effort it takes to make little or no progress on even elementary matters in education; however, we ought to remember that there is also a danger in seeming to make too much progress, too quickly. Sensible conclusions and correct answers are important, but they count most when they are the result of real thinking and real understanding, rather than something more perfunctory or mechanical. Moreover, many of the most difficult situations and problems, relating to so many aspects of the world and life around us, do not yield their secrets very easily, if at all.

If we really understood more about the causes, for example, of ethnic or racial tension, or the forces driving the world economy, or the motives behind a great deal of the puzzling human behavior we see every day, then we might well be in a much better position to guide the course of many events before they become destructive, or simply problematic. But we do not know enough. And even when we do, we may still find it nearly impossible to judge precisely what steps to take in order to produce the best result, assuming that the capacity to take those steps is actually available to us.

From this point of view, the best thing that a good education can do (once we have moved beyond introductory and elementary matters) is to help our students become interested, engaged, and committed inquirers: to learn how to interrogate experience and events; to penetrate beyond the merely apparent or likely; to frame and test hypotheses; to look for relevant evidence and inspect it rigorously; to imagine a range of possible interpretations of an event, or a poem, or a particular person's actions, while recognizing that more than one interpretation may well be plausible.

In addition, education in an excellent school needs to give its students practice, so to speak, in choosing — in coming to conclusions on the basis of all that they can reasonably know, acknowledging that they will rarely, if ever, know enough to be quite certain. Only when students are deciding (as well as analyzing) and then acting on their decisions — whether in an exam or laboratory experiment, or in athletics, or an orchestra, or in relationships with friends — only then will they come to discover the actual values that mean the most to them. And only then can they begin to develop, much more consciously, the values that they want to stand by, and live by.

Helping young people to sort their way through to conclusions and to actions, and helping them to understand and develop their own values, is unquestionably the most difficult and complicated educational challenge that exists. It is also the most significant one. Good results cannot be guaranteed, and no particular kind of school has anything close to a monopoly on success in this hazardous arena.

Nevertheless, I myself believe that a school like Belmont Hill offers the best possible opportunities for exactly the kind of growth I have been describing, essentially because the school has been designed to be a genuine community — with all the implications of that term — rather than just an academy.

By the tone you establish, the expectations you create, and the orientation provided by the steadiness of your sextant, you make clear the fact that education is at bottom a human process that can only be counted a success if people have learned not only a good deal about many fields of knowledge and ways of thinking, but also how to live respectfully and decently — even harmoniously — with one another.

Of course there will always be the inevitable problems of daily life: the sudden outbursts, the ordinary strains, and all the problems that are bound to exist whenever two or three (or more) are gathered together. And, in addition, there must be — especially in a school or university — a full measure of space for serious intellectual disagreement and debate. In the end, however, there also has to be a recognition that no group — certainly no society or nation — can function unless individuals can express and act upon their own convictions while, simultaneously, seeking ways to accommodate the convictions and actions of others. Mutuality of this kind is the foundation of any community, at least any community that places a high value on openness, inquiry, and the development of individual capacities and talents.

There are very few places where these important values, with all their complexities, can be taught and learned — through experience, with guidance, as well as through precept. One of the very few places where this can happen is at a school like Belmont Hill: a school that has viewed itself, from its very beginning, as an institution where all the activities of daily life — the interactions among students, teachers, the headmaster, trustees, coaches, parents, and others — are by definition educational and communal in nature. That is why this school and others like it are so crucial, indeed essential. They have always been important. Now they are indispensable.

We live at a time when very few institutions manage to survive for even a very brief span of time without simply crumbling; or being subject to an act of sudden conglomeration, takeover, or buyout; or suffering the indignity of an involuntary name change, or the chagrin of instantaneous liquidation.

The drama critic Alexander Woollcott once reviewed a newly opened, calamitous piece of theater by saying, "If this play lasts overnight, it should not only be considered a long run, but a revival as well." By my reckoning, Belmont Hill has been going day and night, with a full house, at full tilt, for nearly 30,000 performances already — with tens and tens, indeed hundreds of thousands more performances to come.

To be part of an institution that has grown so progressively strong (from what was already a strong start), and to be participants in the process of building, sustaining, and improving this school: all of that represents something more than just a remarkable achievement. It represents a way of living life, because it requires, as you well know, constant commitment, resources, energy, generosity, stamina, and intelligent purposefulness. Sustaining a school is itself a communal activity, demanding a great deal of faith, lots of hope, and uninterrupted charity. But there is no better cause. Carrying the school forward so superbly, as all of you have done, involves a devotion to precisely those central values which the Belmont Hill School embodies, and that have shaped the lives of its graduates for this past three-quarters of a century.

A Labyrinthine Collegiate Climb

Baccalaureate Address
June 3, 1997

VIRTUALLY ALL normal universities invite a different person every year to say something valedictory to the seniors — something riveting or uplifting, or hazy, impenetrable, and aromatic, or at the very least, something actually anaesthetizing — to ensure that everyone will remain in a state of more or less uninterrupted stupor until graduation (and perhaps for years ever after). At Harvard, however, we have always refused to outsource the Baccalaureate Service. It falls, therefore, to the president of the University — and it falls even more heavily on the collective crania, cerebral cortices, and sensitive auditory systems of all of you who must sit and listen — it falls to the president, year after year, to deliver another astonishing and pulverizing oration to a packed house of ingenious, restless, nonchalant, Harvard conquistadors: yearning, like Ariel, for freedom but, alas, doomed to languish in ritual academic captivity a little longer, clothed in these extravagant costumes, waiting to complete your labyrinthine collegiate climb to full beatification on Commencement morning.

Thus, every year I stand here, watching you become more

seraphic and soporific by the minute, while I myself sink deeper into inarticulate despair: what new sermon from the mount can I possibly come up with this year? What five or ten irresistible commandments, or spectacular rhetorical thunderbolts, can I find to hurl from the heights this time around?

Two or three years ago, I found myself rifling, in search of inspirational passages, through the pages of the *Crimson*, the *Lampoon*, and even the *Wall Street Journal*, looking for nuggets, gems — even rhinestones in the rough — that I might be able to smuggle into a sentence or a paragraph.

I finally found, in the *New York Times*, some reports of what several designated hitters at other graduations had said. One headline urged the senior class to live life to the fullest. That's an original idea, I said to myself — it might be good for two and a half pages, if I use large type and speak very slowly. But then I saw another headline, in even bolder letters, imploring every individual to live up to their full potential. Ah ... even more original, I thought. But it is unfortunately not grammatical, and it is also obscure: I'll never manage to get it past the vigilant Class of 1997. Maybe the sleepy squadrons of 1996, maybe the wayward dreamers of 1998, but not '97 — not that glittering assembly with its 1,392 Rhodes Scholars; sixty-six saxophonists; its NCAA women's basketball and men's baseball virtuosos; its fearless Phillips Brooks House battalions of Crimson berets; its six million campus reporters singing their daily hosannas of praise outside the president's office; its nine tight ends; and its lovable loose cannons.

Since there was no way to slip anything by you, I decided that if I couldn't beat you, I would join you and elect myself an honorary member of your very clever class — which I have done, just this morning, signing my own degree, *summa cum laude*. Now we are at least in the same boat, and, already, I feel much brighter, wittier, and even younger.

In my last round of research, I discovered that confessional speeches are all the rage this year. A large *New York Times* article stated (about a week ago) that graduation speakers really ought to talk about their own personal tragedies. "That is definitely the latest trend," said the *Times*, "That's what students want to hear about. That's the way to have an impact."

I have lain wide awake for the last three nights, searching my psyche for some trace of the tragic, watching the sepulchral light of the moon casting lugubrious shadows as it moved slowly over the huddled objects in my room: the once vibrant electric treadmill, now rusted and fallen into disuse; the large bottle, half empty, of diet cola, reminder of the previous evening's riotous revelry, full of sound and fury, without the consolation of even a single calorie; my tattered academic robe, long ago ransomed for the dull repetitive pattern of paper-thin pinstripes on borrowed blue Brooks Brothers suits — fatal sign of yet another soul cast into darkness, lost in the deep administrative recesses of Massachusetts Hall.

But the more I thought, the more I realized I could never share the Shakespearean depth and Sophoclean shock of these experiences with you — any more than I could confess in public that my Italian grandmother never learned to speak a word of English, and always thought that, because the Fourth of July was so festive, it must be Garibaldi's birthday.

I have nothing devastating to relate, no grand propositions for you — no large theory of life that can help you go with unbounded certainty from the general to the particular. You will probably need some sort of theory in order to make your way through the decades ahead. But I doubt that the theory will be of any use to you, unless it is in close touch with all the nuances and particularities of experience, which will yield their secrets only if you genuinely explore and interrogate them — expanding your range as you go, while trying to clarify and understand, as well as absorb, whatever you encounter. Dr. Johnson once said that "curiosity is the first passion and the last" — by which he meant that there is no stronger or more persistent desire than the human desire to know, to discover as much as we can about who and what we are: where we have come from, where we are going, and what may be the value of all that we choose to do during our brief, susceptible lives.

So, be curious. Start with the assumption that we know very little (if anything at all) about the people and the events which surround us — and which inevitably involve us as participants. Assume that we also know much too little about ourselves. Virginia Woolf's line is worth remembering: "A biography," she wrote, "is considered complete if it merely accounts for six or seven selves, whereas [we know that each of us] may have as many as a thousand."

This recognition is an attitude of mind that sees each of us not only as "I" or "one," but also as a kind of locus — an intersection where shifting feelings, ideas, interests, convictions, passions, compulsions, perceptions, delusions, self-delusions, and illuminations converge; that each of us has any number of conflicting and competing selves which we are always in the process of trying to identify, comprehend, and also harmonize; that we barely arrive at one possible interpretation of even a single set of experiences before we realize how fragile our brave new insights really are: how they can, in fact, be suddenly displaced by a deeper or simply different reading of events — either by ourselves, or someone else.

From this point of view, every significant flicker of experience can make a difference. Every flicker can change the whole look and lighting of a major scene at a crucial moment in your existential drama. Late in life, when he was very ill, Henry James was visited by friends whom he had known for decades. "I have the curious sense," he said, "that I am not the bewildering puzzle to all of you that you are to me." For James, experience was always ambiguous — and therefore tantalizing, frustrating, inviting, bewildering, and also isolating. Right to the end, his closest friends seemed beyond his reach, and his sense of distance was increased, not reduced, by the fact that his friends did not seem to share his own feeling of deep puzzlement. It may not be very hard in life to move beyond the surface of things, learning more, pressing further and further. But behind every door, there is another one.

This is clearly not the place to leave you — isolated, puzzled, fruitlessly pursuing a thousand evanescent selves, just two days before Commencement.

The way out, of course, is to recognize and accept these many complications, including the fact that you yourself are much more complicated than you may realize: that you have actually learned to be — partly unconsciously, partly by imitating others, partly by experimenting with some of those different selves inside you — you have, to a considerable extent, learned and chosen to be what you are in the process of becoming, and what you think you want to become in the future.

If Harvard has helped you at all during these four years, I hope it has stimulated you to keep reimagining the possibilities of your life and the ways that you can give shape to it. Not all of the choices, by any means, are yours to make. But many of them certainly are.

I hope that the roles you choose to play, the person you choose to become, and the drama you are involved in creating will have some real sweep and scope to it; some (heroic) epic entrances; perhaps some foolish lapses into melodrama; a good fair share of wit; some wild, tumultuous exits, followed by scenes of the most unimaginable sentiment — and then, perhaps later, a few blessed moments of unexpected transcendence.

Meanwhile, as you move forward, there will inevitably be any number of long, dark passages, when the parts of your drama — yours and other people's — no longer seem to fit together. You may feel miscast, maybe not large enough for the role, like the notorious Lord Admiral of the British navy, Edward Carson Brown, who failed to distinguish himself — at every single turn — but who was at least perceptive enough to explain, in one of his few memorable pronouncements, that "my only qualification for being put at the head of the navy, is that I [feel] ... very much at sea."

Above all, remember that those passions and interests — and the values they represent — connect you inevitably to everyone you know, and even those you do not know. As you act, try to anticipate the implications of what you are doing; think about the effect on others; do as little harm as possible, and be as charitable as possible — even more charitable than you think you can be. Because without charity, either in giving or in receiving, we are nothing: nothing more than the clamor of sounding brass and tinkling cymbal.

✦ ✦ ✦

My classmates, be generous to yourselves and to others. You will do well. You already have done so very well. Meanwhile, I hope that you will remember us and return often: that you will think of this lovely place — with its Yard, its quadrangles and Houses, its libraries and chapel and trees — that you will think of it as a place that is permanently yours, as a home where you will always be welcome, and always warmly received.

Keeping Our Memory Accurate

Department of Afro-American Studies Thirtieth Anniversary Celebration
April 8, 2000

I RETURNED TO HARVARD in 1991, and can speak at first hand only about this past decade. But I would still like to glance backward a few decades to remember how sparse was the formal knowledge of — and real education in — any aspect of the African American experience. I want to use myself as an example of the kind of ignorance that prevailed at the time.

I entered secondary school in the fall of 1948. It was a very small school — a total of ninety students and eleven teachers — on a remote hillside in rural Connecticut: high academic standards, a demanding curriculum, and an astonishingly dedicated faculty.

Nonetheless, during my four years there, I did not read a single work by an African American, or a single book *about* African Americans, and there were very few references in our American history course textbook to African Americans. Nor were there any African American students in the school.

I do not say this in any spirit of criticism of the school or its teachers. I'm only describing a situation that must have been typical then of hundreds of thousands of students, in thousands of towns throughout the entire United States. I knew essentially nothing about this absolutely central aspect of our collective heritage. In fact, not only did I not know anything, I didn't even (as was once said of a legendary benighted student) suspect anything.

How far had I progressed, if at all, by 1958 or 1968? A little, but not very much. Reading about major events in the press, such as the decision in *Brown v. Board of Education*, and the entire unfolding of the civil rights movement, was one thing. But serious study, actual knowledge in any depth, was a totally different thing. And in that arena, I moved incredibly slowly.

By the 1960s, I had been reading Richard Wright, Ralph Ellison, James Baldwin, Malcolm X, Eldridge Cleaver, and others. But if you had asked me who Zora Neale Hurston was, or Alain Locke, Sojourner Truth, James Weldon Johnson, or even Frederick Douglass and Phillis Wheatley, I would have drawn a complete blank. If there is any solace to be drawn from my own situation (and it is, of course, of no solace), the only explanation I can offer is that schools and colleges at the time provided us with little or no help of any kind.

But here it is essential to be honest. Neither I – nor countless others like me – reached out, or sought with energy on our own to find out more; to understand not only the *terribilità* of our society's past, its history and experience, but also to recognize how little that history had changed. As a result, we failed to see – or acknowledge – how much responsibility we ourselves bore for the continuation of circumstances that remained unjust. Ignorance there was, but also a devastating blindness.

In Martin Luther King's last book, *Where Do We Go from Here?*, published in 1967, he wrote:

> The history books ... have almost completely ignored the contribution of the Negro in American history.... All too many [people] are unaware of the fact that the first American to shed blood in the revolution which freed this country from British oppression was a black seaman named Crispus Attucks. [They] are almost totally oblivious of the fact that it was a Negro physician, Dr. Daniel Hale Williams,

who performed the first successful operation on the heart, ... and that another Negro physician, Dr. Charles Drew, was largely responsible for developing the method of separating blood plasma and storing it on a large scale, a process that saved thousands of lives in World War II. [1]

Similar points could easily have been made about the nation's lack of knowledge concerning the brilliant contributions of African Americans to the music not only of our own country, but of the world. And Ralph Ellison began to construct, at least as early as 1970, a new genealogy for the American language, American speech, and American literature.

In his stunning essay, "What America Would Be Like Without Blacks," Ellison reminded us that Walt Whitman

viewed the spoken idiom of Negro Americans as a source for a native grand opera. Its flexibility, its musicality, its rhythms, free-wheeling diction, and metaphors as projected in Negro American folklore, were absorbed by the creators of our great nineteenth-century literature even when the majority of blacks were still enslaved. Mark Twain celebrated [that same idiom] in the prose of Huckleberry Finn; without the presence of blacks, the book could not have been written. No Huck and Jim, no American novel as we know it. For not only is the black man a co-creator of the language that Mark Twain raised to the level of literary eloquence, but Jim's condition as American and Huck's commitment to freedom are at the moral center of the novel.

In other words, had there been no blacks, certain creative tensions arising from the cross-purposes of whites and blacks would also not have existed. Not only would there have been no Faulkner; there would have been no Stephen Crane, who found certain basic themes of his writing in the Civil War. Thus, also, there would have been no Hemingway, who took Crane as a source and guide. [2]

These few examples only touch the surface of all that was still either unnoticed, or unknown, or consciously omitted and therefore uncelebrated, concerning the history and contributions of African Americans — and of African American experience — to the large pattern of the national and international history in which we all share, and through which we are all so deeply related to one another, through so much of the dreadfulness of the past, as well as through moments of close kinship and love.

Therefore, if we want to grasp at least part of the impact and significance of what has happened since 1970 — shortly after Dr. King wrote his last book, when Ellison wrote the essay from which I just read, and when Harvard's Department of Afro-American Studies was founded — we need to visit the stacks of Widener Library, or bookstores, or visit any number of Web sites, or read our University's course catalogue to see that there has been nothing less than an incalculable expansion, a massive seismic shift with continuous reverberations, in terms of the extent of new knowledge, and the capacity for greater self-knowledge, that now exists in this nation because of the powerful growth of African American studies as a central field of learning during the past three decades.

When we think about major progress in most spheres of life, it is not surprising that we tend to focus on political, legal, economic, societal events — on achievements arrived at through great struggle, conflict, and pain. But there are other very profound, if less dramatic, victories that are also difficult, and every bit as vital (indeed, essential) to our ability to make even elementary sense of our world, of ourselves, of our values, and of our purposes.

From this point of view, new illuminating knowledge gained through persistent, deep research — research that can so often seem fruitless and inconclusive while it is in process, knowledge gained through careful analysis, through imaginative as well as incisive scholarship: these are among our most precious resources. Very few things are as powerful in helping our quest to understand other individuals and groups, or grasp the substantiality of what they have experienced or created. Little else will equip us so well in our effort to keep the human record honest, straight, and clear; to keep memory *accurate* as well as *fresh*; to make the present comprehensible, or to endow the future with potential meaning and hopefulness.

This form of knowledge and understanding, with its own kind of saving power, is what research and teaching — what faculty and universities — can at their best provide to us, so long as we come to the enterprise with minds and hearts that are open and yet disciplined, responsive but also discerning.

Of course, this task never ends. There is always so much more to do. From one perspective, we have barely begun — in the many fields that encompass Afro-American and related studies, and in our human and institutional conditions — the process of genuine education that needs to take place before knowledge becomes understanding, and understanding is transformed into increasingly humane and communal relationships.

From another point of view, however, the distance traveled from the ignorance and blindness of 1970 is immense. And a large proportion of the pioneering work and many of the landmark studies and changes, have come from Harvard's superlative faculty in its Afro-American Studies Department, as well as from a number of the University's cognate departments and programs.

It is not a boast, but rather a simple fact, that Harvard's department leads all others in its brilliance, in its magnetism, in its contributions to learning as well as to public life, in its rich variety, and in the sheer abundance of its inspiring human qualities.

The list of the department's faculty in this year's course catalogue includes a large portion of the world's most distinguished scholars in Afro-American studies, including Anthony Appiah, Lawrence Bobo, Evelyn Brooks Higginbotham, Barbara Johnson, Randall Kennedy, Jamaica Kincaid, Lorand Matory, Marcy Morgan, Orlando Patterson, Werner Sollors, Cornel West, William Julius Wilson, and of course our extraordinary chair, leader, force of nature, and friend, Henry Louis Gates, Jr.

If the Department of Afro-American Studies is now embedded in the heartland of Arts and Sciences at Harvard, as well as in our professional schools, all of the faculty I have just mentioned, and many others from Harvard's past and present, are responsible for that great transformation in knowledge and understanding.

If Harvard undergraduates and graduate students, and so many younger people throughout the world, can now learn and even take for granted far more than I had ever "suspected" half a century ago, then these are the teachers and scholars who have made that possible.

Is there more to be done? Yes — far, far more — and at times the journey ahead can often seem more difficult than the distance traversed, if we mean progress in real understanding, and therefore in the conditions of life for so many African Americans and others in our society. There is still ignorance and blindness — and too often the pathology of hatred and violence — to be overcome.

At the same time, I want to assure you that this university is fully dedicated to the continuous building and expanding of Afro-American studies, in all their richness and complexity.

And Harvard will continue to take ethnicity and race into account, along with many other factors, as it admits students. We will also continue to provide whatever amount of financial aid is required to keep the doors open at the College to talented students from all backgrounds and circumstances.

Finally, if I may speak to our graduates among you, we look forward to seeing you and welcoming you here, again and again, whenever you come: anniversary or no anniversary; in season and out of season; in the best of times or the worst of times. This is your Memorial Church. These are your quadrangles, pathways, and halls of learning. This is your Harvard.

1 Martin Luther King, Jr., *Where Do We Go from Here: Chaos or Community?* (New York: Harper & Row, 1967), 41–42.
2 Ralph Ellison, *Going to the Territory* (New York: Random House, 1986), 109.

Intensity and Form

Sydney Freedberg Memorial Service
April 27, 1998

M Y FIRST MEETING with Sydney Freedberg was one of
those lucky chance encounters that turns out, later in life,
to have been far more significant than I could possibly have
guessed at the time.

I was in my first year of graduate study, and had arrived at Harvard, more or less fresh from Oxford, only several months before.
For some reason, my spring-term collection of seminars in very
early to quite senescent English Renaissance literature included intensive readings in the inspired, but also barely intelligible, verse of
Piers Plowman; Robert Burton's endlessly cheerful *Anatomy of Melancholy*; and John Dryden's *Fables*, written during his declining years
in a style that was an original, but not totally irresistible, mixture
of suppressed neoclassicism and hearty, quaint Chaucerianism.

Searching for comic relief, I found in the pages of the course
catalogue an offering by someone called Professor Freedberg,
with lectures that apparently included a slide projector and color
transparencies, featuring Technicolor samples of selected works
by Masaccio, Piero, Mantegna, Botticelli, and others. So I wandered
over to the Fogg one day, at the appropriate time, masquerading

as a *quattrocento* interloper, and immediately became mesmerized by Sydney's matchless voice, the undulations of that spoken prose, with all those modulated syntactical transitions, that diction and rhetoric shaped to figure forth the patterns of meaning in paintings that Sydney's own style somehow managed both to envelop and to illuminate simultaneously.

After the lecture, I found myself standing outside the Fogg, at the top of the steps, when Sydney emerged for a quick cigarette. We chatted for a few moments — never having met before — and somehow the question of what we were reading came up. Sydney asked me if I had read Günter Grass' *The Tin Drum*. I hadn't. You should, he said. It is very powerful and disturbing. It is an important book.

I was intrigued, surprised, and even moved. This person — a sort of energized Pater, scholarly Vasari, more volumetric Berenson, more full-bodied Wölfflin all rolled into one — this person was reading contemporary German fiction, grounded in the Nazi period and the war. I learned only later, of course, about Sydney's own war experience. But in that first meeting, I felt not only an immediate rapport, but also the sense that there must be any number of levels of complexity within this stylized, imposing, but also approachable Self standing next to me.

We all know that deep reservoirs of feeling and affection, as well as strong urgencies, coexisted in Sydney with an equally strong desire for equilibrium, poise, and balance: unusual intensity, pressing against an equally unusual passion for form. While I could not possibly have understood or articulated much (if any) of this back in 1961 on the steps of the Fogg, I knew that I wanted to see more of this person — to learn more from him, and to try to come to know him better as a friend, if at all possible.

Sydney's book on Andrea del Sarto was published two years after that first meeting, and I still have a pencil mark on page twenty-seven, next to a sentence that discussed "the absence of any unaccustomed spiritual dimension" in Andrea's work. "There is," Sydney wrote, "the tenderest subtlety . . . and there are episodes of excitement, but there is no urgent passion.... Andrea does not have ... the motive — the aspiring tensions of the mind and spirit ... powerfully to develop the resources of his own new variant" of the classical style.[1]

When I read this, I understood (or *thought* I understood) a great deal more about Sydney because his idea of the classical style at its apex was obviously a dynamic one, in which spiritual, moral, and other human passions are constantly in tension with idealized forms — with the grace and fluency of rhythmic lines and shifting patterns.

The apparent incongruity that I first felt between Sydney's Piero or Mantegna on the one hand, and his engagement with Günter Grass on the other, suddenly diminished and soon disappeared. The dynamics of the man were so closely linked not only to the Renaissance painting and style he was so passionate about, but also to contemporary literature and many other aspects of life that were not "classical" in any conventional sense, but that nonetheless possessed urgency — possessed moral and other energies seeking expression in one or another kind of aesthetic form, where form and aspiring energy simply needed one another, if either was to become at all coherent, or reach resolution, or be sustainable.

All of Sydney's books stand in our library, on a convenient shelf, as tokens of friendship, true *souvenirs* — reminders of what we learned from him, of what he himself achieved, and of what he meant to us. As a person, scholar, and connoisseur, he was all of a piece: formidable but affectionate; exacting and self-exacting, but generous, human, and very deep. He cared about art because he cared about life. All of us who were fortunate to be his friends are now diminished — greatly diminished — by his loss. The world seems just that much less intriguing, less welcoming, less intricate and surprising, less affectionate, and surely less grand in the quality and capaciousness of its aspirations.

1 S.J. Freedberg, *Andrea del Sarto* (Cambridge: Harvard University Press, 1963), 27–28.

Something Luminous

Harry Levin Memorial Service
October 20, 1994

I AM HERE to say a few words about Harry Levin, mainly in my role as one of his countless students. I first sought him out not long after I came to Harvard, from Oxford, already focused on Elizabethan literature.

I needed a dissertation advisor who would not only be open-minded and patient, but also indulgent: because while I was quite sure that I wanted to write on the poetry of Philip Sidney, I was far from having any particular topic in mind. I knew only that Sidney's work interested me, and that his poetry seemed to me to be very important.

To my astonishment, that was enough for Harry. He immediately agreed to supervise me — purely "on spec," as we might say, more or less sight unseen. It all happened very quickly and graciously, and I came away from my meeting with him almost wishing that he had said no instead of yes. For, after all, if he was willing to take a chance on me, that meant I had no choice but to deliver. And at that moment, deliverance in any tangible shape or form seemed very far off indeed.

As events turned out, he was the ideal supervisor. He would

listen very attentively to my rather disconnected perceptions and ideas with his head slightly tilted, and an expression that seemed to indicate real curiosity on his part. He always gave me the reassuring impression that I might actually say something interesting and more or less intelligent. And he seemed hopeful on one's behalf: hopeful that the conversation on any given day would be enlivened by a new insight or remark worth remembering.

The chance of achieving that result was, of course, very remote. Since Harry had read virtually everything, and since his own mind had already raced far beyond the edges of whatever literary space I was just beginning to explore, there were certainly not many — if any — surprises one could ever hope to offer him.

His own advice, meanwhile, was always tentative rather than prescriptive. There were no sudden showers of lists of articles or books one was told to consult. Of course it was important to be reading widely and learning everything possible about the entire Elizabethan period and beyond. But there was always the conviction, which Harry so strongly communicated, that the poetry itself — in my case, Philip Sidney's own work — mattered first and last, and that if one stayed with the poetry long enough, it would sooner or later yield up its secrets.

Looking back, I can now see how his entire way of teaching and advising was so consistent with his own approach to literature and criticism. In his essays and books, he could be systematic and press an analytical argument when he felt it was necessary. But more than anything, he was guided by his extraordinary sensibility, by those wonderful antennae always scanning and picking up the least flicker of any significant literary vibration in the atmosphere. Those qualities, so intuitive and finely tuned, made him the best possible supervisor for a young and uncertain student like myself.

They also insured, almost by definition, that there would be no Levin "school" of criticism or followers, no obvious legacy in terms of a transferable critical methodology or apparatus, because no one could really emulate him. How does one emulate an original and unerring sensibility? He wrote with unselfconscious elegance and style; and that, too, precluded imitation.

We are left in the end with essays and books of literary criticism that are in fact unique, because they are so clearly the mark of this particular mind and man: work that continues to stimulate us with its learning, its stunning insights, its sudden aperçus, its bright illuminations.

In 1974, after Edmund Wilson's death, Harry wrote an eloquent tribute to Wilson. Toward the end of the essay, he quoted two couplets that Wilson had once sent to a number of friends in the form of witty but serious New Year's resolutions and advice. Reading these lines, one can see why Harry plucked them out of all of Wilson's writings, and why they might have had a special meaning for Harry himself: because they do seem to embody so much of his own character, his own attitudes, his own perspective on both life and literature.

> *Beware of dogmas backed by faith;*
> *Steer clear of conflicts unto death.*
>
> *Keep going; never stoop; sit tight;*
> *Read something luminous at night.*[1]

---

1 Harry Levin, *Memories of the Moderns* (New York: New Directions, 1980), 197.

Consequential Minds and Presences

On the Occasion of Receiving an Honorary Degree
Oxford University, November 23, 1998

I F THERE IS any academic approximation of the *ne plus ultra*, it
is surely an honorary degree from Oxford. I have rarely before
suffered from any delusions of adequacy in my works and days.
But if there is anything at all that might tempt me to succumb, it
would be just this experience of being awarded a Doctorate of
Civil Law – or indeed any other sort of law – *Oxoniensis*. For this
experience, and for this occasion, I thank you.

History, in this case stretching back more than three and a
half centuries, is not always kind or convenient. Harvard's debt to
Oxford is in many ways profound, but if we think for a moment
about origins, then I fear that my own university must be seen –
in its early relationship to Oxford – as nothing less than a renegade, indeed, an apostate.

You may (or perhaps may not) remember that the first meeting of the stockholders of the newly chartered Massachusetts
Bay Company was held in the town of Cambridge, England, in
August of 1629. And by far the largest number of educated people
who sailed to New England, especially to Massachusetts, in the

1630s had been spawned by Britain's most feverish and notorious nurseries of puritan learning – Emmanuel College, Trinity College, and similar unreliable resorts at Cambridge University.

Of the original twelve Overseers appointed in 1638 to look after the newly born Harvard College, seven had degrees from Cambridge, four had no degrees but had either brothers or sons who had attended Cambridge, and one – only one of the those first twelve apostles – was an Oxford man: John Davenport of Merton.

And Davenport – one might almost have guessed – turned out to be among the most disputatious, restless, fractious, and choleric of the twelve. He lasted only one year on the Overseers, and then left precipitously to found a new city in an utterly obscure, desolate place somewhere to the south of Cambridge: a place called – as fate would have it – New Haven, Connecticut, ultimately the home of President Levin's formidable and now, under his wise rule, altogether unfractious institution of learning, which still houses within it a College named Davenport.

So it was that even the one, single, lone Oxonian particle at Harvard left not the slightest electrical trace or charge there, but ultimately made its only lasting, visible – indeed imperishable – mark on the body politic of our cousins at Yale.

There is one final twist to this brief saga. In 1636, the very year in which Harvard was founded as a puritan congregational College, Archbishop Laud was the reigning High Church Chancellor of Oxford, and he received King Charles I in suitable splendor on a state visit, precisely here, in these very precincts.

In fact, as we know, Oxford became (for a while) King Charles' Anglo-Catholic military headquarters during the early years of the Civil War – while Harvard and Massachusetts were sending radical puritan colonists back across the sea to serve as reinforcements on behalf of Mr. Cromwell's effort to unseat King Charles and (yes) even to vanquish Brasenose, Balliol, and all our other local collegiate haunts.

As a result of these discomforting events, the city where Angelica and I now reside is called not Oxford, Massachusetts, but Cambridge. And John Harvard's name is to be found on the graduate rolls not of New College or Christ Church or Magdalen, but of Emmanuel College, Cambridge.

Fortunately, the memory of all that distant contentiousness had dissipated by the time I entered Oxford in 1956. The 1950s were an unusual historical moment: they seemed distinctive then, and they continue to seem so in retrospect. There were still lingering traces of the aftermath of World War II: modest scarcities; very little heat, and certainly not any hot water in my New College rooms; a muted spartan spirit; and a sense that the very great weight of experience — from the previous half century of war and economic devastation — had certainly not yet been lifted.

But if there were ample residual skepticism and wariness, born of experience, there was also a feeling that much of the world had now been given a new lease on life, with a touch of revived innocence and even some qualified confidence about what might be done to make the future different from the past.

Most of all, it was a time of consequential minds and presences, before the era when entire new systems of universities had been created; before the number of academics working in every conceivable field of learning — across nations, and around the world — had grown to such vast proportions; before ever-increasing specialization; before the professionalization of methodology, the stultifying effects of untethered theory, and the advent of great avalanches of academic manuscripts and articles cascading annually into print.

In short, it was in many respects an age of innocence, not in terms of the quality and power and incisiveness of the minds at work, but in terms of the relative lack of heavy and elaborate machinery employed in the process of production. There was, so to speak, a very great deal of output for a modest amount of required input. The yield was high, and the number of interlocutors still small enough to constitute a genuine community of people engaged in the most serious – but not humorless – forms of creative and disciplined study, as well as continuous conversation.

In 1956, W. H. Auden had just been installed as Professor of Poetry, and I went immediately to Blackwell's to buy one of those little pamphlets – another sort of modesty and innocence in presentation – containing Auden's first major lecture, "Making, Knowing and Judging."

During my years at New College, Isaiah Berlin gave his inaugural lecture – another pamphlet, entitled "Two Concepts of Liberty." George Kennan was the Eastman Professor in 1957–58, and I remember listening to his Reith Lectures on the BBC in the fall of 1957. There was Hugh Trevor-Roper's inaugural lecture as Regius Professor of History, and J. L. Austin giving the lectures that would eventually become the wonderful little volume called *Sense and Sensibilia.*

Meanwhile a young John Bayley was my main tutor in English literature, with Lord David Cecil offering regular classes in literary criticism at New College, and Christopher Tolkien doing his best to teach me the stresses and strains of Anglo-Saxon.

The little pamphlets and the books from Blackwell's began to pile up rather quickly – especially since almost everything seemed to cost either one and sixpence, or at most two and six. One read, one talked, one traveled, looked, listened, and sometimes learned.

Was it really so unusual a time – so refreshingly bright and exhilarating – or was it mainly because I was one and twenty and very much in the mood for exhilaration? I rather think that there was in fact something special about that particular moment: it was, as Henry James might have said, "the real thing." Not that today isn't also perfectly real – and also excellent. But it is a reality and an excellence that exist on the further side of another intervening half century of experience – experience that has especially transformed the nature of academic and university life around the globe, including our modes of inquiry.

Allow me to close by simply expressing my deepest thanks: for the honor you have bestowed; for the indulgence you have shown to the renegade apostate past of Harvard; for the rich experience of the comparatively innocent and always inspiring Oxford I knew as a student — and for the continuing power and warmth of the Oxford that I know today, and that I continue to treasure dearly.

Passion As Task

Address to Celebrate the Close of the University Campaign
Sanders Theatre, May 13, 2000

A FEW YEARS AGO, in this very theatre, we began a major
undertaking together, and we did so without knowing quite
how, or perhaps even whether or when, we might finish.

There were certainly enough challenges when we set out, and
if we had thought about them too long, we might well have
decided not to go forward at all. Ralph Waldo Emerson, Class of
1821, once remarked that any great or substantial performance
requires at least "a little fanaticism in the performer." He might
have added that a tinge of naïveté, and a touch of the quixotic, can
also come in handy.

Early on in the campaign, Fred Glimp sent me a *New Yorker* car-
toon showing a puzzled, slightly stunned, and exasperated banker
sitting at his desk, staring at a piece of paper and saying: "A billion
is a thousand million? Why wasn't I informed of this?"

Too much information, too soon, is not necessarily a good
thing. A certain amount of blessed innocence can sometimes
enable us to play stunning cadenzas, create sublime soufflés, and
even soar well beyond the most aerial of fund-raising goals.

The chief problem with such performances — or in fact any performance — is that they may not, of course, actually succeed. "The play," wrote Heywood Hale Broun about an ill-fated work, "opened at 8:40 sharp and ended at 10:40 dull." "I saw the piece under extremely unfortunate conditions," said George S. Kaufman about another bit of drama doomed to oblivion. What were the unfortunate conditions? "The curtain," said Kaufman, "was up."

There is always a risk that the show (or the soufflé) will flop, and ours certainly had no guarantee of success. We faced, almost inevitably, a profusion of potential difficulties. We knew, for instance, that thousands of Harvard graduates and friends had not really been visited — perhaps not even fleetingly waved at — by anyone from the University for quite a long while previous to the fund drive. Then, after so many degrees of separation, they found themselves suddenly lavished with decanal, provostial, presidential, and even loftier ministrations. What could possibly have accounted for this unexpected superflux of warmth and jollity?

One thing that certainly did not account for it was anything resembling the Reverend Mr. Collins' behavior in *Pride and Prejudice*. You may remember that at one point in the novel, Collins became unaccountably more demonstrative than ever before, because he had begun to have marital designs on one of Mr. Bennet's daughters. Alert to the Reverend's transparent motives as well as his extravagant manner, Mr. Bennet turned at one point and said, "May I ask whether these pleasing attentions proceed from the impulse of the moment, or are the result of previous study?"

In the case of our own campaign, we can answer candidly that there was simply no time — even if we had wanted it, which we did not — for "previous study" or rehearsal. Our impulses were very much "of the moment," and they sprang, sometimes quite awkwardly, from our collective concern for — and commitment to — the University.

Nonetheless, there was some worry — given the extraordinary size of our goal — that alumni and others might just run away in droves, or find ways to avoid engaging in conversation, at the very appearance of a dean, or indeed of anyone who looked even remotely "developmental." Bob Stone's long and large shadow quickly became one of the icons of the fund drive: instantly recognizable far in the distance, it allowed plenty of time for people to dive off their respective boulevards into the surrounding shrubbery, or simply scatter indiscriminately.

Even if the streets were sometimes emptied, and the echoing squares deserted, legions of Harvard loyalists nonetheless did rally around: our national campaign chairs; our honorary campaign chairs; our Major Gifts Committee chairs and members; our many campaign advisory committees and chairs for the professional schools and other important units; the Committee on University Resources and its remarkable executive committee; the Harvard College Fund and its chairs; the Harvard Alumni Association; reunion class agents and secretaries; the Board of Overseers; the Corporation; literally thousands of individual volunteers, abroad as well as in this country; and, indispensably, our extraordinary professional development staff and its consummate leadership.

✦   ✦   ✦

This immense assembly was, in my entire experience, the most talented, dedicated, effective, and numerous multitude ever gathered together on behalf of a single university. And, clearly, it required at least that much firepower to overcome the last challenge that I want to mention: to wit, the widespread perception that Harvard did not, perhaps, need any more money or resources than it already possessed.

This issue was, of course, a serious one. What may be less well known is that the perception was far from new. In fact, it has a quite long and interesting history, and I want to take a few moments to discuss it, because it can help to place our present situation in a useful perspective. It can also increase our understanding of the unusual – in fact, historic – significance of the campaign we have just concluded.

Glancing backward, here is a sample of what we can find:

> *The President [of Harvard] has long been impressed with a con-*
> *viction that the wealth of the University is greatly overestimated by*
> *her friends and by the public…. She is not wealthy; partly because*
> *she has control over only a limited portion of her income. The*
> *greater part of her funds are given on strict and inviolable condi-*
> *tions, and are not applicable to the new emergencies of the times.*[1]

That was President Thomas Hill in 1868. Hill was one of our more astute presidents, and he wanted Harvard to become and remain the preeminent institution of its kind in the nation. Why were more resources necessary? Recent increases in the number of students, Hill explained, had led to the need for more classrooms and recitation halls, more financial aid, and more scientific equipment.

For example, the Rumford Professor (who was then a chemist) was in the awkward position of having to borrow most of his labo-ratory equipment from a local manufacturer before each lecture, and then cart it all back immediately afterward. This practice, along with other logistical marvels, contributed only moderately to President Hill's efforts to increase productivity at the University.

Quite apart from a shortage of equipment, there was always the threat of a potential dearth of students, difficult as that may be for us to imagine today. Larger numbers of students were essential to the academic health and strength of the College. But because each student cost more to educate than the tuition that was charged, the arithmetic never seemed to work out quite as cleverly as our predecessors had hoped. President Hill acknowl-edged in one of his reports, "The very prosperity of the College creates its poverty."

The year 1867 was not necessarily an optimal moment for as-sessing Harvard's financial situation. If we make another probe, however, we find the following:

> *An opinion appears to be prevalent in the country that Harvard is*
> *a rich institution which has only to ask for money in order to obtain*

*it in limitless amounts, but unfortunately the work she is doing
today exceeds her resources, even with the most rigid economy.*[2]

That was President Lowell in 1911, a president who is generally
regarded as having reigned at a time when it was possible to have
all of one's cake and to eat it, too. After all, Mr. Lowell built more
buildings (with more colonnades and cupolas, as well as more
pilasters, with a greater *mélange* of Palladian, Mannerist, and neo-
Georgian portals and porticos) than any other president in Harvard's history. Yet, as he confessed more than once in his annual
reports, the University was in deficit a great deal of the time, and
even "ordinary" faculty salary increases were enough to make the
deficit grow.

Finally, one last piece of presidential lamentation:

*Two legends are now current in certain circles in the United States:
one is to the effect that the days of private philanthropy are over;
the other is that Harvard, unlike other universities, is so rich it
needs no more money. Both [legends] are demonstrably false.*[3]

That was President James Conant in 1948, and he followed this
opening statement by saying that the University's endowment —
largely restricted and therefore inflexible, with very little of it
available to the President and Fellows — covered just 25 percent of
Harvard's operating budget; that salaries needed to be raised; that
the cost of scientific and other facilities was increasing rapidly;
and that tuition had recently grown by more than 30 percent and
could not continue at such a pace. "The question which is upper-
most in the minds of all college presidents today," said Conant,
"[is] how to meet the increased costs [of higher education]."

✦   ✦   ✦

If we take the statements made over the course of about a century
by Presidents Hill, Lowell, and Conant, it is worth asking whether
we can account for so persistent a presidential impression con-

cerning Harvard's relative poverty, in the face of so strong a general public perception concerning Harvard's considerable wealth. How did such an apparent paradox come to haunt this very modest institution of ours, and what was the reality of the situation?

The beginning of an answer can be found in an essay written, not so long ago, by Oscar Handlin. "Harvard College," wrote Handlin,

> *was always poor, strapped by a meager endowment.... Mismanagement by Treasurer John Hancock (Class of 1754) and the disturbances of [the Revolutionary] war wiped away [even the few endowed funds that existed]. In the nineteenth century, despite Harvard's longevity, prestige, and reputation, the total [income from endowment] remained small and vulnerable ... less than $200,000 in 1845.*[4]

If circumstances were relatively dire in 1845, they were somewhat – but *only* somewhat – better sixty years later. For instance, in 1904, a plaintive and obviously frustrated President Charles Eliot found himself facing his seventh deficit in nine years, and he decided – fearless fellow that he was – to cut the salary budget of the Faculty of Arts and Sciences in order to bring things into balance. He did so, and he even survived. But in the following autumn, the undergraduate student body contained 118 fewer matriculants than predicted, and the loss in tuition revenues was substantial enough to leave the president still paddling about in an unappealing pool of crimson-red ink.

Therefore, the University's financial strength and stability were very long in coming. They were mainly a product of the last three-quarters of the twentieth century. Even then, however, the change was gradual, and there were any number of setbacks. In fact, we have almost certainly forgotten just how recent was the creation of certain programs that today may seem absolutely essential, eternal, and integral to everything we do.

For instance, some years after World War II, President

Conant reported that tuition still continued to rise rapidly and that more and more students were applying for financial aid, creating a great deal of stress and strain for the College.

> *To meet this steadily worsening situation we have, in the last two years, greatly expanded the use of loans and student employment.... Scholarship stipends have been trimmed.... Perhaps even more serious, we have been forced to restrict undesirably the number of candidates for admission to whom we could give scholarship help. We are now making scholarship awards to a significantly smaller proportion of our students than either Yale or Princeton is, and we are losing scores of promising boys because of our inability to help.*[5]

That was January 1952. There was no Harvard policy of need-blind admissions and need-based aid — not even an expectation (just forty-eight years ago) that the University could ever hope to achieve such a policy. And although it may seem preposterous, we are said to have been losing scores of talented students, simply because of a lack of money, to two other notorious institutions that were less exotic, mythic, and polynomial than Harvard.

✦   ✦   ✦

So, what are we to conclude? There does seem to have been something genuine about Harvard's relative poverty — whether in John Hancock's day, or President Hill's, or President Lowell's, or even as recently as President Conant's. But does that mean the legend of relative wealth was a total illusion?

Not really. If we look more closely, we can see that the University decided, about a century and a half ago, to begin to press beyond the limits of what nearly all other American colleges or universities were prepared to do, either in terms of quality or quantity, of depth or breadth, of intellectual variety and scope and reach. In fact, Harvard decided to pursue all the different aspects of its multifarious agenda simultaneously.

It was not necessarily surprising, therefore, that revenues for the operating budget seemed always one or two steps (at least) behind expenditures, and that the endowment – not large to begin with, and always heavily restricted – had a very difficult time reaching the point where it began to be at all consequential in size.

Let me offer one or two examples of this process, in slightly greater detail, to observe what actually happened. The way in which Harvard approached the creation of its library, for instance, can give us – in a snapshot – some idea of how the University's financial dynamics tended to work. Beginning in the mid-nineteenth century, our library already had a reputation as the best college library in the United States, even though it had virtually no funds for the actual purchase of books. People and institutions had simply begun to send materials to us, free of charge.

During the mid- to late nineteenth century, we received – in a short space of time – 1,500 volumes from a Dr. Henry Wales: volumes "mostly on philology, in German, Italian and Oriental literature." Then from somewhere in outer darkness arrived an interesting collection of modern (not ancient) Latin poetry, together with "sixty-two volumes and nineteen pamphlets, largely of the same character."

From the Midwest came eighty-four volumes of the legislative documents of the State of Ohio. From across the Atlantic, fifty-four volumes of duplicates from the imperial library in Berlin; then a singular copy of the Koran from someone in Calcutta, and a fine collection of manuscripts in the language of the Delaware Indians. Baptist societies, Sunday School societies, and all manner of bibliomaniacs sent us their most *recherché* treasures. Finally, the City of New York sent us ninety-four volumes of its own imperishable bureaucratic prose, together with an apparently accurate map of itself.

All this (and much more) came pouring in, and we accepted it all, creating near-crisis conditions. President Eliot reported one year that there were "42,000 [uncatalogued] volumes kept in 16 different buildings, of which only four are fireproof." Stacks of books in the aisles of the main College library made the place more or less impassable. There was a perpetual shortage of staff as well as space. In other words, Harvard was determined to have an unparalleled university library collection, even if there was no place to put it, and even if faculty and students could not actually find — and gain access to — the books they were looking for.

Nor was the financial problem solved — in fact, it was for a while made worse — when Widener Library was eventually constructed. Archibald Coolidge, the chair of the Library Council and himself a great benefactor, wrote:

> For me the tremendous question is one of finance. How are we going to move into the new building, how are we going to run it when we are in, how can we buy any more books, or catalogue them.... I feel rather hopeless and bewildered.... Even my private finances are crippled.[6]

In a public statement after the dedication of Widener, Coolidge wrote that the new library offered "unequalled opportunities." But, he added, the "dark side to the picture is the cost of running ... such a Library as Harvard now possesses." When asked by a friend how much money was expended on the construction of the new library, Coolidge replied that he did not know, and he doubted that he — or anyone — would ever know. Nor, given the nature of the predicament, was it clear that he even *wanted* to know.

Nevertheless, Coolidge added, "We need not now enter into the question of ways and means. In its Library, as elsewhere, Harvard has to accept the burden of its greatness.... Whatever difficulties such a possession brings with it, they must and will be overcome."

✦　✦　✦

We can see something like this pattern repeated in nearly every part and parcel of the University, decade after decade. When the renowned Professor Louis Agassiz was brought from Switzerland to Harvard, for instance, little did the President and Fellows suspect the full extent of what they were about to unleash. Professor Agassiz believed that the *Jardin des Plantes* was the premier research facility of its kind in the world, and nothing less than a New England equivalent of that Parisian phenomenon could possibly be adequate for Harvard.

Soon afterward, Professor Agassiz began — on many occasions — storming the Caribbean seas and the vast Gulf of Mexico in search of every conceivable specimen that could be seized. Like a marauding, benign conquistador — or a curatorial Captain Ahab — he pursued his objects with irresistible force and passion.

In 1867, for example, President Hill reported that Harvard's collections had "been made rich by the return of Professor Agassiz from Brazil, bringing with him an untold wealth [of objects] gathered principally in the Valley of the Amazon." This new hoard, said President Hill, has "been repacked in fresh alcohol, but it is still in a state comparatively useless, crowded in barrels and kegs in the cellar, for want of room to bring them into sight."

And this, of course, was only the beginning. At various times in the next decades, Agassiz acquired tens of thousands of items, including — in one good year — "a mass of fossil vertebrates, mainly mammalian,… from Wyoming, Kansas, and Texas"; an "important collection of Solenhofen fossils…, and an immense and very valuable collection of the Silurian fossils of Bohemia."

With the help of his own separate board of trustees, and his own private financial means, Agassiz built his own version of the *Jardin des Plantes* — what we in Cambridge now affectionately call the Museum of Comparative Zoology — and he added exhibition room after room, wing after wing, without any financial contributions from Harvard.

Eventually, of course, the professor and his board deeded their entire establishment — together with its unfortunately insufficient endowment – to the President and Fellows. It would have been churlish to have greeted this act of munificence with anything less than an ecstatic chorus of hosannas. Yet President Eliot's subsequent annual reports reveal how difficult it was to swallow, in its entirety, the whole of the MCZ. Fifteen years after Harvard had accepted responsibility for the Museum, Eliot praised its cornucopia of curiosities, but he also recorded – as he put it – "three unwelcome facts."

First, the Museum desperately needed more exhibition space, including an "aquarium and a live-stock room" to house various sorts of not-yet fossilized living creatures. This particular lacuna presented an unusual challenge for an otherwise tranquil university that had been designed mainly for the care and nourishment of ordinary human beings. Second, as always, more staff were needed for the Museum. And third, the MCZ owed the University $24,113.79, a debt incurred when the Corporation loaned the Museum enough money to construct its most recent addition of an unspecified number of cubic feet.

+   +   +

Whether we consider the growth of the library, or Mr. Agassiz's Museum, or Harvard's expansion of departments, professional schools, and other important empires unto themselves, we can find the same sweeping forward movement, across a broad institutional front, with expenditures nearly always outpacing revenues.

This approach to university growth and educational aspiration was obviously very risky. And it is clearly not a methodology that could usefully guide us today. But the theory that lay behind it was fundamentally simple. It seemed to Harvard and its leaders that it was far better – in those earlier expansionist times – to try to be unsurpassingly superb and to live, if necessary, close to the ragged edge than to be supremely safe, without ever discovering where the edge might possibly be.

If this was a hazardous course to take, it was nevertheless

rooted in the deep conviction that if one could create something absolutely excellent, people would eventually be drawn to it, would value it, would identify with it, would contribute to it, and would cherish it. And that is precisely what happened. The hazard turned out, in the end, to be a hazard of good fortune.

Harvard was, in a real sense, constantly racing to catch up with itself, even as late as the 1950s, when our financial aid program — and a good deal more — was struggling against difficult pressures. And this unusual situation helps to explain why, given all that the University had undertaken, built, and achieved in the century that preceded the 1950s, it was possible for Harvard to look very wealthy in terms of its facilities — its array of schools and libraries, departments, laboratories, and museums: it was possible for Harvard to look as if it had, in effect, everything one could possibly want or need, while at the same time it was equally plausible for the University to be nearly always behind in terms of its ability to support financially the exceptional quality, scale, and variety of all that it had created. The very prosperity of the University, as President Hill had suggested, contributed to its feeling, if not of poverty, then at least of considerable financial difficulty and stringency.

✦   ✦   ✦

Since the late 1950s and early 1960s, several developments have obviously happened — step by step — to change Harvard's situation significantly. In this regard, the significant contributions made during the presidencies of Nathan Pusey and Derek Bok were obviously crucial to establishing a genuinely firm foundation for Harvard's financial health. There is, however, a final reason that can help us to explain why we felt so relatively "less well off" just four or five decades ago, and how we have come to reach the different position in which we now find ourselves.

That reason has to do — overwhelmingly — with all of you in this room, and your fellow graduates and friends who are not present. You have provided, through this watershed University-wide campaign, the extra and indispensable resources to undergird all of Harvard more strongly and indisputably than ever before.

You have shared the conviction that the edge — not the ragged edge, but the edge and outermost limit of knowledge, learning, and inquiry — is precisely the region that Harvard must explore; that what the University has already achieved in terms of excellence should be not only sustained but extended, because in education, that is what motivates all of us: the strong desire to press forward, and to peer more deeply, in order to gain the clearest possible understanding of reality and of ourselves.

For your conviction, and for your abiding generosity, I want, on behalf of the entire University community, to express profound gratitude. You had a goal, a task, that was greater in magnitude and far more formidable than any other in the history of philanthropy. You surpassed the goal by an amount so great that it would, in itself, represent an extraordinarily ambitious target for all but a handful of the world's educational and cultural institutions.

In this, and in so many other ways, you have set a singular standard, demonstrating beyond any possible doubt the significance and fundamental value to society (as well as to individuals) of education and research, of learning in all its dimensions, across the wide span of the liberal arts and sciences and their closely related fields of knowledge in the professional schools. And you have done this in an intensively collaborative way, conceiving of the University as a single institution that must — now and in the future — function as a unity, as well as a collegium of distinctive individual parts.

If we ask, therefore, why this campaign has been genuinely historic in its significance, we can see that it has consolidated in an unprecedented way the educational and financial strength of Harvard University in its entirety. It has, in effect, brought to culmination a process of moving Harvard from the more precarious predicament described by President Conant less than fifty years ago to our current position. That move — viewed in the light of the long span of the University's history — has been a very recent one, far more recent than we might have suspected. And you who are here in this hall, together with others, have made the decisive difference in guiding us from those less settled seas of an earlier era to this more sunlit haven of time that we are blessed with today.

✦   ✦   ✦

There will, inevitably, be moments in the future — just as there have been in the past — when other challenges will arise, and we (or others) will be asked for help to guide Harvard and to keep it strong. Indeed, there may possibly be far more difficult days ahead than we have witnessed in earlier eras. But I draw great hope from several sources.

First, I am an optimist — not a foolish one, I think, because there is after all some pertinent evidence to draw upon. Great universities have been durable and resilient for many centuries, and if there is any lesson to be drawn from their history — and there may not be a lesson — I believe it can be stated quite simply. Aspiration and excellence are our essential guardians, because all of us need — and therefore all of us will stand ready to support — examples of the best that can be achieved. If we remain unwilling to settle for less than the best, I am confident that we will remain all that we are today — and more, far more, in the future.

Next, I believe that the bonds of friendship that Harvard inspires, and the loyalty it receives, are extraordinary in their kind. I say, in all candor, that the breadth of your vision; your ability to distinguish between what is genuinely significant, and what is simply endemic to the vexations of our common sublunary existence (exasperating as those vexations may often be); and, perhaps most of all, your depth of understanding concerning the University's central purposes, its values, its commitment to free thought and free expression, and its passion for learning: all of these qualities — which you have demonstrated so consistently — are remarkable, and have inspired you to create an enlightened fellowship and strong friendships powerful enough to carry this vessel of ours not only through periods of calm in future times, but also through all the storms that lie ahead, however turbulent they may be.

If such bonds of fellowship and friendship did not exist, and had not existed in the past, it would be hard to explain what could conceivably have led so many hundreds of thousands of people to commit so many human and financial resources, on such a massive scale — over so many centuries of time — to create, nurture, and watch over such a cloistered and yet disarmingly open and engaged a university as this one. Unless we felt that the University's quest for knowledge, as well as its pursuit of excellence, was a shared venture in which we had all participated, it seems impossible to comprehend how something as imaginative, sweeping, and compelling as Harvard could ever have come into being, and commanded such continuous affection and commitment.

Finally, I believe that adversity (at least *some* degree of adversity) is not necessarily a bad thing: indeed, it can often be a salutary thing. Henry James, Harvard Law School's most famous dropout, once wrote about his own craft and his own sense of circumstance: "We work in the dark," said James, "we do what we can — we give what we have. Our doubt is our passion, and our passion is our task."

Those words have haunted me for many years, because they seem to me to dramatize a marvelously moving, quietly heroic, and wonderfully generous response to a profound predicament. To work in the dark, with doubt as a companion, but not to diminish one's passion for the task; to do whatever one can, and to give what one has: this situation represents a mode of action under continuous adversity, which in turn elicits a mode of faith and commitment sustained by continuous passion. The energy and determination in James' lines are tangible, and they would not — could not — exist except for the consciousness of doubt and darkness.

Let us live with some measure of doubt, but let us also be

confident and passionate. Let us do whatever we can, now and in the future, whatever the circumstances may be. Meanwhile, as a gentle reminder of earlier, darker days — days that were also met with energy and courage — I want to close with a passage written not long before the United States entered the Second World War. The passage appeared in a spring 1941 issue of the *Harvard Alumni Bulletin*. The moment was a menacing one, when the possibility of brutal defeat in Europe and beyond seemed very real. And with such a defeat, of course, would certainly come the devastating destruction of peoples and institutions, including universities as independent centers of free inquiry and speech, of impassioned pursuit and discovery.

> *Up the river sweep the beams and half-beams of homeward suburban cars against the slower-moving glitter of inbound Boston traffic. The Weeks Bridge, a pretty Georgian fragment thrown across the Charles, and her less beautiful elder sister to the west, flank the batteries of increasing window light from the Houses and the Business School. It is Monday evening ... and the graceful Lowell tower emerges in the gloom, touched off by ... modern reflectors, cunningly concealed. Cambridge is a city of spires now, even by night, and at other times there are three of them ablaze at once.... A pretty sight, with spring so faintly stirring in the night air: a moment of security, almost, in a world so pitifully insecure.*
>
> *The lights of Harvard's Cambridge come on with a greater front and a steadier shine than they did for our more somnolent ancestors....*
>
> *Light has always been one of the first symbols of colleges and learning. Centuries and electrons have not changed us there. The point is that at Harvard the lights can still come on — in fair weather or in rain, in a time of free thinking, or of the soul's own darkness, when [we] shall save [our] birthright only by a masterful resolve.*[7]

That darkness, nearly sixty years ago, was very great, as was the need for masterful resolve. But, as Henry James suggested, there is a profound sense in which we always work in the dark, we always need and desire beacons of hope to bring us light. And there is really never a moment when our resolve can afford to be less than masterful.

Thank you for your own masterful resolve during these past few years. Thank you for your friendship and companionship. Thank you for assuring that, at Harvard, "the lights *can* still come on — in fair weather or in rain, in a time of free thinking, or of the soul's own darkness." Thank you, finally, for the brightness that you have brought to the University through all that you have accomplished during these last years that we have shared together.

1 Thomas Hill, *Report of the President to the Board of Overseers, 1867–68*, 4.

2 A. Lawrence Lowell, *Report of the President to the Board of Overseers, 1909–10*, 23.

3 James B. Conant, *Report of the President to the Board of Overseers, 1947–48*, 11.

4 Oscar Handlin, *Glimpses of the Harvard Past* (Cambridge: Harvard University Press, 1986), 48.

5 James B. Conant, *Report of the President to the Board of Overseers, 1950–51*, 19.

6 W. Bentinck-Smith, *Building a Great Library: The Coolidge Years at Harvard* (Cambridge: Harvard University Library, 1976), 90.

7 "Editorial: The Lights Come On," *Harvard Alumni Bulletin*, March 22, 1941, 701.

Self-Education

President's Associates Dinner Remarks
November 17, 2000

I HAVE RECENTLY been thinking a great deal about Harvard, and about universities. And I thought I would simply share with you some ideas reaching as far back as the seventeenth century, and then forward to this very academic year.

I have a simple theme. I want to suggest that, insofar as education and teaching are concerned, matters have improved considerably over the past three hundred and more years. I will also say something about our current undergraduates and what it is like to teach them, since I tried doing precisely that earlier this year.

For many decades after the founding of Harvard College, the faculty consisted almost entirely of students who had very recently graduated (people we would now call graduate-student teaching fellows), with the sole exception of the president, who was often the lone adult in the professorial ranks. The undergraduates, meanwhile, were not always completely charming. In fact, they seemed at times so intractable that when Increase Mather, minister of the largest church in Boston, was invited to be president of Harvard, he replied, a little indelicately: "What? Should I [give up] preaching to 1500 souls … [in order] to expound to 40 or 50 children, few of them capable of [any] edification" whatsoever? So Mr. Mather, along with several others who were approached, decided that there were much greener pastures to be found elsewhere, as compared to whatever grass and clover were then growing in Harvard Yard.

Early in the eighteenth century, a young Boston newspaper reporter named Benjamin Franklin found great pleasure in regularly excoriating Harvard, whose students he regarded as ignorant and arrogant, as well as lazy and languid. Fashionable dress seems to have been one of their most intense preoccupations — a charge that appears to be at least partly borne out by the fact that, in 1754, Harvard College felt compelled to pass a new ordinance declaring that "every candidate for his degree [must] appear in black, or dark blue, or grey clothes, and that no one wear any silk nightgowns."

We know at least as much about student discipline in those earlier eras as we do about anything academic. It does seem to have been the case, however, that plane geometry was about as far as most Harvard eighteenth- and even early nineteenth-century students progressed in mathematics. We know this because, toward the end of senior year, Harvard undergraduates engaged in an annual, solemn nighttime ritual in the Yard, presumably chanting and gesticulating as they went. At the conclusion of this festival rite, they buried, ceremoniously, a copy of Euclid's *Elements*, bidding it *adios* forever.

We also know, from the diary and letters of a bright Princeton undergraduate of the same era, that his class succeeded in covering only about a dozen pages of his chemistry textbook after an entire year of study. And having gone to Princeton partly because of his strong interest in history, he found that there was absolutely no instruction in that subject during the whole of his first two terms — and not much in sight as he looked further down the road.

Given the fact that Harvard, Princeton, and some other colleges clearly graduated some intelligent, literate, well-informed, and capable leaders during the eighteenth and nineteenth centuries, we might well wonder how that could possibly have happened.

There are several reasons, but one in particular was important. Many of the gaps and other deficiencies of the cramped, prescribed curriculum, and often deadly teaching methods, did not cause nearly as much intellectual damage as we might imagine, because recent research on this subject has shown that student-organized debating societies, essay societies, literary and other publications, and similar activities created many of the most valuable and powerful learning experiences for undergraduates.

In fact, at Princeton, the two major debating societies had, in their own buildings, quite large libraries consisting of recent and contemporary books in philosophy, literature, history, religion, and other subjects: many of the books, in other words, that the college library was not itself acquiring.

So the students essentially created their own informal and lively curriculum, their own reading habits, and their own methods of teaching and learning — methods that were based mainly on discussion, argument, questioning, criticizing, and debating. Henry Adams, who graduated from Harvard in 1858, was absolutely withering about the College's formal curriculum and instruction. But looking back, half a century later, he wrote about his election in his senior year as Class Orator for Commencement. After his speech, one elderly gentleman commented on Adams' "perfect self-possession":

> *Self-possession indeed! [wrote Adams.] If Harvard College gave nothing else, it gave calm. For four years each student had been obliged to [present himself] daily before dozens of young men who knew each other to the last fibre. One had done little but read papers to Societies, or act comedy in the Hasty Pudding, not to speak of all sorts of regular exercises, and no audience in future life*

would ever be so intimately and terribly intelligent as these.... Self-possession was the strongest part of Harvard College, which certainly taught men to stand alone.... Whether this was, or was not, education, Henry Adams never knew. He was [however] ready to stand up before any audience in America or Europe, with nerves rather steadier for the excitement, but whether he should ever have anything to say, remained to be proved.[1]

How Harvard managed to transform itself from the ossified methods of the 1850s or the 1750s into a different kind of college for serious and stimulating learning is an intriguing tale, but one that is much too long and complicated to relate on this occasion. But part of the answer was that Harvard found ways, in effect, to institutionalize in its formal curriculum and pedagogy many of the lively and energetic forms of learning that the students themselves were already practicing.

The prescribed course system, which allowed for very little student choice, was completely changed by President Eliot's creation of the "free elective system," which meant that the College soon needed a different kind of faculty, with much deeper knowledge across a much wider range of subjects. The "recitation system" of instruction (where students essentially memorized material and then "recited" what they knew in class) was gradually displaced by discussion groups designed to be, as President Eliot said, "Socratic" in nature.

Then, late in the nineteenth century, the teaching of science was also totally revamped. In 1886, the departments of chemistry, physics, botany, and zoology established experimental courses for entering freshmen. These departments, President Eliot wrote, "will be studying the difficult problem" of how "to teach a science of observation by experimental methods to young persons whose mental training has been received almost exclusively through book-study of languages and mathematics."

So in subject after subject, the student was placed in the position of being a much more active, inquiring, exploring agent: a co-participant in experimentation, or in library research for a seminar paper, or in any number of other activities.

By 1932, President Lowell was in a position to write about the nature of teaching and learning at Harvard in a way that would have been unthinkable a century earlier:

> *Teachers can impart facts — not, perhaps, better than an earnest student can get them from books — they can explain, present points of view, and, if the pupil is not too reluctant, they can stimulate and inspire; but unless the student desires, or is provoked, to learn, he will profit little. He must be made to educate himself, working out things by his own effort.... To absorb and give back the information and ideas of the teacher may win good [grades] in many courses, but for training and fortifying the mind it is less valuable than power acquired by voluntary exertion in pursuit of an object. In short, the essence of all institutions of higher learning should be self-education under guidance.*[2]

So, in the space of about sixty or seventy years, Harvard College adopted and articulated a new vision for undergraduate education — a massive change that we now take more or less for granted. This is not to say, however, that everything worked as planned. In fact, President Lowell also wrote, more than once, about the fact that everyone

> *who has taught a freshman course in a subject requiring the use of books dealing with large questions is aware of the fact that freshmen can read paragraphs, or a few pages covering a definite point, but that they can rarely read a book; that is, they have not the habit of sustained thinking needed to grasp and hold a continuous line of thought and take in its full meaning.*[3]

In short, we had our vision and our defined standards, but there was still a very great deal to do in terms of actually achieving the goals that we had set for ourselves.

Well, how are we managing today? As you might expect, matters are (and always will be) rather less than perfect. But the situation is encouraging and exciting. To find out whether our current freshmen could read more than a paragraph in a sustained and intellectually coherent way — or write more than a paragraph — I decided to teach a mini-course to a dozen entering freshmen this past September, during the week *before* freshman orientation. We met for two hours every morning and two hours every afternoon for a week, with three papers due between Tuesday and Thursday. This was an intellectual version of Outward Bound and similar programs that we offer freshmen during that same week. Our seminar subject was lyric poetry — all sorts of poems from different periods, but a good deal of difficult twentieth-century verse.

I want to say a few words about how the students in our seminar coped with one very short poem, but before that, let me give you some sense of what these students were like, in their own words. In answer to a question concerning the kind of poetry that interested them, and whether they read any poetry in any languages other than English, I received answers such as:

> *I read poetry in French — mostly Racine, Hugo, and Apollinaire. I speak some Italian and made one enjoyable abortive attempt to read Dante's* Inferno *in the original. This summer I have had a lot of fun reading (slowly)* The Canterbury Tales *in the original, so in some sense I might be able to add Middle English to my list [of languages].*

Then in response to a question concerning how they spent their last three summers, I received: "Double Session Football Camp"; "Youth Fellowship to Israel"; "Playing tennis and playing piano"; "Computer graphics programming"; "Five-Star Basketball Camp"; "Community Service Program on St. John's Island, South Carolina," and so on.

I found myself, therefore, with a dozen public-spirited, athletic, poetry-readers, and the first poem that we discussed — a beguiling little bit of off-hand conversation – provoked quite strong reactions in the seminar.

This Is Just to Say

I have eaten
the plums
that were in
the icebox

and which
you were probably
saving
for breakfast

Forgive me
they were delicious
so sweet
and so cold[4]

Some students read the poem as a subtle but devastating exposé of human evasiveness and selfishness. The speaker is seen as trying to pass off his actions as a perfectly natural and understandable midnight raid on the icebox, with only a brief conventional apology to the other person – perhaps his wife. The speaker (according to this reading) doesn't seem to care that the plums were probably chosen to be shared at breakfast. He seems entirely insensitive, except that he's alert enough to realize he should at least admit to having done something that perhaps he should not have done.

Other students disagreed: the poem is not a profound moral drama. Rather, the poet is trying to record and present ordinary behavior that occurs every day between people who know each other very well and understand each other. There were the plums. The speaker was suddenly attracted to them. He disposed of them, and then he wrote a note to explain what happened. It shows the strength of the relationship and the easy trust between these two people, rather than exposing any great selfishness that threatens to divide them.

There were other readings and other views, and we talked for at least an hour, trying to see what we could make of these elusive lines that at first sight seemed so transparent. We did agree that this was a very carefully crafted poem and that it would be possible to trace the ways in which the lines are organized: the number of syllables in each word and line, the subtle patterning, the careful placement of key words and phrases — in short, the thoughtfully composed, subliminal order.

But what, after all, did we think the poem is "about"? We decided that something important *did* happen here: a form of transgression (eating the plums) followed by an appeal for forgiveness, with the two words "Forgive me" placed strategically and conspicuously as the first line of the last stanza.

At the same time, we concluded that the poem did not seem to be an exposé of deep selfishness on the speaker's part. There *is* a sense in which this is a minor, modest transgression, well within the range of our ordinary, imperfect, everyday lives. In fact, as readers, we are almost invited to participate in eating the plums: the last three lines of the poem seem almost to celebrate — certainly to appreciate — the deliciousness and sweetness of the fruit. The objects of this world evoke desire. In that sense, they may be hazardous. On the other hand, we cannot very well do without them, and the poem seems to suggest that we are not wrong to respond to their beauty and to experience their bounty.

We sensed, in other words, a delicate balance in this situation. The daily ritual of a relationship — the expectation that things will be shared, and the important symbolic act of "breaking fast" together — has been momentarily disrupted. And yet, there is also an instantaneous act to repair the damage, with a note that is itself a gentle confession. We sense that forgiveness will be forthcoming, because the transgression is seen and felt to be understandable, even natural.

We even raised the possibility that there is here a very distant echo of Genesis, the Garden, and the Fall: forbidden fruit, indulgence, dislocation, and the need to find a way to reconcile. But if so, this is a *pianissimo* version, and these rather innocent plums are not at all tragic in their implications.

Further discussion led us to think about the poem as a metaphor for the very nature of human relationships – the way in which human communities must function if they are to remain healthy: every day there are innocent or less innocent temptations, potential falls and necessary repairs. The students talked about *their* experience of learning to live together as a new community – soon to be part of a much larger university community in which they themselves would be constantly sending and receiving signals or messages that would have to be patiently read and interpreted, and that might possibly begin with a line such as, "This is just to say."

In effect, therefore, the poem, and our seminar, became one way of thinking about Harvard as a human place, as well as an academic place. And our few lines of verse seemed to reassure all of us that it was natural – in fact, inevitable – to stumble, and equally possible and natural to recover or restore equilibrium. Indeed, this process was central to the experience of learning, of growing, and of building relationships that would ultimately be more durable because they had been so fully tested.

There have been many wonderful moments during these past ten years at Harvard. And this week of teaching – of watching young people reach more deeply to understand words, implications, and meanings – was as important an experience as any I have had. I can now (should there have been any doubt) wholeheartedly testify that matters really *have* improved over these last three hundred years: our freshmen can, rather remarkably, read *many* paragraphs, entire volumes, and a great deal of difficult poetry with sustained intensity and comprehension. For this, and for so much more, Harvard is deeply and gratefully in the debt of friends such as you who have come together on this occasion, because it is your continuous engagement, interest, and generosity that make it possible, year after year, for us to bring such extraordinary students to this extraordinary College and University.

1 Henry Adams, *The Education of Henry Adams: An Autobiography* (Boston: Houghton Mifflin, 1918), 69.

2 A. Lawrence Lowell, *Report of the President to the Board of Overseers, 1931–32*, 7.

3 A. Lawrence Lowell, *Report of the President to the Board of Overseers, 1923–24*, 7.

4 William Carlos Williams, "This Is Just to Say," *Collected Poems, 1909–1939, Volume 1* (New York: New Directions Publishing, 1986), 1: 372.

POINTING OUR THOUGHTS

has been set in ITC Golden Cockerel, a digital version of a face designed by Eric Gill for Robert Gibbings' Golden Cockerel Press. The type was first used for the publisher's 1931 edition of the *Four Gospels of Lord Jesus Christ*, often named as one of the most beautiful books from England. Like other type designs by Gill, Golden Cockerel is based on his inscriptional lettering, not on more traditional calligraphic models. The result is a face of notable heft, with a dense color on the page and sharp serifs reminiscent of the carver's chisel. The book has been printed in an edition of five thousand copies on Mohawk Superfine paper by The Stinehour Press, Lunenburg, Vermont, and bound by Acme Bookbinding in Charlestown, Massachusetts.

✦   ✦   ✦

Designed by Carl W. Scarbrough